The Collected Works of
Langston Hughes

Volume 10

Fight for Freedom and
Other Writings on Civil Rights

Projected Volumes in the Collected Works

The Poems: 1921–1940

The Poems: 1941–1950

The Poems: 1951–1967

The Novels: *Not without Laughter*
  and *Tambourines to Glory*

The Plays to 1942: *Mulatto* to *The Sun Do Move*

The Gospel Plays, Operas, and Other
  Late Dramatic Work

The Early Simple Stories

The Later Simple Stories

The Essays

Fight for Freedom and Other Writings on Civil Rights

Works for Children and Young Adults: Poetry,
  Fiction, and Other Writing

Works for Children and Young Adults: Biographies

Autobiography: *The Big Sea*

Autobiography: *I Wonder as I Wander*

The Short Stories

The Translations

The Sweet Flypaper of Life

An Annotated Bibliography of the
  Works of Langston Hughes

The Collected Works of

Langston Hughes

Volume 10

Fight for Freedom and
Other Writings on Civil Rights

Edited with an Introduction
by Christopher C. De Santis

University of Missouri Press
Columbia and London

Copyright © 2001 by Ramona Bass and Arnold Rampersad, Administrators
    of the Estate of Langston Hughes
Introduction copyright © 2001 by Christopher C. De Santis
Chronology copyright © 2001 by Arnold Rampersad
University of Missouri Press, Columbia, Missouri 65201
Printed and bound in the United States of America
All rights reserved
5 4 3 2 1   05 04 03 02 01

Library of Congress Cataloging-in-Publication Data

Hughes, Langston, 1902–1967
   [Works. 2001]
   The collected works of Langston Hughes / edited with an introduction by
Christopher C. De Santis
      p. cm.
   Includes bibliographical references and indexes.
   ISBN 0-8262-1371-5 (v. 10 : alk. paper)
      1. African Americans—Literary collections. I. De Santis, Christopher C. II. Title.
PS3515.U274 2001
818'.5209—dc21   00066601

⊗™This paper meets the requirements of the
American National Standard for Permanence of Paper
for Printed Library Materials, Z39.48, 1984.

Designer: Kristie Lee
Typesetter: Bookcomp, Inc.
Printer and binder: Thomson-Shore, Inc.
Typefaces: Galliard and Optima

Contents

Acknowledgments

The University of Missouri Press is grateful for assistance from the following individuals and institutions in locating and making available copies of the original editions used in the preparation of this edition: Anne Barker and June DeWeese, Ellis Library, University of Missouri–Columbia; Teresa Gipson, Miller Nichols Library, University of Missouri–Kansas City; Ruth Carruth and Patricia C. Willis, Beinecke Rare Book and Manuscript Library, Yale University; Ann Pathega, Washington University.

The *Collected Works* would not have been possible without the support and assistance of Patricia Powell, Chris Byrne, and Wendy Schmalz of Harold Ober Associates, representing the estate of Langston Hughes, and of Arnold Rampersad and Ramona Bass, co-executors of the estate of Langston Hughes.

The editor gratefully acknowledges the Department of English and the College of Arts and Sciences at Illinois State University for providing research grants that helped in the completion of this volume. Ron Fortune, Chair of the Department of English, has been particularly supportive of faculty research and deserves special recognition and thanks. Jane Lago, Managing Editor of the University of Missouri Press, expertly guided this volume to completion; her editorial comments on the introductory material and advice about the final contents of the volume were invaluable. The editor also acknowledges Susan Kalter for her meticulous reading of the introduction to this volume and Arnold Rampersad for his generosity of spirit and for providing a superlative model of Hughes scholarship to which others might aspire.

Chronology
By Arnold Rampersad

1902 James Langston Hughes is born February 1 in Joplin, Missouri, to James Nathaniel Hughes, a stenographer for a mining company, and Carrie Mercer Langston Hughes, a former government clerk.

1903 After his father immigrates to Mexico, Langston's mother takes him to Lawrence, Kansas, the home of Mary Langston, her twice-widowed mother. Mary Langston's first husband, Lewis Sheridan Leary, died fighting alongside John Brown at Harpers Ferry. Her second, Hughes's grandfather, was Charles Langston, a former abolitionist, Republican politician, and businessman.

1907 After a failed attempt at a reconciliation in Mexico, Langston and his mother return to Lawrence.

1909 Langston starts school in Topeka, Kansas, where he lives for a while with his mother before returning to his grandmother's home in Lawrence.

1915 Following Mary Langston's death, Hughes leaves Lawrence for Lincoln, Illinois, where his mother lives with her second husband, Homer Clark, and Homer Clark's young son by another union, Gwyn "Kit" Clark.

1916 Langston, elected class poet, graduates from the eighth grade. Moves to Cleveland, Ohio, and starts at Central High School there.

1918 Publishes early poems and short stories in his school's monthly magazine.

1919 Spends the summer in Toluca, Mexico, with his father.

1920 Graduates from Central High as class poet and editor of the school annual. Returns to Mexico to live with his father.

1921 In June, Hughes publishes "The Negro Speaks of Rivers" in *Crisis* magazine. In September, sponsored by his father, he enrolls at Columbia University in New York. Meets W. E. B. Du Bois, Jessie Fauset, and Countee Cullen.

1922 Unhappy at Columbia, Hughes withdraws from school and breaks with his father.

1923 Sailing in June to western Africa on the crew of a freighter, he visits Senegal, the Gold Coast, Nigeria, the Congo, and other countries.

1924 Spends several months in Paris working in the kitchen of a nightclub.

1925 Lives in Washington for a year with his mother. His poem "The Weary Blues" wins first prize in a contest sponsored by *Opportunity* magazine, which leads to a book contract with Knopf through Carl Van Vechten. Becomes friends with several other young artists of the Harlem Renaissance, including Zora Neale Hurston, Wallace Thurman, and Arna Bontemps.

1926 In January his first book, *The Weary Blues,* appears. He enrolls at historically black Lincoln University, Pennsylvania. In June, the *Nation* weekly magazine publishes his landmark essay "The Negro Artist and the Racial Mountain."

1927 Knopf publishes his second book of verse, *Fine Clothes to the Jew,* which is condemned in the black press. Hughes meets his powerful patron Mrs. Charlotte Osgood Mason. Travels in the South with Hurston, who is also taken up by Mrs. Mason.

1929 Hughes graduates from Lincoln University.

1930 Publishes his first novel, *Not without Laughter* (Knopf). Visits Cuba and meets fellow poet Nicolás Guillén. Hughes is dismissed by Mrs. Mason in a painful break made worse by false charges of dishonesty leveled by Hurston over their play *Mule Bone.*

1931 Demoralized, he travels to Haiti. Publishes work in the communist magazine *New Masses.* Supported by the Rosenwald Foundation, he tours the South taking his poetry to the people. In Alabama, he visits some of the Scottsboro Boys in prison. His brief collection of poems *Dear Lovely Death* is privately printed in Amenia, New York. Hughes and the illustrator Prentiss Taylor publish a verse pamphlet, *The Negro Mother.*

1932 With Taylor, he publishes *Scottsboro Limited,* a short play and four poems. From Knopf comes *The Dream Keeper,* a book of previously published poems selected for young people. Later, Macmillan brings out *Popo and Fifina,* a children's story about Haiti written with Arna Bontemps, his closest friend. In June, Hughes sails to Russia in a band of twenty-two young African Americans to make a film about race relations in the United States. After the project collapses, he lives for a year in the Soviet Union. Publishes his most radical verse, including "Good Morning Revolution" and "Goodbye Christ."

1933 Returns home at midyear via China and Japan. Supported by a patron, Noël Sullivan of San Francisco, Hughes spends a year in Carmel writing short stories.

1934 Knopf publishes his first short story collection, *The Ways of White Folks.* After labor unrest in California threatens his safety, he leaves for Mexico following news of his father's death.

1935 Spends several months in Mexico, mainly translating short stories by local leftist writers. Lives for some time with the photographer Henri Cartier-Bresson. Returning almost destitute to the United States, he joins his mother in Oberlin, Ohio. Visits New York for the Broadway production of his play *Mulatto* and clashes with its producer over changes in the script. Unhappy, he writes the poem "Let America Be America Again."

1936 Wins a Guggenheim Foundation fellowship for work on a novel but soon turns mainly to writing plays in association with the Karamu Theater in Cleveland. Karamu stages his farce *Little Ham* and his historical drama about Haiti, *Troubled Island.*

1937 Karamu stages *Joy to My Soul,* another comedy. In July, he visits Paris for the League of American Writers. He then travels to Spain, where he spends the rest of the year reporting on the civil war for the *Baltimore Afro-American.*

1938 In New York, Hughes founds the radical Harlem Suitcase Theater, which stages his agitprop play *Don't You Want to Be Free?* The leftist International Workers Order publishes *A New Song,* a pamphlet of radical verse. Karamu stages his play *Front Porch.* His mother dies.

1939 In Hollywood he writes the script for the movie *Way Down South,* which is criticized for stereotyping black life. Hughes goes for an extended stay in Carmel, California, again as the guest of Noël Sullivan.

1940 His autobiography *The Big Sea* appears (Knopf). He is picketed by a religious group for his poem "Goodbye Christ," which he publicly renounces.

1941 With a Rosenwald Fund fellowship for playwriting, he leaves California for Chicago, where he founds the Skyloft Players. Moves on to New York in December.

1942 Knopf publishes his book of verse *Shakespeare in Harlem.* The Skyloft Players stage his play *The Sun Do Move.* In the summer he resides at the Yaddo writers' and artists' colony, New York. Hughes also works as a writer in support of the war effort. In November he starts "Here to Yonder," a weekly column in the Chicago *Defender* newspaper.

1943 "Here to Yonder" introduces Jesse B. Semple, or Simple, a comic Harlem character who quickly becomes its most popular feature. Hughes publishes *Jim Crow's Last Stand* (Negro Publication Society of America), a pamphlet of verse about the struggle for civil rights.

1944 Comes under surveillance by the FBI because of his former radicalism.

1945 With Mercer Cook, translates and later publishes *Masters of the Dew* (Reynal and Hitchcock), a novel by Jacques Roumain of Haiti.

1947 His work as librettist with Kurt Weill and Elmer Rice on the Broadway musical play *Street Scene* brings Hughes a financial windfall. He vacations in Jamaica. Knopf publishes *Fields of Wonder,* his only book composed mainly of lyric poems on nonracial topics.

1948 Hughes is denounced (erroneously) as a communist in the U.S. Senate. He buys a townhouse in Harlem and moves in with his longtime friends Toy and Emerson Harper.

1949 Doubleday publishes *Poetry of the Negro, 1746–1949,* an anthology edited with Arna Bontemps. Also published are *One-Way Ticket* (Knopf), a book of poems, and *Cuba Libre: Poems of Nicolás Guillén* (Anderson and Ritchie), translated by Hughes and Ben Frederic Carruthers. Hughes teaches for three months at the University of Chicago Lab School for children. His opera about Haiti with William Grant Still, *Troubled Island,* is presented in New York.

1950 Another opera, *The Barrier,* with music by Jan Meyerowitz, is hailed in New York but later fails on Broadway. Simon and Schuster publishes *Simple Speaks His Mind,* the first of five books based on his newspaper columns.

1951 Hughes's book of poems about life in Harlem, *Montage of a Dream Deferred,* appears (Henry Holt).

1952 His second collection of short stories, *Laughing to Keep from Crying,* is published by Henry Holt. In its "First Book" series for children, Franklin Watts publishes Hughes's *The First Book of Negroes.*

1953 In March, forced to testify before Senator Joseph McCarthy's subcommittee on subversive activities, Hughes is exonerated after repudiating his past radicalism. *Simple Takes a Wife* appears.

1954 Mainly for young readers, he publishes *Famous Negro Americans* (Dodd, Mead) and *The First Book of Rhythms.*

1955 Publishes *The First Book of Jazz* and finishes *Famous Negro Music Makers* (Dodd, Mead). In November, Simon and Schuster publishes *The Sweet Flypaper of Life,* a narrative of Harlem with photographs by Roy DeCarava.

1956 Hughes's second volume of autobiography, *I Wonder as I Wander* (Rinehart), appears, as well as *A Pictorial History of the Negro* (Crown), coedited with Milton Meltzer, and *The First Book of the West Indies.*

1957 *Esther,* an opera with composer Jan Meyerowitz, has its premiere in Illinois. Rinehart publishes *Simple Stakes a Claim* as a novel. Hughes's musical play *Simply Heavenly,* based on his Simple character, runs for several weeks off and then on Broadway. Hughes translates and publishes *Selected Poems of Gabriela Mistral* (Indiana University Press).

1958 *The Langston Hughes Reader* (George Braziller) appears, as well as *The Book of Negro Folklore* (Dodd, Mead), coedited with Arna Bontemps, and another juvenile, *Famous Negro Heroes of America* (Dodd, Mead). John Day publishes a short novel, *Tambourines to Glory,* based on a Hughes gospel musical play.

1959 Hughes's *Selected Poems* published (Knopf).

1960 *The First Book of Africa* appears, along with *An African Treasury: Articles, Essays, Stories, Poems by Black Africans,* edited by Hughes (Crown).

1961 Inducted into the National Institute of Arts and Letters. Knopf publishes his book-length poem *Ask Your Mama: 12 Moods for Jazz. The Best of Simple,* drawn from the columns, appears (Hill and Wang). Hughes writes his gospel musical plays *Black Nativity* and *The Prodigal Son.* He visits Africa again.

1962 Begins a weekly column for the *New York Post.* Attends a writers' conference in Uganda. Publishes *Fight for Freedom: The Story of the NAACP,* commissioned by the organization.

1963 His third collection of short stories, *Something in Common,* appears from Hill and Wang. Indiana University Press publishes *Five Plays by Langston Hughes,* edited by Webster Smalley, as well as Hughes's anthology *Poems from Black Africa, Ethiopia, and Other Countries.*

1964   His musical play *Jericho–Jim Crow*, a tribute to the civil rights movement, is staged in Greenwich Village. Indiana University Press brings out his anthology *New Negro Poets: U.S.A.*, with a foreword by Gwendolyn Brooks.

1965   With novelists Paule Marshall and William Melvin Kelley, Hughes visits Europe for the U.S. State Department. His gospel play *The Prodigal Son* and his cantata with music by David Amram, *Let Us Remember,* are staged.

1966   After twenty-three years, Hughes ends his depiction of Simple in his Chicago *Defender* column. Publishes *The Book of Negro Humor* (Dodd, Mead). In a visit sponsored by the U.S. government, he is honored in Dakar, Senegal, at the First World Festival of Negro Arts.

1967   His *The Best Short Stories by Negro Writers: An Anthology from 1899 to the Present* (Little, Brown) includes the first published story by Alice Walker. On May 22, Hughes dies at New York Polyclinic Hospital in Manhattan from complications following prostate surgery. Later that year, two books appear: *The Panther and the Lash: Poems of Our Times* (Knopf) and, with Milton Meltzer, *Black Magic: A Pictorial History of the Negro in American Entertainment* (Prentice Hall).

The Collected Works of

Langston Hughes

Volume 10

Fight for Freedom and
Other Writings on Civil Rights

Introduction

"I grew up with the NAACP," Hughes reminisced in his postscript to *Fight for Freedom*. "I learned to read with *The Crisis* on my grandmother's lap." In his sixtieth year, Hughes's memories of childhood were peopled with heroes and heroines of the long struggle for racial equality in the United States. His grandfather, Charles Langston, had been tried in 1858 for protecting a fugitive slave; another relative died with John Brown at Harpers Ferry. Hughes's grandmother, Mary Langston, ensured that the boy was well versed in the lives and exploits of Nat Turner, Frederick Douglass, Ida B. Wells Barnett, Mary White Ovington, and W. E. B. Du Bois, among others. Equally vivid in Hughes's memories were the painful incidents of racial discrimination that made him, even as a child, all too aware of the necessity for the National Association for the Advancement of Colored People. Recalling the Fourth of July speeches that celebrated "liberty and justice, freedom and democracy" which he heard as a boy, Hughes "knew they did not apply to me because I could not even buy an ice cream soda at the corner drug store where my mother bought the family soap. I could not go to the movies in Lawrence, Kansas, because there was a sign up: COLORED NOT ADMITTED."

When Hughes accepted a commission to write the official history of the NAACP in 1960, he could acknowledge with a guarded optimism that the nation had made positive strides in civil rights for African Americans since the association's founding in 1909. The horrific lynchings of black men and women, an issue of the gravest importance for the NAACP, had decreased substantially over the course of a half-century campaign waged against such crimes. Inter- and intrastate travel on public forms of transportation, long a mainstay of racial segregation and discrimination, had become far more civil as a direct result of the NAACP's working together with organizations such as the Congress of Racial Equality (CORE), the Southern Christian Leadership Conference (SCLC), and the Student Nonviolent Coordinating Committee (SNCC). The battle over segregation in public schools, another major campaign in which the NAACP was invested, had resulted in the beginnings of the painfully slow process of integration. Other NAACP campaigns involving African American voting rights, restrictive covenants in housing, and discrimination in places of employment had also met with some success. Still, Hughes recognized that the struggle was far from over. Nearing the end of a distinguished literary career that had spanned more than forty years, he approached the task of writing *Fight for Freedom: The Story of the NAACP* as a dual opportunity. First, he would reaffirm his own commitment to the NAACP and its leaders, some of whom, over the years, had befriended Hughes and supported him both personally and professionally during times of crisis. Second, he would attempt to demonstrate that the NAACP remained vitally important in the early 1960s, when its leaders were increasingly being criticized by more militant individuals and organizations for their conservative approach to combating racial injustices. The result is a book that may strike some readers as more of a scorecard for the NAACP's accomplishments than an objective history of the association. Hughes had not always approached the subject of the NAACP with uncritical praise, however, and a consideration of his early relationship to the association and the turbulent middle years of his writing career is necessary to understand why he did so in *Fight for Freedom.*

Hughes was only nineteen years old in 1921 when, accompanied by his mother, he first visited the New York NAACP offices. Previous to this visit he had been in correspondence with Jessie Redmon Fauset, the literary editor of the NAACP's *Crisis* magazine, who had accepted and published one of his finest poems, "The Negro Speaks of Rivers." During his visit Hughes met Fauset and W. E. B. Du Bois, whose eloquent words of strength, protest, and defiance in *The Souls of Black Folk* and in his *Crisis* editorials were among the earliest Hughes remembered from his childhood. Although Hughes was terrified by the prospect of meeting Du Bois—a living hero in the young writer's eyes—the introduction went well, marking the beginning of a strong relationship to Du Bois, Fauset and the NAACP.[1] Only a few years after this important meeting, Hughes was a well-known and highly regarded personage among NAACP dignitaries, especially those who were part of the burgeoning literary and artistic community at the center of the Harlem Renaissance. Indeed, when he arrived at an NAACP-sponsored benefit dance in 1924 after a long stay in Africa and Europe he was treated as a celebrity, attracting the attention of Walter White, assistant secretary of the NAACP, and Mary White Ovington, one of the group's founders. There, too, Hughes

---

1. See Arnold Rampersad, *The Life of Langston Hughes,* 2 vols. (New York: Oxford University Press, 1986), 1:19, 48, 53.

again brushed elbows with Du Bois and was introduced to James Weldon Johnson, executive secretary of the NAACP and a fellow writer whom Hughes greatly admired.[2]

During the peak years of the Harlem Renaissance immediately following this event, the NAACP's *Crisis* was an integral part of Hughes's developing career as a writer, both as a publishing outlet for his poems and essays and as a source of encouragement to allow him to focus more exclusively on writing. A 1925 *Crisis*-sponsored literary contest yielded cash prizes to Hughes in two categories, the essay and poetry. (The contest was funded in part by Amy Spingarn, the wife of Joel E. Spingarn, chairperson of the NAACP board of directors and soon-to-be president of the association. Five years later Hughes would dedicate his novel *Not without Laughter* to the Spingarns.)[3] More important, the 1920s witnessed Hughes's rise from obscurity to being "virtually the house poet of the most important journal in black America."[4] In addition to providing a forum for Hughes to gain an increasingly international reputation, the leaders of the NAACP ensured that the young writer was introduced to important people in New York's artistic community. In *Fight for Freedom* Hughes would look back fondly on the many "cultural soirees" that James Weldon Johnson, Jessie Fauset, and Walter White hosted at their Harlem apartments:

> Celebrities of both races who often attended included the Carl Van Vechtens, the Clarence Darrows, and the young Paul Robesons; Miguel Covarrubias and Aaron Douglas, the artists; Charles S. Johnson, the sociologist; Rebecca West, the English novelist; and Salvador Madariaga, the Spanish philosopher. Walter White's parties too, on Edgecombe avenue in what was then Harlem's most fashionable apartment building, brought together brilliant company—Sinclair Lewis, Willa Cather, Rudolph Fisher, Heywood Broun, George Gershwin—and perhaps included more stars of the theater than the other gatherings did.

The stock market crash of 1929 largely brought to an end this festive atmosphere that pervaded the artistic and intellectual community at the height of the Harlem Renaissance. With the Great Depression looming over America, the patronage for black artists wasn't as generous, prizes

---

2. Rampersad, *Life*, 1:96–97; see also Faith Berry, *Langston Hughes: Before and Beyond Harlem* (Westport, Conn.: Lawrence Hill and Co., 1983), 56.

3. Rampersad, *Life*, 1:113, 189; Berry, *Before and Beyond Harlem*, 63–64.

4. Rampersad, *Life*, 1:48.

offered to promising writers by journals were fewer, and the stipends for submissions were decreased. In spite of mounting financial worries, Hughes adhered to his goal of making a living by writing. However, while his 1926 manifesto, "The Negro Artist and the Racial Mountain," sounded a joyful note of youthful rebellion against those who would attempt to stifle the artist, Hughes's writings of the 1930s reflected a more serious, politically committed state of mind. Racial violence, economic hardship, and the daily humiliation of segregation that African Americans suffered in the South and elsewhere outraged Hughes. Taking his status as one of the preeminent creative voices in African America very seriously, Hughes accepted the responsibility to speak out against these injustices in his writing and to fight them in his daily life, at whatever cost to his reputation or personal welfare.

The Scottsboro incident of 1931 set the tone for much of Hughes's radical poetry and prose in the years following the Harlem Renaissance. It also provoked a temporary split between Hughes and the NAACP. On March 25, 1931, a deputy sheriff in Alabama, responding to a call regarding a fight between black and white teenagers who had hitched a ride on an open railroad freight car traveling through the state, led an armed white mob in arresting nine African American youths, ranging from thirteen to twenty years of age. The black youths were transported to a jail in Scottsboro, the Jackson County seat, and charged with the rape of two white women who had been traveling on the freight train. Eight of the youths, who insisted they had never seen the women prior to their arrests, were put on trial within two weeks of the incident. They were quickly convicted by all-white juries and sentenced to death. The trial of the ninth of the "Scottsboro boys," as they came to be called, ended in a mistrial because the jurors and the prosecution disagreed about a death sentence. In March 1932 the Alabama Supreme Court reversed the conviction of the youngest of the nine youths, and in November 1932 the U.S. Supreme Court overturned guilty verdicts against the other seven. The next four years saw a series of retrials, appeals—some of which reached the U.S. Supreme Court again—and more retrials, even though Ruby Bates, one of the alleged victims, recanted her charges of rape on the witness stand and admitted she had fabricated the entire story. In the end, none of the youths was put to death for the alleged crime.[5]

---

5. See Dan T. Carter, *Scottsboro: A Tragedy of the American South* (1969; Baton Rouge: Louisiana State University Press, 1990), and James Goodman, *Stories of Scottsboro* (New York: Vintage, 1995).

Immediately after the original death sentences were handed down by the juries, the International Labor Defense—a legal defense organization controlled by members of the Communist Party—offered to defend the nine youths, convinced that its participation in the case would not only help the defendants but also bring both recognition to its antilynching crusade and new members to the party. The ILD persuaded some of the teenagers' parents that it was in the best position to defend their sons effectively, quickly obtaining signed agreements granting the organization full control over the case. NAACP officials, by contrast, hesitant to act until details of the case were better known, had avoided public comments on the indictments of the Scottsboro boys. After the teenagers were convicted, however, the association rallied. According to Mark Naison, "the NAACP recoiled in horror at the thought of Communists handling their appeal." Failing to convince the youths' parents to repudiate the ILD's participation in the case, NAACP executives began to wage a drawn-out battle against the Communist Party that alienated many African Americans and abated only when the ILD agreed to allow the NAACP to fundraise in behalf of the defendants.[6]

The Scottsboro case certainly did not compel Hughes to embrace the radical Left—he had immersed himself in Max Eastman's *The Liberator* as a high school student. Yet, in William J. Maxwell's words, it "melted Hughes's remaining resistance to imagining himself as a black bolshevik writer, one willing to produce for Communism's benefit."[7] Hughes viewed the Scottsboro case as an impending mass lynching and embraced the Communist Party as the only entity that seemed able, or at least willing, to help the nine youths. Committed to lecturing and fund-raising on behalf of the Scottsboro boys, Hughes also wrote a series of essays that voiced his disappointment in the Communists' opponents. In "Southern Gentlemen, White Prostitutes, Mill-Owners, and Negroes," included in this volume, he struck a tone of disgust and defiance in posing a challenge to African Americans in general but, more specifically, to those who had

6. *Communists in Harlem during the Depression* (Urbana: University of Illinois Press, 1983), 58, 83.

7. See Maxwell's *New Negro, Old Left: African-American Writing and Communism between the Wars* (New York: Columbia University Press, 1999), 134, and Rampersad, *Life,* 1:215. At some point in the early 1930s Hughes also assumed the presidency of the Communist League of Struggle for Negro Rights (though he would always insist that he was never a member of the Communist Party). Maxwell and Rampersad are in disagreement over the year Hughes became president, the former claiming that it was before the Scottsboro incident and the latter speculating that it was probably not before 1934.

remained silent about Scottsboro because of ideological differences with the ILD:

> But back to the dark millions—black and half-black, brown and yellow, with a gang of white fore-parents—like me. If these 12 million Negro Americans don't raise such a howl that the doors of Kilby Prison shake until the 9 youngsters come out (and I don't mean a polite howl, either), then let Dixie justice (blind and syphilitic as it may be) take its course, and let Alabama's Southern gentlemen amuse themselves burning 9 young black boys till they're dead in the State's electric chair.

Hughes was equally critical of NAACP executives who, far from remaining silent, had publicly voiced their strenuous opposition to the Communist Party and the ILD. His friend Walter White, who had succeeded James Weldon Johnson as executive secretary of the NAACP, was one of the most vocal, spearheading the campaign to wrest control of the Scottsboro case from the Communist Party. According to biographer Arnold Rampersad, Hughes "detested [White] for opposing the communists," and while he did not express his opinions openly, he "would write two articles highly critical, even nasty in tone, about White" and other prominent African Americans who supported the NAACP's attack on the ILD.[8] Hughes apparently never published these essays, both written in 1932, but in "Brown America in Jail: Kilby" he alluded to the NAACP's well-publicized critique of the Communists for attempting to appeal directly to the governor of Alabama for the immediate release of the Scottsboro boys: "Listen Communists, don't send any more cablegrams to the Governor of Alabama. Don't send any more telegrams to the Supreme Court. What's the matter? What's all this excitement about, over eight young niggers? Let the law wash its hands in peace." Two years later he would register a more general critique of conservative African American leaders and educators in "Cowards from the Colleges," wryly noting that "with demonstrations in every capital in the civilized world for the freedom of the Scottsboro boys, so far as I know not one Alabama Negro school until now has held even a protest meeting."[9]

In the interval between the 1930s and the publication of *Fight for Freedom* in 1962, Hughes's interpretation of the NAACP's role in the

---

8. *Life,* 1:218.

9. See below in "Other Writings on Civil Rights" for the full texts of these and the other essays quoted below and not otherwise cited in the footnotes.

Scottsboro case would change dramatically. Granting the often bitter conflict between the association and the ILD a scant two sentences in the book, Hughes is unequivocal in his support for the former and pointedly harsh toward the latter:

> This became one of the famous criminal cases of the 1930's, the NAACP's initial efforts in behalf of the boys being nullified by the intervention of the Communists. The latter, seeking to exploit the matter for their own ideological purposes, misrepresented the NAACP as being in league with "the lyncher bosses" and persuaded the boys to abandon the NAACP-provided counsel, which included Clarence Darrow and Arthur Garfield Hays.

Hughes declined to mention that Darrow and Hays agreed to help the defendants somewhat late in the case, and only after the lawyers initially recruited by Walter White had withdrawn their participation because of strong popular support for the ILD. Rather, he ends the brief treatment of this negatively charged moment in the NAACP's history in a manner that erases the crucial role of the Communist Party in the case: "None of the boys were executed; eventually, as the result of NAACP negotiations, they were successively released."

Hughes's dramatic shift away from the radical Left and back into the fold of the NAACP was not the result of his having been commissioned to write the association's official history. It had occurred much earlier, in the wake of a series of events that compelled him to rethink both his creative output and his reputation in the eyes of other African Americans. On the heels of his activism on behalf of the Scottsboro boys, Hughes made two trips that, both directly and indirectly, would influence this process of self-redefinition. In 1932 he traveled to the Soviet Union as part of a group of twenty-two young African Americans to make *Black and White,* a motion picture commissioned by the Meschrabpom Film Corporation of the Worker's International Relief. Although the film was never completed, Hughes chose to remain in Russia for one year. Like his outrage over the Scottsboro case, his experiences in the Soviet Union found an outlet in some of his most powerful and controversial writings. Hughes greeted Moscow with unbridled optimism, similar to his youthful exuberance upon first arriving in New York City: "Moscow and freedom! The Soviet Union! The dream of all the poor and oppressed— like us—come true."[10] In "Goodbye, Christ," by contrast, a poem that

10. "Moscow and Me," *International Literature* 3 (July 1933): 62.

right-wing reactionaries would use to demonize him for many years after its initial publication in the *Negro Worker,* Hughes struck a defiant tone, embracing Marxist ideology and dismissing what he believed to be the hypocritical state of organized religion in the United States:

> Goodbye,
> Christ Jesus Lord God Jehova,
> Beat it on away from here now.
> Make way for a new guy with no religion at all—
> A real guy named
> Marx Communist Lenin Peasant Stalin Worker ME—[11]

Like his experiences in the Soviet Union, Hughes's six-month tenure in Spain as a correspondent for the *Baltimore Afro-American* during the Spanish Civil War enabled him to draw connections between the lives of black people in America and those of oppressed people throughout the world. As Rampersad has pointed out, the time spent in Spain reinvigorated Hughes's sense of himself as a poet of the people, a vulnerable position given the dehumanizing racial situation in the United States: "Langston's spirit, dulled and blunted by poverty and disappointment in America, became honed again under the pressure of the anti-fascist struggle in wartime Spain. As the foreboding grew that an even greater war was coming to Europe, he would begin to feel life with an intensity he had not known since his first weeks in the Soviet Union."[12] That intensity found an outlet in Hughes's poetry and fiction, in his nonfictional prose, and in his speeches, the latter represented most powerfully in July 1937, shortly before he left for Spain. Addressing the Second International Writers Congress in Paris—in a speech he would later publish in the *Crisis* under the title "Too Much of Race"—Hughes was both impassioned and optimistic in his critique of fascism around the world:

> The Fascists know that we long to be rid of hatred and terror and oppression, to be rid of conquering and of being conquered, to be rid of all the ugliness of poverty and imperialism that eat away the heart of life today. We represent the end of race. And the Fascists know that when there is no more race, there will be no more capitalism, and no more war, and no more money for the munition makers, because the workers of the world will have triumphed.

11. "Goodbye Christ," *The Negro Worker* 2 (November–December 1932): 32.
12. *Life,* 1:341.

When Hughes published the first volume of his autobiography, *The Big Sea*, three years later, such passionate, radical ideology was largely absent. In fact, Hughes wrote of his life and career up to 1931 only, consciously omitting the turbulent decade that had compelled his transformation from the blues poet extraordinaire of the Harlem Renaissance to the radical voice of the proletarian masses. The Nazi-Soviet Nonaggression Pact of 1939 was a significant factor in the repression of his radicalism. That pact was announced only a year after Hughes and other writers had signed the supportive "Statement of American Progressives on the Moscow Trials."[13] Indeed, when Hughes appeared before Senator Joseph McCarthy's Senate Permanent Sub-Committee on Investigations on March 26, 1953, to explain and account for his "un-American," radical past, he offered a prepared statement that alluded to his disappointment with the pact and effectively repudiated his radical writings. Asked by Roy Cohn, chief counsel to McCarthy, to describe the period in which he sympathized with the Soviet Union and to state when that period ended, Hughes replied:

> There was no abrupt ending, but I would say, that roughly the beginnings of my sympathies with Soviet ideology were coincident with the Scottsboro case, the American depression, and that they ran for some 10 or 12 years or more, certainly up to the Nazi-Soviet Pact, and perhaps, in relation to some aspects of the Soviet ideology, further, because we were allies, as you know, with the Soviet Union during the war. So some aspects of my writing would reflect that relationship, that war relationship.[14]

If his disillusionment with radical socialist ideology after the Nazi-Soviet Pact was a contributing factor in Hughes's decision to write with a less overtly political agenda after 1939, equally decisive were growing concerns about his seemingly chronic poverty and his reputation as a major creative voice in African America. According to biographer Faith Berry, there was nothing Hughes feared more than public ostracism: "Like a turtle, he withdrew into a public shell whenever he felt threatened. In his craving for public approbation and affection, he sometimes let himself be guided by what was expedient."[15] Hughes's mettle in this

13. See Rampersad, *Life*, 1:374, and Berry, *Before and Beyond Harlem*, 286–87.
14. United States, State Department Information Program, "Testimony of Langston Hughes, Accompanied by his Counsel, Frank D. Reeves," March 26, 1953, p. 74.
15. Berry, *Before and Beyond Harlem*, 297.

respect was severely tested in November 1940 when a luncheon in California at which he had hoped to publicize *The Big Sea* was cancelled when Aimee Semple McPherson, the head of a fundamentalist religious organization, sent a contingent of picketers to spread awareness of Hughes's impious "Goodbye Christ," in which he had sarcastically mentioned the evangelist. Shaken by the protest, Hughes was mortified to discover a month later that the *Saturday Evening Post,* which also came under fire in the poem, had reprinted "Goodbye Christ" without his permission.[16] Anticipating by over a decade the repudiation of his radical socialist writings before McCarthy's investigating committee, Hughes immediately sent a press release concerning the poem to friends, publishers, and foundations. After cataloging in this statement the systems of global oppression that prompted his satirical words in the early 1930s, Hughes wrote the poem off as an error of youth:

> Now, in the year 1941, having left the terrain of "the radical at twenty" to approach the "conservative of forty," I would not and could not write "Goodbye, Christ," desiring no longer to *épater le bourgeois*. . . . I have never been a member of the Communist Party. Furthermore, I have come to believe that no system of ethics, religion, morals, or government is of permanent value which does not first start with and change the human heart. Mortal frailty, greed, and error, know no boundary lines.[17]

With Hughes's acknowledged turn toward conservatism came a desire to improve conflicted relationships, particularly with the NAACP. He was also preoccupied with commemorating his longevity as a writer and reestablishing himself as a regular voice in the journal that helped launch his career. Twice in just over a month he reminded his friend Arna Bontemps that he was nearing the twentieth anniversary of his professional writing career, dating it from the publication of "The Negro Speaks of Rivers" in the June 1921 *Crisis*.[18] Having been a regular contributor to the *Crisis* during the 1920s, in the 1930s Hughes published very little in the NAACP's official journal. As Berry notes, his first overt step toward bridging the ideological gap that had come between himself and

16. See ibid., 295–96, and Rampersad, *Life,* 1:390–92.
17. Langston Hughes, "Statement Concerning 'Goodbye, Christ,'" January 1, 1941, in *Good Morning Revolution: Uncollected Social Protest Writings by Langston Hughes,* ed. Faith Berry (New York: Lawrence Hill and Co., 1973), 135.
18. Hughes to Bontemps, February 14 and March 22, 1941, in *Arna Bontemps–Langston Hughes Letters, 1925–1967,* ed. Charles H. Nichols (New York: Dodd, Mead and Co., 1980), 75, 77.

the association during the Scottsboro trials was an essay written "especially for *The Crisis,* in observance of his twentieth year as contributor to the NAACP magazine."[19] Far different from his radical prose of the 1930s, "The Need for Heroes" is didactic in tone. It emphasizes a moral responsibility among black writers to chronicle the strongest individuals and best achievements of the past and present rather than the faults and defeats of African America. Hughes also used the essay to comment on the representation of African Americans in the American entertainment industry, an issue of vital importance to the NAACP:

> It is the social duty of Negro writers to reveal to the people the deep reservoirs of heroism within the race. It is one of the duties of our literature to combat—by example, not by diatribe—the caricatures of Hollywood, the Lazy Bones of the popular songs, the endless defeats of play after play and novel after novel—for we are not endlessly funny, nor always lazy, nor forever quaint, nor eternally defeated.

Lest the association miss his gesture of goodwill in sending this essay to the *Crisis,* Hughes agreed to a request by Walter White, whose anticommunist rhetoric he had denounced in the early 1930s, to write a poem in celebration of the NAACP's thirty-second annual convention in Houston.[20] While certainly not an example of his best work, "NAACP" demonstrated that Hughes's disagreement with the association's handling of the Scottsboro case was a thing of the past, replaced by a strong belief in the organization's potential to effect social change:

> The Jim Crow car's still dirty.
> The color line's still drawn.
> Yet up there in Washington
> They're blowing freedom's horn!
> The NAACP meets in Houston.
> Folks, turn out in force!
> We got to take some drastic steps
> To break old Jim Crow's course.[21]

After these early gestures of reconciliation, Hughes continued his attempts to strengthen his relationship with the NAACP. In 1944 he published a column in the *Chicago Defender* about a dinner in honor of

19. Berry, *Before and Beyond Harlem,* 299.
20. Rampersad, *Life,* 1:56; Berry, *Before and Beyond Harlem,* 300.
21. "NAACP," *Crisis* 48 (June 1941): 201.

Walter White's twenty-fifth anniversary with the NAACP. His former disdain for White's conservatism was only dimly evident in his observation that "among all those distinguished lawyers, judges, politicians, ladies, and race leaders, looks like to me there should have been some labor, too." Still, his radical past continued to haunt him. The FBI had targeted Hughes as a subversive after the incident in 1940 with Aimee McPherson, maintaining a file that listed him as a member of the Communist Party and a potential threat to Caucasians. He was also hounded by the House Un-American Activities Committee (HUAC)—established in 1938 to investigate subversive political groups and individuals in the United States—for his membership in radical organizations. Hughes took various steps to counter the accusations against him and to prove just how politically moderate he was, among them aligning himself with the NAACP, a decidedly anticommunist organization under Walter White's leadership.[22] If his wartime columns in the *Chicago Defender* protesting segregation in the armed forces or praising the Red Army positioned him firmly on the political Left, he balanced them with a 1945 column in which his humorous fictional character and alter ego, Jessie B. Semple, joined the NAACP: "I have just joined the National Organization for the Association of Colored Folks and, Jack, it is FINE." Moreover, although Hughes would protest in his *Defender* column W. E. B. Du Bois's 1951 indictment for subversive activities, he repeatedly declined requests from Du Bois and others for a stronger commitment to radical Left causes. Instead, he focused on praising the NAACP in the *Defender* and fundraising on its behalf.[23]

These activities served him well when he was subpoenaed by a United States marshal in 1953 to appear before McCarthy's investigating committee. Understandably fearful of McCarthy's Cold War witch-hunts, Hughes immediately consulted his longtime legal adviser, NAACP President Arthur Spingarn, and Lloyd K. Garrison, an official of the NAACP's National Legal Committee. Garrison advised Hughes on the potential implications of the impending hearing while another lawyer with ties to the NAACP, Frank D. Reeves, actually represented Hughes before the investigating committee. In addition to providing him with legal

22. For information on Hughes's troubles with HUAC, see Rampersad, *Life*, 2:90–98.
23. Ibid., 2:198–99.

counsel, "the NAACP assumed Langston's expenses for the hearing, in return for the extensive work he had done for the organization in the past."[24] Perhaps in gratitude to the NAACP for its support during this trying period, Hughes again made an offering to the *Crisis*. Published in May 1953, "Langston Hughes Speaks" summarized the statement he had earlier prepared to defend himself before McCarthy's committee. Balancing a rejection of Communism with a recitation of his family's historic role in the struggle for civil rights, the statement could only further endear Hughes to the more conservative officials of the NAACP:

> I am not now and have never been a member of the Communist Party, and have so stated over the years in my speeches and writings. But there is in my family a long history of participation in social struggles—from my grandfather who went to prison for helping slaves to freedom and another relative who died with John Brown at Harpers Ferry to my great uncle, John M. Langston, only Negro representative in Congress from Virginia following the Reconstruction, and who had supported Abraham Lincoln in his recruiting Negro troops, and spoken for freedom on the same platform with Garrison and Phillips.

Six years later, in 1959, Hughes would celebrate the fiftieth anniversary of the NAACP in his *Chicago Defender* column, reaffirming his personal commitment to the association: "For most of my life I have been a member of the NAACP, but sometimes when funds were low, or when I was out of the country, my membership lapsed. However, as soon as I have had a dollar or two, I renewed my membership in one branch or another throughout the country."

Hughes's return to the good graces of the NAACP after the stormy period of the 1930s was completed on June 26, 1960, when he received the association's highest honor, the Spingarn Medal. Awarded the medal by Arthur B. Spingarn himself at the association's fifty-first convention in Minneapolis, Minnesota, Hughes had been chosen by the selection committee for being "generally recognized in America, Europe, Asia, Africa, Central and South America as a major American writer and considered by many the poet laureate of the Negro race."[25]

24. Ibid., 2:221.
25. Award citation quoted in Warren D. St. James, *NAACP: Triumphs of a Pressure Group, 1909–1980,* 2d ed. rev. (Smithtown, N.Y.: Exposition Press, 1980), 293–94.

In his speech before the large contingent of delegates at the convention, Hughes accepted the medal "in the name of the Negro people who have given me the materials out of which my poems and stories, plays and songs, have come; and who, over the years, have given me as well their love and understanding and support." Hughes was elated to receive this award, which he had long coveted. Indeed, his sincere gratitude toward the NAACP would be reflected on nearly every page of the official history of the association he published two years after the award ceremony.

Hughes had already met with some success in the field of historical writing when he began work on *Fight for Freedom*. A series of books for children and adolescents on African American history, music, and culture was well received, as was *Pictorial History of the Negro in America,* a book he had coauthored with Milton Meltzer. Hughes also provided historical commentary and analysis on a range of issues directly affecting African American readers in his weekly newspaper column. *Fight for Freedom* is unique among Hughes's nonfictional writings, however, for its sustained historical treatment of a single subject. Beginning with the social, political, and economic contexts that led to the founding of the NAACP in 1909 and ending with a summary of its targeted goals for 1963, Hughes attempted a history that would be comprehensive in scope and singular in its purpose of highlighting the ways in which the association had a direct and positive impact on racial justice in the United States.

In some respects, *Fight for Freedom* is very much a part of a long and distinguished literary tradition that persistently challenged dominant representations of African Americans as either uncivilized beasts of burden or helpless victims of a racially oppressive social order. From the slave narratives of Harriet Jacobs and Frederick Douglass and the powerful novels of Frances Ellen Watkins Harper and Pauline Hopkins in the nineteenth century, to the revisionary historical writings of Du Bois and John R. Lynch in the early twentieth century, black writers have rewritten history to demonstrate a vital, defiant African America of citizens working for social change rather than submitting to the status of passive objects. From its first page, *Fight for Freedom* engages in this cultural work of historical revision. Hughes introduces the NAACP as a powerful and influential American institution, one of the most "talked-about," "written-about," and "damned" organizations in the country. The association's leaders and members are constantly in motion, constantly agitating for social justice, constantly demanding that the nation live up to its democratic ideals to the extent that "not a week goes by but that somewhere the lawyers of the NAACP are in court defending its members against arrest, fines, or imprisonment." In these early pages, Hughes reconfigures the idea of the "Negro problem"—a vague something with which whites must always deal, against which they must always react— into a "white problem"; the NAACP becomes both an active agent and a vehicle through which individuals enact self-determination, openly refusing to be a problem that someone else needs to solve. Hughes demonstrates that this will-to-power was not a twentieth-century phenomenon, but rather the admirable legacy of heroic individuals demanding freedom and justice: Cinque, the African chieftain's son who led the famous mutiny of slaves aboard the schooner *Amistad;* Nat Turner, the freedom fighter who struck fear into the white South with his well-organized rebellion; John Brown, who proved in his raid at Harpers Ferry that he was willing to die to secure the freedom of others; Ida B. Wells Barnett, whose fearless exposé of lynchings nearly cost her her own life; and many others, black and white, who set the stage for the NAACP to do its historic work.

Hughes documents that work chronologically in a history that focuses on the individuals who had the greatest impact on the NAACP and the issues with which the organization was most concerned during its first fifty years. As such, the book is a virtual catalog of interesting people, troubling events, and joyful victories. Hughes strikes a balance in this respect between biography and cultural history. Major figures throughout the NAACP's history are well represented in the book's numerous biographical vignettes. Choosing high praise over objectivity, Hughes makes no attempt to hide his great admiration for two of the association's founders, W. E. B. Du Bois and Mary White Ovington. Other NAACP officials, including Joel and Arthur Spingarn, William Pickens, James Weldon Johnson, Walter White, Thurgood Marshall, Kivie Kaplin, Roy Wilkins, and Medgar Evers, receive equally laudatory treatment. In contrast to his praise for the leadership behind the association is Hughes's unconstrained disgust for the many incidents of racial violence, prejudice, and discrimination that motivate the NAACP to act. Hughes gives particular emphasis to the NAACP's long-term campaign against lynching, often describing in horrific detail the crimes committed to terrorize African Americans into submission. Hughes also chronicles the association's fight against the malicious misrepresentation of African Americans in the American entertainment industry and its legal battles over residential segregation ordinances, segregation and discrimination in the United States armed forces, and inequities in health services and public transportation.

Twenty years prior to the publication of *Fight for Freedom,* Hughes had begun writing nonfictional, journalistic prose about these same issues as a regular columnist for the *Chicago Defender,* one of the nation's most influential African American newspapers. In these columns, Hughes projected a narrative voice that often shifted in tone. This voice rarely sounded academic; for all that he did accomplish, Hughes never aspired to be a professional historian, nor was he trained as one. While *Fight for Freedom* reads at times like a standard academic history, more often one cannot help but discern the inimitable, varied, and sometimes blues-tinged voice that made Hughes's *Chicago Defender* columns so popular. Similarly, Hughes's prose style itself often varied from column to column, as it does at times in *Fight for Freedom.* Hughes was fond of blending anecdotes—often related in a dialogue between two personas, and sometimes rendered in African American folk vernacular—with descriptive narration. These variations in voice and style paradoxically point to both strengths and weaknesses in *Fight for Freedom.* At their best, they remind readers—in the midst of some of the most heartbreaking moments in the nation's history—of the blues maxim "laughing to keep from crying." Whatever his subject, Hughes always found redemption in humor. At their worst, these variations make *Fight for Freedom* read like a newspaper society column, as when Hughes devotes four pages of text to Kivie Kaplan's NAACP Life Membership Campaign, complete with a long roster of names.

These stylistic variations did not go unnoticed by Hughes's contemporaries, whose reviews of *Fight for Freedom* reveal critical debates similar to those he faced throughout his career as a professional writer. On the one hand were critics who celebrated the very characteristics that had long endeared Hughes to a broad, popular audience: clear, unaffected language that could be folksy without being trite; subtle yet sharply pointed commentary on racial discrimination and violence; and finally a blues sensibility that balanced even the most painful experiences with humor. On the other hand were those who bemoaned a lack of keener analysis in Hughes's writing. For these critics, *Fight for Freedom* was at best an introductory history of the NAACP. At worst, the book served as little more than an uncritical advertisement.

Arna Bontemps published the most eloquent review of *Fight for Freedom* in the February 1963 *Crisis.* Referring to the story of the NAACP as an "American epic," Bontemps situates Hughes as the "singularly appropriate" poet to write its history. Hughes had grown up with the NAACP, Bontemps notes, and the poem that had launched Hughes's career, "The Negro Speaks of Rivers," became for Bontemps, "along with the Du Bois editorials and Jean Toomer's 'Song of the Son,' the voice of the Association itself." The poet and literary critic J. Saunders Redding also noted the epic nature of the NAACP's history. Redding surmised "that probably no one else could do as well" as Hughes in terms of capturing the "human-ness and the drama" behind the association's achievements with passion and, when appropriate, humor. Both in response to and anticipatory of critics who faulted the book's lack of documentation and Hughes's often uncritical praise for the NAACP, Redding's November 1962 review in the *Baltimore Afro-American Magazine* elevates *Fight for Freedom*'s emphasis on human-interest storytelling over "dry as dust" historical or sociological treatises: "Certainly the story of the NAACP was no job for the formal historian or the sociologist, either of whom might easily and perhaps excusably have missed the drama of it."[26]

Other reviewers who praised *Fight for Freedom* perceptively noted Hughes's intention of demonstrating the repetitive nature of racial history in the United States. Writing for the *Chicago Tribune*, Era Bell Thompson, a managing editor of *Ebony*, lauded both the historical consciousness of Hughes's book and its timeliness: "In 1905 . . . Dr. W. E. B. Du Bois said what Rev. Martin Luther King is saying in 1962: 'We want manhood suffrage and we want it now.'" Similarly, a reviewer for the *New York Herald Tribune* stressed the importance of *Fight for Freedom* in the context of ongoing battles for civil rights, calling it "a valuable handbook for such diverse insurgents as African nationalists, sit-ins and Freedom Riders, Southern historians and Muslims." Irving Dilliard aptly summarized the tenor of many reviewers' enthusiasm for *Fight for Freedom* in a single line in the *Saturday Review*: "Somebody ought to put it in every library in the country!"[27]

Very few reviews of *Fight for Freedom* were outright negative, but one reviewer was compelled to dismiss both the book and its author

26. Bontemps, "Marching Song," *Crisis* 70 (February 1963): 121–22; Redding, "Langston Hughes Brings Out Tears, Laughter in 'The NAACP Story,'" *Baltimore Afro-American Magazine,* November 10, 1962, p. 4.

27. Thompson, "The Most Damned Group of Respectable Citizens," *Chicago Tribune,* September 9, 1962, pt. 4, p. 4; H.F.W., Sr., "The Week in Nonfiction," *New York Herald Tribune Book Review,* September 23, 1962, p. 13; Dilliard, "A Poet Asks: How Long Is a While?" *Saturday Review* 45 (September 29, 1962): 32–33.

for a single offending page. Hughes recounts the story of Westley W. Law, a letter carrier in Savannah, Georgia, who was fired from his job in 1961 over allegations of misconduct and inefficiency. At the time Law was president of the Georgia branch of the NAACP and a member of the association's Board of Directors, which quickly protested his dismissal "on trumped-up charges" via a telegram to President John F. Kennedy. Kennedy encouraged the Savannah postmaster to reconsider his criticism of the letter carrier, and Law was soon reinstated. Of the incident, Hughes reported that "only the stern pressure and vigilance of the [NAACP] was responsible for nipping in the bud this ignominious persecution of a Negro letter carrier." In a review for the *Charleston Evening Post* entitled "NAACP Story Glosses Over Many Topics," Manning Rubin charged Hughes with willfully omitting important details of "the notorious Law case," particularly those concerning Law's alleged shortcomings on the job. "This treatment of the Law incident," Rubin pointedly suggests, "gives you an idea of what to expect in reading *Fight for Freedom*."[28]

The most consistent critiques lodged against *Fight for Freedom* pertained to Hughes's partisanship and methodology, particularly the dearth of scholarly documentation and critical analysis in the telling of the history. While Rubin's critique focused on a specific passage from the text, the historian George B. Tindall was much broader in his dismissal of *Fight for Freedom*. Published in the December 1962 *Progressive*, Tindall's scathing review concedes that the book is more skillfully written than Robert L. Jack's 1943 *History of the National Association for the Advancement of Colored People*. Nevertheless, Tindall labels *Fight for Freedom* "a superficially researched publicist's tract for the NAACP rather than a critical history." Tindall rightly notes Hughes's avoidance of anything that might suggest internal conflict within the NAACP. Conspicuously absent in Hughes's history, for example, is "the important policy struggle of the Thirties between the integrationists and the Du Bois group that supported separate economic development as the basis for future gains." A more recent policy crisis, resulting from the direct action movement's impatience with the NAACP's traditional legal approach, constitutes a missed opportunity for Hughes to analyze the association's effectiveness in the early 1960s. Writing for the *National Guardian*, Len Holt was not quite so dismissive of *Fight for Freedom* but still found the

28. "NAACP Story Glosses Over Many Topics," *Charleston Evening Post*, August 31, 1962, p. 8B.

book to be overgenerous in its support for the NAACP and uncritical in its approach: "Where is the analysis of why things happen to the NAACP, instead of the simple recitation of its history?" Even in some of the most positive reviews, critics were reluctant to give the book unqualified praise. Haynes Johnson, writing for the *Washington Star* in 1962, found much to value in the book, but suggested that Hughes's reticence in critiquing the NAACP or chronicling more fully its internal struggles and fight to remain viable to a more militant generation of African Americans gave *Fight for Freedom* the air of "a campaign tract."[29]

Contemporary readers of *Fight for Freedom* will likely note that these critiques are not unwarranted. Hughes did not approach this book as a scholar, and those expecting a well-documented study that analyzes the difficult political decisions and internal conflicts of the NAACP will not find it in this volume. Nor is *Fight for Freedom* a dispassionate history. As Hughes makes clear in his postscript, the NAACP is inextricably linked to his earliest awareness of how racial difference was made a liability in the United States rather than a cause for celebrating America's diversity. The association defied this aspect of American culture at every turn. In this respect, the actions of the NAACP are always ultimately beneficial, its leaders always heroic. Hughes thus privileges the victories of the association over the defeats, and some readers may feel they are getting only part of the story.

Yet readers interested in a basic history of the NAACP's first fifty years, narrated by a master storyteller who knew firsthand many of the people and events about which he wrote, will not be disappointed. Hughes tells the stories of these people and events in the familiar manner with which he related aspects of his own life story in *The Big Sea* and *I Wonder as I Wander,* interspersing historical facts with compelling anecdotes that often frame subtly ironic commentaries on various themes. The result is a history that also provides a lens through which to view Hughes's attitudes in the early 1960s toward the ways in which the NAACP addressed the vital social, cultural, political, and economic issues central to its agenda. Readers interested in how these attitudes varied over the course of a long writing career now have access, for the first time, to a single edition that includes both *Fight for Freedom* and other nonfictional

29. Tindall, "Books: The Unfinished Emancipation," *Progressive* 26 (December 1962): 63–64, 66; Holt, "In Praise of NAACP," *National Guardian* (October 8, 1962): 9; Johnson, "A History of the NAACP by Hughes," *Washington Star,* August 26, 1962, p. E5.

writing related to Hughes's relationship with the NAACP. Thus, as a unique contribution to the oeuvre of an African American writer whose full significance to American literature, history, and culture will continue to be defined well into the twenty-first century, *Fight for Freedom and Other Writings on Civil Rights* constitutes an indispensable text.[30]

30. For more on issues related to the NAACP, see Leonard C. Archer, *Black Images in the American Theatre: NAACP Protest Campaigns—Stage, Screen, Radio and Television* (Brooklyn, N.Y.: Pageant-Poseidon, 1973); Christopher C. De Santis, ed., *Langston Hughes and the* Chicago Defender: *Essays on Race, Politics, and Culture, 1942–62* (Urbana: University of Illinois Press, 1995); Minnie Finch, *The NAACP: Its Fight for Justice* (Metuchen, N.J.: Scarecrow Press, 1981); Kenneth W. Goings, *The NAACP Comes of Age: The Defeat of Judge John J. Parker* (Bloomington: Indiana University Press, 1990); Charles Flint Kellogg, *NAACP, a History of the National Association for the Advancement of Colored People* (Baltimore: Johns Hopkins University Press, 1967); Edward B. Muse, *Paying for Freedom: History of the NAACP and the Life Membership Program, 1909–1987* (Baltimore: National Association for the Advancement of Colored People, 1986); Wilson Record, *Race and Radicalism: The NAACP and the Communist Party in Conflict* (Ithaca, N.Y.: Cornell University Press, 1964); Barbara Joyce Ross, *J. E. Spingarn and the Rise of the NAACP, 1911–1939* (New York: Atheneum, 1972); Mark W. Tushnet, *The NAACP's Legal Strategy against Segregated Education, 1925–1950* (Chapel Hill: University of North Carolina Press, 1987); Carolyn Wedin, *Inheritors of the Spirit: Mary White Ovington and the Founding of the NAACP* (New York: Wiley, 1998); Sondra Kathryn Wilson, ed., *In Search of Democracy: The NAACP Writings of James Weldon Johnson, Walter White, and Roy Wilkins (1920–1977)* (New York: Oxford University Press, 1999); and Robert L. Zangrando, *NAACP Crusade against Lynching, 1909–1950* (Philadelphia: Temple University Press, 1980).

A Note on the Text

This edition of *Fight for Freedom* is based on the original edition published by W. W. Norton and Company in 1962. The texts of "One More Conference," "Emmett Till, Mississippi, and Congressional Investigations," and "Remarks by Langston Hughes in Acceptance of the 45th Spingarn Medal" are based on Hughes's file copies housed in the Yale Collection of American Literature at the Beinecke Rare Book and Manuscript Library, Yale University. The essays and newspaper columns included in this volume are based on photocopies from the original sources. In preparing *Fight for Freedom and Other Writings on Civil Rights,* I have made silent corrections of obvious misspellings and typographical errors, unless Hughes intentionally altered standard spelling and usage to convey African American folk vernacular. These corrections are not substantive, but are rather attempts to regularize inconsistent typesetting in the originals. Stylistic inconsistencies among the various works included have been allowed to stand.

Although Hughes's bibliography and appendix to *Fight for Freedom* are dated, they are included without alteration to preserve the original text as a product of a specific period in history. The footnotes to my introduction indicate more recent sources for readers interested in pursuing the story of the NAACP beyond 1962.

Fight for Freedom

The Story of the NAACP

(1962)

The sins of omission are many in this necessarily small book about a *big* subject. But some day there will be a full and definitive study of the NAACP. Some day, too, there will be an America that will have no need of an NAACP. This volume is dedicated to the Youth Councils of the NAACP that help so greatly to bring about a truly democratic America.

Contents

Acknowledgments

The author is greatly indebted to the published works of Carter G. Woodson, John Hope Franklin, J. Saunders Redding, Mary White Ovington, W. E. B. Du Bois, James Weldon Johnson, Walter White, Roi Ottley, Arna Bontemps, Francis L. Broderick, Henry Lee Moon, and Florence Murray, and to the archives of the National Association for the Advancement of Colored People, for much of the information used in this book.

His thanks go also to Arthur Spingarn, Roy Wilkins, Thurgood Marshall, Jack Greenberg, and Mrs. Amy Spingarn for information and materials not otherwise available, as well as for helpful conferences relative to some of the subject matter; to George Bass and Jesse De-Vore for invaluable research assistance; and to John Morsell for editorial assistance.

1

The First Decade

Five Famous Letters

The most *famous* initials in America are N.A.A.C.P.

The most *talked-about* non-political organization in America is the N.A.A.C.P.

The most *written-about* voluntary association in America is the N.A.A.C.P.

The most *damned* group of respectable citizens and, on the other hand, one of the most praised groups in America, is the N.A.A.C.P.

These initials—N.A.A.C.P.—stand for the National Association for the Advancement of Colored People.

Since even when used as a unit—NAACP—as is now customary, this combination of letters is not a natural syllabic sound—like NATO, for example—the initials are pronounced in full, letter by letter. By group effort in recent years the men and women behind these five letters have changed the legal and social history of the United States and they are still effecting monumental changes today.

Because of its amazing national leverage, the NAACP is continuous front-page news. No day goes by but that somewhere in the United States—in the press, in magazines, in the *Congressional Record,* in newsreels, on radio and television—these initials are printed, visualized, or broadcast. Not a week goes by but that somewhere the lawyers of the NAACP are in court defending its members against arrest, fines, or imprisonment.

More NAACP members have undergone arrest in recent years than have members of the Communist party. Yet the NAACP has never been labeled a subversive organization—except by extreme reactionaries, race-baiters, and the Ku Klux Klan.

In some southern communities it is tantamount to a crime to belong to the NAACP. But former United States Senator Lehman is on its Board of Directors, as are Ralph Bunche of the United Nations, and Eleanor Roosevelt. Robert C. Weaver, Administrator of the Housing and Home Finance Agency, is a former Board chairman. Nelson A. Rockefeller, governor of New York, is a life member, and so is Richard Cardinal Cushing of Boston.

More suits brought before the Supreme Court in Washington by lawyers of the NAACP have been decided favorably than is true of suits by any other similar organization petitioning the court.

More nationally prominent Negroes—many of them are in *Who's Who*—belong to the NAACP than to any other single organization. Yet the NAACP is interracial, having thousands of white adherents. Mary White Ovington, one of its founders, was a white woman. Its long-time president (since 1940), Arthur B. Spingarn, is not a Negro, nor is Lloyd Garrison, chairman of its National Legal Committee. The chairman of its Life Membership Committee is Kivie Kaplan. And one of its most consistent donors is an American-born Chinese. The NAACP practices the integration it preaches. Its composition is truly American.

What the NAACP Is

The National Association for the Advancement of Colored People defines itself as an organization seeking "to end racial discrimination and segregation in all public aspects of American life."

Both in influence and in size of membership, the NAACP is the foremost civil-rights organization in the United States. Its national office in New York directs some 1500 local branches with nearly 400,000 members across the country.

At the time of its founding more than half a century ago, one of the NAACP's major objectives was the abolition of lynchings—which have about disappeared from American soil. Another priority goal then, as now, was equal education for every child and the opening of all publicly supported institutions to all who wished to study. A pressing objective has always been the extension and protection of every citizen's right to vote, but specifically that of the Negro who is so often denied this basic democratic right in the Deep South. Freedom to purchase property and to live in the area of one's choice, to travel without being segregated, to secure meals and lodgings in restaurants and hotels that are open to the general public, and to read books in libraries, sit in public parks, look at pictures in museums, and watch animals in zoos have been and are vital concerns of the NAACP. A further concern is to inform all America of the un-American difficulties its Negro citizens have experienced, and to make clear that these continuing difficulties are not only a blot on the shield of democracy but a hindrance to the development of a large segment of its human potential which America can ill afford to neglect.

Through its legal defense work, the NAACP seeks court rulings to uphold constitutional rights so often breached by state or local laws and to prevent the unfair enforcement of local statutes in regard to Negroes. It seeks new civil-rights legislation where needed. Through its magazine, *The Crisis,* its press service, and its mass meetings and speakers' bureaus, it seeks to explain its objectives to all who read or listen. In every way possible, it attempts "to create a climate of public opinion in favor of equal rights and human brotherhood."

How It All Began

Because of certain historical factors stemming from slavery (over which those of us living today had no control) the United States inherited something called the race problem. It has often mistakably been called the Negro problem. But this perhaps is a misnomer, for if Negroes are a problem to white Americans, whites are even more of a problem to Negroes. To deal with this double-edged problem is one of the functions of the NAACP.

Historically, it was *white* people who brought Africans to the western world against their will and sold them on the docks to other whites. A booming slave trade was soon established; and for more than two hundred years the clank of slave chains could be heard from New Orleans to Boston and all the ports between. Auctioneers offered men, women, and children to the highest bidders. From 1619 to 1861, the crack of whips compelled Negro people to go where white people wished them to go, do what the whites ordered them to do, work at any tasks assigned them, eat whatever food they were given—in short, to live and die entirely at the whim of their masters. Their children were born into slavery. A slave had no rights his master was duty-bound to respect. Because some people in America still think that a Negro has no rights a white man is duty-bound to respect, there is need for the NAACP.

The captive Africans aboard ship on the long voyage across the Atlantic Ocean to the New World in the 17th and 18th centuries often came from various tribes speaking different tongues; nor did they know where they were headed. Even so, there are records of organized revolts on the earliest of the slave ships. One well-documented and famous mutiny was that of the Mendi slaves aboard the schooner *Amistad* in 1839. Led by

Cinque, an African chieftain's son, the Mendi took over the schooner in Caribbean waters, recharted its course, and eventually landed in New Haven. Ardent abolitionists carried the Mendi's fight for freedom all the way to the United States Supreme Court. No less a person than John Quincy Adams argued their case. The Supreme Court eventually decided in their favor, and the Negro captives of the *Amistad* and their leader Cinque returned to Africa free men. Another successful slave revolt on the high seas occurred in 1841 on the *Creole* sailing from Virginia to New Orleans. The 130 captives aboard took over the *Creole* at sea and guided the boat into the harbor at Nassau. There they were allowed to remain, free in spite of charges of stealing and of threats of war against that British colony by the United States government.

Not all slaves, however, were as astute or as lucky as those on the *Amistad* and the *Creole*. Hunger strikes and mass suicide aboard ship were more common than revolts. Slaves chained together sometimes leaped overboard in mid-ocean—valuable human cargo that went voluntarily to the sharks in the sea rather than to the sharks of the slave system. No African wanted to be a slave. Some preferred death rather than slavery, and many did die before reaching land.

Other slaves were scarcely on shore before they began to plan their escape. Some ran away from the southern plantations and joined the Indians in the swamps. Others just ran, without knowing where they were going. The runaways were pursued by slave-catchers with dogs. If captured they were whipped severely; some were killed. Because it was hard for a Negro bondsman to gain freedom *alone,* it was inevitable that secret organizations of slaves came into existence whose whispered objective was freedom.

In the century or so before the Civil War, hundreds of widely scattered slave revolts took place, some of them carefully organized. In New York City, 31 slaves were put to death in 1741 for planning a revolt. In Virginia, during the summer of 1800, Gabriel Prosser stealthily banded together more than 1000 slaves to rise against the planters. His intent was to march on Richmond, killing and burning along the way; but a great September storm frustrated his plans, and he and many of his followers were put to death. In Charleston in 1822, Denmark Vesey died on the scaffold with 36 other Negroes when his plans for a rebellion were discovered. In 1831 the whole South was thrown into a state of panic when black Nat Turner and his well-organized freedom seekers massacred some 60 Virginia slaveholders. More than 100 slaves were executed for conspiring to be free. The seeds of Negro organization, carefully planned as these revolts indicate, were sown long before physical freedom came.

The earliest Negro organizations permitted by white Americans were religious. Although slaveholders in some communities permitted Negroes to have churches, in most of the South any gathering of Negroes whatsoever was prohibited. Such regulations were enforced with special vigor after the great revolts of the 1800's; as a result, even religious organizations were almost impossible. But prior to 1800 there were Negro churches in Virginia and Georgia, and in 1805 a Negro Baptist church existed at Mound Bayou, Mississippi. From these Negro churches eventually developed fraternal, social, and civic organizations, with the church serving as a meeting place. In general, however, Negro churches and their pastors were looked upon with disfavor by whites in the slaveholding states, because any organization of Negroes could be dangerous. Indeed, any persons concerned with ameliorating the lot of the Negro were suspect by those seeking to maintain the status quo—just as today the NAACP is suspect by those who resist change.

Before the NAACP

The earliest active groups of Negro people to band together openly *on behalf of Negro rights* had, perforce, to be in the North. The first National Negro Convention was held in Philadelphia in 1830. Its concern was "the oppression of our brethren in a country whose republican constitution declares *'that all men are born free and equal.'*" And its assembled delegates earnestly requested "brethren throughout the United States to co-operate with us by forming societies auxiliary to the Parent Institution." For a number of years thereafter, these National Conventions concerned with race relations were held regularly; although largely attended by Negroes, eventually some prominent whites, such as the abolitionist William Lloyd Garrison, took part. Interestingly enough, more than a hundred years before the NAACP secured its epoch-making school desegregation decision from the United States Supreme Court, Negro delegates meeting at Troy, New York, in 1847 urged Negro students to seek admission to white colleges.

In 1849 a State Convention of Colored Citizens of Ohio resolved to aid escaped slaves. Further, it asked for educational rights "in common with others, for we pay school taxes in the same proportion," and it stated its belief that Negroes were "entitled to all privileges—moral, mental, political and social—to which other men attain." In subsequent years numerous regional Negro organizations having much the same objectives came into being—except that after Emancipation, slavery itself was no longer an issue.

The conditions of life for Negroes after the brief period of promise during Reconstruction were in many ways almost as unbearable as under slavery. The white-robed Ku Klux Klan spread violence up and down the highways of the South. Peonage reduced Negro workers to near-bondage again, mobs drove Negro voters from the polls, and the lynch rope kept Negro men from being men. The problems of self-protection, the ballot, civil rights, and full freedom occupied their attention from the First California Negro Convention in 1855 through the Convention of Colored Men of Texas in 1883, the meetings of the Young Men's Progressive Association of New Orleans in 1878, and the Macon, Georgia, Consultation Convention in 1888, to the National Afro-American League founded at Chicago in 1890. Each new Negro organization found itself faced over the years with the same old problems—the tragically tangled skein of race relations—that the NAACP is still trying to solve today.

The Niagara Movement

Even so scholarly a group as the American Negro Academy, founded in Washington in 1897 with the express purpose of "the promotion of literature, science and art," found itself impelled to include among its objectives "the defense of the Negro against vicious assault." For the word *assault* might literally mean physical attack against even intellectuals of color. Fresh in the memories of those framing the Academy's initial statement might well have been the expulsion from Memphis of Ida B. Wells, a brilliant young Negro journalist whose newspaper offices were demolished after she exposed the names of various members of a lynch mob.

Among the founding members of the American Negro Academy was William Edward Burghardt Du Bois. It was Du Bois who in 1905 issued a personal call from Atlanta:

> The time seems more than ripe for organized, determined and aggressive action on the part of men who believe in Negro freedom and growth. . . . I write you to propose a conference during the coming summer for the following purposes: 1. To oppose firmly the present methods of

strangling honest criticism, manipulating public opinion and centralizing political power by means of the improper and corrupt use of money and influence. 2. To organize thoroughly the intelligent and honest Negroes throughout the United States for the purpose of insisting on manhood rights, industrial opportunity and spiritual freedom. 3. To establish and support proper organs of news and public opinion.

As a result of the Du Bois proposal there assembled at Niagara Falls (on the Canadian side because no hotels were open to Negroes on the American side) a group of 29 Negro professional men, ministers, editors, and teachers from various parts of the country. They formed an organization known as the Niagara Movement.

At its second annual meeting a year later (held at Harpers Ferry in tribute to the militant abolitionist, John Brown), more than 100 prominent Negroes were present. Du Bois stated their objectives in his keynote speech: "We want full manhood suffrage and we want it now. . . . We want discrimination in public accommodation to cease. . . . We claim the right of freemen to walk, talk, and be with them that wish to be with us. . . . We want the Constitution of the country enforced. . . . We want our children educated. . . . And here on the scene of John Brown's martyrdom we reconsecrate ourselves, our honor, our property to the final emancipation of the race which John Brown died to make free. . . . We are men! We will be treated as men. And we shall win."

The members of the Niagara Movement held their third meeting in historic Faneuil Hall in Boston in 1907. The following year public rallies were held in New York, Cleveland, Minneapolis, Baltimore, and Washington. Meanwhile, there was in process of formation a group which enabled most members of the all-Negro Niagara Movement to join forces with a similar-minded band of white Americans dedicated to the same objectives. They met together in New York in 1909 in a National Negro Conference which within a year became the National Association for the Advancement of Colored People.

Half a Man

The idea of the NAACP really began with a letter written by Mary White Ovington. A young social worker, free-lance writer, and humanitarian, Miss Ovington was also a woman of independent means who, beneath a most feminine exterior, had a will of her own. In the summer of 1906 she was assigned by the *New York Evening Post* to cover the second annual meeting of the Niagara Movement. What she saw and heard at Harper's Ferry impressed her deeply, for her concern over the years had become the same as that of the Negroes assembled there.

When shortly before the turn of the century Mary White Ovington finished her studies at Radcliffe (then generally known as the Harvard Annex for Women), she assisted in establishing the Greenpoint Settlement in Brooklyn where for seven years she worked with the underprivileged. In 1904 she became a researcher on the staff of Manhattan's Greenwich House, conducting a four-year survey of the Negro in New York City. This survey resulted in her first book, *Half a Man,* which revealed that there was a race problem not just in the South but in the North as well. Not only for purposes of her study but because of a deep interest in Negroes, especially children, Miss Ovington moved into the Tuskegee apartments on San Juan Hill. In this Negro neighborhood in Manhattan's West Sixties bordering the infamous Hell's Kitchen, there were racial skirmishes almost daily; sometimes even Negro children were attacked by older whites. Here all the problems of a segregated community became Miss Ovington's problems—racial violence, inadequate police protection, the blindness of political officials to vice and crime, underpaid workers, the mothers whose work as domestic servants left their children with no one to look after them all day, the young people with aspirations but little to which they might aspire. Even in New York, the young social worker discovered, the Negro was half a man.

Then Dr. Du Bois invited Miss Ovington to attend the Atlanta Conference at Atlanta University. In Georgia she first saw legal segregation—but she also met Negro men like Dr. Du Bois and Dr. Crogman who *walked* wherever they went in Atlanta rather than ride on the Jim Crow cars. She saw that city's tumble-down shanties—"worse than New York's tenements"—and the woefully inadequate schools for Negro children, and learned how voting restrictions kept Negro citizens from having any voice in politics. She noted that southern white men did not remove their hats when talking to Negro women, yet always did so in the presence of white women. She learned too that where prejudice was greatest, more Negroes had been forced to go into business for themselves, many with considerable success, but that white mobs had no more respect for Negroes who got ahead in business than they did for the poor and illiterate.

When Miss Ovington visited Atlanta again in 1906 after the race riots, she saw the wreckage of Negro homes and businesses. In the rural areas of Alabama she found sharecroppers working under conditions not unlike those of slavery. She learned how Negro women were abused by white men, and how Negro males, fighting to protect their women, might be lynched without anyone ever being punished for the crime. The horror of these conditions caused Miss Ovington to decide, as she later wrote, to "give what strength and ability I had to the problem of securing for the American Negro those rights and privileges into which every white American is born." To this objective she devoted the rest of her life.

Call to Action

The letter which eventually led to the founding of the NAACP was written to William English Walling by Mary White Ovington immediately after she read his moving account of the Springfield, Illinois, race riots in the *Independent*. Walling's story vividly described how for two days a mob surged through the streets of that city in the summer of 1908 looting and burning Negro homes; they lynched a Negro barber and an 84-year-old man for no reason at all except that the prisoners the whites were looking for were not in the jail. The mob seriously injured some 70 persons, and drove hundreds of Negroes from the city. All this violence occurred near the Lincoln mansion and less than two miles from the Great Emancipator's grave. Walling concluded his article, which he called "Race War in the North," by invoking "the spirit of the abolitionists, of Lincoln and of Lovejoy" to help alleviate the repressive conditions of the Negro. "Who realizes," he asked, "the seriousness of the situation, and what large and powerful body of citizens is ready to come to their aid?"

In her letter to Walling, Miss Ovington suggested that they explore what could be done to remedy the deplorable state of race relations in the North and South. In the decade preceding the Springfield riots there were over 1000 lynchings in the United States. In 1901 alone, 105 Negroes were publicly done to death by mobs in mass orgies of violence; they had no protection from the police and their lynchers were not brought to trial. Since 1900 an epidemic of race riots had swept the country from Texas and Georgia as far north as Pennsylvania, Ohio, and Illinois, causing millions of dollars' worth of property damage and killing or wounding hundreds of people. All this violence, added to the everyday handicaps which Negroes already suffered, presented a dire picture indeed.

To discuss this sorry situation, three people met in Walling's apartment in Manhattan in the first week of the new year 1909. These three—Miss Ovington, a wealthy Northerner who had made a thorough study of racial problems; William English Walling, a southern journalist with liberal racial views; and Henry Moskovitz, a Jewish social worker—all were concerned with democracy and the Negro. They decided to issue a call for a conference to be signed by a number of prominent Americans. It would be released on February 12, 1909, the 100th anniversary of Abraham Lincoln's birth. Written by Oswald Garrison Villard of the *New York Post*, the call read in part:

> The Celebration of the Centennial of the birth of Abraham Lincoln, widespread and grateful as it may be, will fail to justify itself if it takes no note of and makes no recognition of the colored men and women for whom the Great Emancipator labored to assure freedom. . . . If Mr. Lincoln could revisit this country in the flesh, he would be disheartened and discouraged. He would learn that on January 1, 1909, Georgia had rounded out a new confederacy by disfranchising the Negro, after the manner of all the other Southern States. He would learn that the Supreme Court of the United States, supposedly a bulwark of American liberties, had refused every opportunity to pass squarely upon this disfranchisement of millions. . . . He would learn that the Supreme Court . . . had laid down the principle that if an individual State chooses, it may "make it a crime for white and colored persons to frequent the same market place at the same time, or appear in an assemblage of citizens convened to consider questions of a public or political nature in which all citizens, without regard to race, are equally interested."
>
> In many States Lincoln would see the black men and women, for whose freedom a hundred thousand soldiers gave their lives, set apart in trains, in which they pay first-class fares for third-class service, and segregated in railway stations and in places of entertainment; he would observe that State after State declines to do its elementary duty in preparing the Negro through education for the best exercise of citizenship. Added to this, the spread of lawless attacks upon the Negro, North, South, and West—even in the Springfield made famous by Lincoln . . . could but shock the author of the sentiment that "government of the people, by the people, for the people, should not perish from the earth."
>
> Silence under these conditions means tacit approval. . . . Hence we call upon all the believers in democracy to join in a National Conference for the discussion of present evils, the voicing of protests, and the renewal of the struggle for civil and political liberty.

This document was signed by sixty persons of distinction—among them, Jane Addams, the famous founder of Hull House; Francis J. Grimké, Washington's militant Negro minister; John Dewey of Columbia University; William Lloyd Garrison of Boston; the Reverend John Haynes Holmes; Alexander Walters, bishop of the African Methodist Episcopal Zion Church; Rabbi Stephen S. Wise; Ida B. Wells Barnett; J. G. Phelps Stokes, the philanthropist; Lincoln Steffens, the famous journalist; Mary E. Woolley, president of Mount Holyoke College; Ray Stannard Baker; Mary Church Terrell; Lillian D. Wald; Brand Whitlock, mayor of Toledo; and Dr. W. E. B. Du Bois.

Birth of the NAACP

The conference that resulted from this call began on May 30, 1909, with an interracial reception at the Henry Street Settlement in New York, and ended on June 1 with a mass meeting at Cooper Union. From these sessions there emerged an organization called the National Negro Committee, consisting of 40 persons. It held four well-attended public meetings during the year and enrolled many additional members.

At the second annual meeting of the National Negro Committee in May, 1910, a new name was chosen, the National Association for the Advancement of Colored People. As such, the organization was incorporated under the laws of the State of New York, and its purposes officially recorded: "To promote equality of rights and eradicate caste or race prejudice among the citizens of the United States; to advance the interest of colored citizens; to secure for them impartial suffrage; and to increase their opportunities for securing justice in the courts, education for their children, employment according to their ability, and complete equality before the law." Among those signing the papers of incorporation were Mary White Ovington, W. E. B. Du Bois, Oswald Garrison Villard (a grandson of William Lloyd Garrison), John Haynes Holmes, and Walter E. Sachs. Although the NAACP did not receive its name until May, 1910, and was not incorporated until the following year, the date of its founding has always been considered to be the date of the call written by Villard—February 12, 1909, the centennial of Lincoln's birth.

The first president of the NAACP was Moorfield Storey, the distinguished Boston lawyer; William English Walling became chairman of the Executive Committee; John E. Milholland, treasurer; Oswald Garrison

Villard, disbursing treasurer; Frances Blascoer, executive secretary; and W. E. B. Du Bois, director of publicity and research. Thanks to Oswald Garrison Villard, the NAACP obtained a rent-free office in the *Evening Post* building on Vesey Street. From the beginning the organization and its workers were interracial. Its Board of Directors included eight former members of the Niagara Movement.

Within three months after its organization the NAACP opened its first local office in Chicago. That summer also its legal work, which was eventually to have so great an effect upon American racial patterns, began, when NAACP lawyers filed a petition of pardon for a Negro sharecropper in South Carolina. This man had been given the death penalty for slaying a constable who burst into his cabin after midnight to charge him with breach of contract. The young NAACP initiated an intensive publicity campaign by means of press releases and pamphlets exposing acts of racial injustice and setting forth the Association's objectives. The first issue of its official organ, *The Crisis,* appeared in November under the editorship of Dr. Du Bois.

Du Bois and *The Crisis*

William Edward Burghardt Du Bois was born in Massachusetts. After graduating from Fisk University in Nashville, he studied at the University of Berlin and received his Ph.D. in sociology at Harvard. His doctoral dissertation, *The Suppression of the African Slave Trade to the United States of America,* was published in 1896 as the first volume in a newly inaugurated series, the Harvard Historical Studies. A significant piece of scholarship, it is still in circulation. More than a dozen books—essays, fiction, scholarly studies—have come from his pen since then, the most famous being *The Souls of Black Folk,* published in 1903 and frequently reissued. For more than half a century Dr. Du Bois was considered the dean of Negro writers and the foremost intellectual of his race. Thousands of young Negro men and women have been guided and inspired by his example as writer, editor, speaker, teacher, and interpreter of the race problem.

After fourteen years of teaching and research at Atlanta University, Du Bois threw in his lot with the newly founded, financially insecure NAACP. As was true of Mary White Ovington, the plight of the Negro people was the thing closest to his heart. In *The Souls of Black Folk* Du Bois wrote: "The problem of the Twentieth Century is the problem of the color line—the relation of the darker to the lighter races of men in Asia and Africa, in America and the islands of the sea." To this problem he devoted his enormous erudition, his years of sociological training, and his gift of words. His mouthpiece was *The Crisis,* the magazine of the NAACP. *The Crisis* took its name from "The Present Crisis," a poem by the abolitionist James Russell Lowell:

> . . . to side with Truth is noble when we share her wretched
>   crust,
> Ere her cause bring fame and profit, and 't is prosperous to
>   be just;
> Then it is the brave man chooses, while the coward stands
>   aside,
> Doubting in his abject spirit, till his Lord is
>   crucified . . .

As a result of his brilliant editorials in *The Crisis,* that periodical achieved unprecedented circulation among Negro readers and attracted the attention of many whites as well. The initial issue of 1000 copies was soon exhausted. By the end of its first year it had 12,000 readers. Eventually its circulation rose to more than 100,000. It spotlighted distinguished Negro "Men of the Month" and in "Following the Color Line" featured news of race problems and progress around the world. There was a month-to-month résumé of NAACP activities, and each year a roundup with photographs of Negro college graduates, records of advanced degrees, Phi Beta Kappa selections, and other academic achievements. Reviews of books and plays relating to Negro life were an important part of the contents. Young writers published their poems and stories in *The Crisis.* The poet-novelist, Jessie Redmon Fauset, was appointed to the staff as managing editor. Harvard-trained Augustus Granville Dill was business manager.

In the first issue Du Bois stated that *The Crisis* would stand for "the highest ideals of American democracy, and for reasonable but earnest and persistent attempts to gain these rights and realize these ideals." *The Crisis* became America's leading publication devoted to the Negro, a position it held for well over a quarter of a century. When it became self-supporting, with its staff paid from its own income rather than with Association funds, *The Crisis* became the only magazine in the country devoted to social service that was not dependent upon subsidy. Its founding was one of the great contributions of the NAACP to national cultural life.

The Early Years of the NAACP

Every time a Negro was arrested, the alleged lawbreaker was customarily identified in the press by race. Other Americans—Irish, German, Italian—when haled into court were never labeled ethnically by the newspapers. But headlines continually read: NEGRO STEALS CLOCK; NEGRO HOLDS UP MAN; BLACK THUG WAYLAYS TEACHER; and so on. At the same time, the press seldom published any news of a favorable nature relative to Negro achievements. During its first year of existence, the NAACP set about to remedy this situation. One gratifying result was that the Associated Press promptly ordered that there be no stress on race or religion in its crime stories. Eventually most of the major newspapers in the country ceased to identify non-white legal offenders by race and began to capitalize the word *Negro;* northern publications sometimes even carried news about Negroes other than that taken from police blotters.

The first case the Legal Committee of the NAACP handled that concerned housing involved a group of Kansas City Negroes whose newly purchased homes in a formerly white neighborhood were bombed. With this case they began to lay the groundwork for future court attacks on residential segregation. A campaign against the exclusion of Negro lawyers from the American Bar Association was initiated. The services of the William J. Burns detective agency were utilized to uncover the facts in the mob burning of a Negro laborer in Coatesville, Pennsylvania, and the data were turned over to the governor with a petition calling for the arrest and conviction of the lynchers.

NAACP intervention in 1912 prevented the discharge of Negro firemen on the Southern Railroad when the white Railroad Brotherhoods sought to displace them. On the civil-rights front, a Negro denied entrance to Palisades Amusement Park just across the river from New York was not only awarded $300 damages through the efforts of the NAACP, but was given a season ticket to the park as well. Ever since then, the park has been open to Negro patrons, although further action was necessary to open up the swimming pool and the dance pavilion.

News of these early victories was spread across the country in the Negro press as well as in the columns of *The Crisis,* whose paid circulation had grown to 24,000 within two years. From Boston, Baltimore, and the District of Columbia to as far west as Tacoma, Washington, a new branch of the NAACP was opened almost every month. By the end of 1913 the National Association for the Advancement of Colored People had 24 branches in the United States, and its budget had increased to

$16,000. But violence and racial discrimination were increasing, not diminishing. That year 79 persons were lynched. In 1912 the count was 63—an average of more than one mass murder a week. An expanded NAACP was a national necessity.

In January, 1914, Dr. Joel E. Spingarn, distinguished professor of English at Columbia University, was elected chairman of the Board of Directors. A man of means, he was able to give a great deal of his time and effort to the young organization. His charm and culture enabled him to interest others like himself in its objectives—persons with influence in high places or with access to the media of public opinion. As a scholar steeped in the humanities, he had the interest of all human beings at heart. As an American, he wished to see his country free of racial stigmas. Within the month, Joel Spingarn held conferences and addressed meetings in eight cities, spreading the gospel of the NAACP throughout the Middle West, soliciting support, recruiting members, and creating good will.

His brother, Arthur B. Spingarn, then associated with Charles Studin, took over supervision of the legal work of the NAACP. For twenty-seven years thereafter Arthur Spingarn served as chairman of legal defense without charge to the Association, and often persuaded other distinguished attorneys to lend their services without remuneration. The Spingarn-Studin offices were the rent-free legal headquarters of the NAACP for a number of years.

Mary White Ovington, with her highly competent Negro secretary, Richetta Randolph, kept NAACP office hours from 9 to 5 every day. Dr. Du Bois often worked around the clock, conducting surveys, editing *The Crisis,* speaking and traveling in the interests of the Association. The early years were not easy ones for the devoted few in charge of the national work of the NAACP. But they were gratifying in that these workers could see that their organized efforts were beginning to produce results in more ways than one. By the end of 1914 there were 50 branches of the NAACP in the United States.

The Long Haul

Off to a good start, the young Association still had a long haul. The going was far from easy. Powerful philanthropists, mostly of the Booker T. Washington school of thought, gave the NAACP no aid. Conservative whites and even some prominent Negroes attacked it as "radical." They charged that its program of complete equality was impractical, if not utopian. Some even said that the NAACP platform did race relations in America more harm than good. Few newspapers anywhere gave its activities sympathetic coverage. It was denounced violently in the South. In some cities *The Crisis* could not be sold openly. And there were places in the South where it was impossible to organize branches for fear of mob reprisals. Even so, the Sixth Annual Conference of the NAACP was held in Baltimore, and the Roman Catholic Cardinal Gibbons sent it a personal message of support.

At this conference it was reported that during the preceding year the NAACP had filed a friend-of-the-court brief in a suit to invalidate the State of Oklahoma's "grandfather clause." (Most southern states had enacted laws which exempted from rigorous tests persons whose parents or grandparents were eligible to vote prior to 1860.) This notorious piece of legislation permitted poor and illiterate whites to vote but denied the same right to Negroes. The Supreme Court invalidated this clause in what was hailed as the court's most important decision affecting Negro citizens in twenty-five years.

In its first armed services case, the NAACP secured the release from military prison of a Negro soldier who had been unfairly court-martialed in Honolulu. In Washington a mass meeting of more than 6000 persons was held near the White House to protest increasing discrimination in federal employment under President Woodrow Wilson.

During the months that followed, *The Crisis* for the first time published the voting records of all Congressmen on anti-Negro bills; and all candidates campaigning for national office received from the NAACP questionnaires regarding their stand on civil rights. These procedures, once initiated, became part of the NAACP's activities from then on. The Washington branch of the NAACP was designated the watchdog for any anti-Negro legislation brought before Congress or any hostile action on the part of the executive branch of the government that might come to light. It was discovered that there was then a plan afoot to segregate Negro railway mail clerks into separate units under white foremen, but this plan was abandoned following an NAACP protest. A survey that was published later concerned the separate but supposedly "equal" accommodations for Negroes in rail travel in the South. These Jim Crow accommodations of course were found to be anything but equal. The facts were made available to Congressmen and the public.

From the Los Angeles branch early in 1915 there came to the national office reports of the release in Hollywood of a vicious anti-Negro film,

The Birth of a Nation, based on Thomas Dixon's novel, *The Clansman, An Historical Romance of the Ku Klux Klan,* which pictured Negroes after Emancipation in a viciously distorted light. Negro leaders of the Reconstruction were depicted as venal and uncouth. In one of the most horrifying scenes in the film, a Negro bent on rape chased a beautiful white woman to her death over a cliff. The nightriders of the Ku Klux Klan were portrayed as noble protectors of white womanhood and southern honor. This major Hollywood production with thousands of dollars' worth of publicity behind it was destined to be shown in theaters across the nation. The NAACP felt that such showings at a time when mob violence and race hatred were on the upgrade would do incalculable harm. Protest meetings and picket lines were organized. This constituted the NAACP's first campaign against the malicious misrepresentation of the Negro people in films, on the stage, and in fiction. This campaign had little effect on the film's distribution, but in some cities the worst of its anti-Negro footage was cut, and in a few others it was banned. However, most film critics on the major newspapers hailed the picture as a masterpiece, and its continued showing for many years presented a distorted view of Negroes to the world.

Under Arthur Spingarn's direction, the NAACP Legal Committee endeavored to defeat residential segregation ordinances in St. Louis and in Dallas. President Moorfield Storey successfully argued before the Supreme Court against a Louisville residential segregation ordinance. In St. Louis a temporary injunction was secured restraining officials from enforcing such ordinances. The NAACP planned to take the matter of white primaries into court as soon as a suitable test case presented itself. But Arthur Spingarn did not stay cloistered in his law offices, nor was he concerned with court activities alone. When the National Council of Social Workers removed Negro speakers from its program in Memphis in 1914 out of deference to southern prejudice, Spingarn, with William Pickens and others, marched with signs in front of where it was meeting, picketing the conference. This was probably the first interracial picket line in the South.

Black and White Together

In 1915 William Pickens was appointed director of branches for the growing NAACP. He traveled north and south coordinating activities, recruiting members, and making speeches. A genial, very dark South

Carolinian "man of the people" with a powerful voice, a jolly face, and a smile "like a lighthouse in the sea," Pickens became one of the most popular platform orators in America. Although he had received his Phi Beta Kappa key at Yale, Pickens never lost the common touch and was not averse to using colloquial English in his talks. He had at his command a vast number of humorous stories to send his audiences into gales of laughter. One story he used effectively in his membership drives concerned a Negro coachman who loved to show off his skill with the whip as he drove his white employer down the road. From his seat he would skillfully flick flies off his horse's ears without disturbing the horse. The coachman could even flick a bee from a flower along the road as the carriage went by, or a caterpillar off a leaf. One day the carriage passed a tree on whose branches hornets were swarming from a nest in the crook of a limb near by.

"Let's see you flick a few of those hornets off the end of that limb," his boss said.

"*Oh, no sa-ah-h-h!*" cried the Negro. "I never bother hornets!"

"Why not?" asked the white man.

"They's organized!" answered the Negro.

Pickens would then go on to point out to his audience the value of organization—obviously meaning the NAACP. "But," he would continue with a shrug, "I can't *make* you folks join this great association that is fighting for your rights and mine. It's true that a man can lead a mule to water—but he can't make him drink. Nobody can *make* you join the NAACP. I can't, nobody can. You don't *have* to join. So far as I know, the only things you *have* to do are eat, drink, sleep, stay black, and die—but you can do all these things better—and be *protected in your right to do them*—if you join the NAACP." Pickens recruited many Negro members.

Among the Negroes most active in voluntary service in the Association during its formative years were Dr. F. N. Cardozo of Baltimore; Neval Thomas, George W. Cook, the Grimké brothers, and Mary Church Terrell of Washington; Dr. William Sinclair, whose father had been lynched in South Carolina; George Crawford of New Haven; the Reverend Walter H. Brooks of St. Marks Methodist Church in New York, the Reverend Hutchins C. Bishop of St. Philips Protestant Episcopal Church, the Reverend Adam Clayton Powell, Sr., Bishop Alexander Walters of the AME Zion Church, Bishop John L. Hurst of the African Methodist Episcopal Church, and Dr. V. Morton Jones, woman physician and director of the Lincoln Settlement in Brooklyn.

At a meeting held in New York City early in 1917 to select members of the Board of Directors, 60 persons, Negro and white, were present. *The Crisis* noted that in contrast to the meetings held in its early years, Negro distrust of the sincerity of the whites had disappeared. "Just as one saw that that distrust had vanished, so one recognized a solidarity not only between a few colored and white members, but among thoughtful colored people of the country. . . . One felt that not only among the talented tenth, but among the mass of the race there was a growing confidence in the ability, a growing sense of the dignity, of the colored people." The NAACP gained confidence from its part in this increase of self-respect discernible among the Negro masses and in the increase in interracial solidarity visible within the organization itself.

The Amenia Conference

Booker T. Washington never became affiliated with the NAACP. His philosophy of racial gradualism seemed to many to be in opposition to the methods of the Association. For a generation the famous pioneer of industrial education at Tuskegee had been the darling of American conservatives, while Du Bois was emerging as the knight-in-armor of the liberals and so-called radicals. When Booker T. Washington died in 1915, Du Bois became the foremost spokesman of the Negro people in the United States. His fiery editorials in *The Crisis* were quoted more and more often, even in the *Congressional Record,* and his influence had grown to a point where the *New York Sun* called him "the leading factor in the race question." When Joel Spingarn in 1916 called for a policy-making conference of Negro and white leaders and Dr. Du Bois and Spingarn wrote personal notes urging them to come, 50 distinguished men and women accepted the invitation.

Although not officially an NAACP convention, and by no means limited to its members, such a gathering of prominent persons could hardly have been assembled except at its instigation. This three-day conference was held in August at Troutbeck, the country home of Dr. and Mrs. Joel Spingarn near Amenia, New York, only a few miles from Great Barrington, Massachusetts, where Du Bois was born.

Those who attended the Amenia Conference ranged all the way from southern conservatives like Booker T. Washington's long-time secretary, Emmett J. Scott, to the often-termed "extreme" Negro radical, William Monroe Trotter, whose newspaper, the *Boston Guardian,* promulgated a program of action far more militant than that of the NAACP. The conference was opened by Governor Charles S. Whitman of New York. Other white people attending included Oswald Garrison Villard and the beautiful Inez Milholland, daughter of John Milholland, one of the organizers of the great Race Congress in London in 1911 which Du Bois had attended.

From the Amenia Conference there emerged no precise manifestoes and no formal program of action, but there was a general agreement as to the basic procedures for the bettering of race relations in this country. It was affirmed that old controversies should be forgotten, that Negro leaders should work together for the good of everyone, that political freedom was needed for all regardless of party affiliations, and that education in every form, academic and industrial, should be encouraged for Negro youth. The "peculiar difficulties" involved in working for racial betterment in the South were recognized, and it was agreed that a variety of methods aimed toward the same end might be required in different parts of the country. When the Amenia Conference adjourned, a further unity of liberal thought among progressive Negroes and whites had been achieved.

Cause for a Holiday

In 1916, Woodrow Wilson, a Southerner and a Democrat, was elected President of the United States for the second time. In spite of campaign promises favoring Negro rights, under his administration segregation had grown apace in the national capital and in federal offices. Racial violence had in no wise diminished anywhere in the country, and neither the federal nor state governments made any attempt to bring white lynchers to justice. Lynchings were usually done quite openly and the lynchers appeared proud of their savagery. After making a speech against mob violence at the Ethical Culture Hall in New York, John Haynes Holmes, an NAACP board member, received in the mail a picture postcard from the South showing a lynched Negro surrounded by his killers. Their faces were plainly visible in the photograph. In spite of this clear identification (usual in most lynchings), local authorities never brought anyone to trial. Since lynching was not a federal offense, the federal authorities did nothing, either. For this reason, the NAACP attempted to get Congress to enact a federal anti-lynching law. On the wall of the Association's New York office there was a lynch map of the United States; a pin was stuck in the map at every place where there had been a mob murder. The lower part of this map was black with pins.

In the spring of 1916 there was a lynching of such horror that people throughout America were shocked—even those who were not interested in Negro welfare. On a sunny day in Waco, Texas, 10,000 men, women, and children cheered when Jesse Washington, a 19-year-old Negro mental defective, was burned alive in the public square. Youngsters were held high to watch his agony as the flames crackled. Innumerable photographs were taken of this gruesome spectacle with its carnival atmosphere. The NAACP sent to Texas a white undercover investigator whose findings concerning this human barbecue were published in a special 8-page supplement to *The Crisis* entitled "The Waco Horror." "Washington . . . was dragged through the streets, stabbed, mutilated and finally burned to death in the presence of a crowd of 10,000. . . . After death what was left of his body was dragged through the streets and parts of it sold as souvenirs. His teeth brought $5 apiece and the chain that had bound him 25¢ a link."

Philip Peabody had given the Association $1000 to initiate an anti-lynching fund. President Moorfield Storey immediately contributed a second $1000, and smaller contributions came from hundreds of NAACP members. Within a few months $11,269 had been raised. Renewed pressure was exerted in Washington on behalf of a bill against lynching. That year, 1916, the NAACP distributed more than 200,000 pieces of literature pointing out that the United States of America was the *only* civilized country in the world where human beings were publicly burned alive—without judge, jury, or trial of any sort.

During that year 59 persons—more than one a week—were done to death by mobs: 52 Negro men, 3 white men, 3 Negro women, and a Mexican. The following year, 1917, the year the United States entered the war in defense of democracy, there were 47 lynchings on our democratic soil. It was so unusual for an official entrusted with law enforcement to take any action against a mob that the NAACP presented a silver loving cup to Sheriff Eley of Lima, Ohio, "for devotion to duty in preventing the lynching of a colored prisoner." The presentation was made by the governor of Ohio himself.

In 1919 Missouri Representative L. C. Dyer, at the request of the NAACP, introduced in the House a bill designed to make lynching a federal offense. His proposed legislation never survived southern filibusters in the Senate, though the House passed it in January, 1922, by a vote of 230–119. The year before, five men were lynched on one day in

Valdosta, Georgia. All told, there were 67 hangings or burnings in 1918–19 during the month of May alone. The tally for the year included two women and six children, for mobs did not limit themselves to lynching men or Negroes exclusively. Of the 84 people lynched in 1919, four were white men, two were Mexicans, and one was a woman. Mob violence had gotten entirely out of hand; however, Washington seemed strangely unconcerned. Had it not been for the count kept by the NAACP and the agitation it carried on against such barbarities, the world might never have known to what extent the crime of mass murder had entrenched itself in the United States. In some communities a lynching was a cause for a holiday.

The Shame of America

A major contribution to awakening the national conscience regarding lynching was the publication in 1919 of the findings of an exhaustive review of lynching records. This startling study was entitled *Thirty Years of Lynching in the United States, 1889–1918.*

Within these thirty years, 3224 men and women had been lynched. In only 19 percent of these cases had rape or other sex offenses even been alleged—although the South justified lynching as a "necessary" means of protecting white women from Negro assault. Since 1889 only seven states had not had at least one lynching. Ten states had had more than 100 each. Georgia topped the list with 386. The greatest contributor to mob murder was the South from Texas to the Atlantic seaboard, Kentucky to the Gulf. No lynchings were recorded in four New England states.

In tabulating this study, Martha Gruening and Helen Boardman combed the files of newspapers for three decades. One section of the study, "The Story of One Hundred Lynchings," described the most horrifying hangings, burnings, and shootings. Some incredible things were reported. One Negro being roasted at the stake did not lose consciousness until his lower limbs had been burned away; three Negroes were forced to stand on the rail of a bridge with ropes about their necks, then whipped until they jumped; an insane man in Louisiana was surrounded by a mob and killed as he hid in a tree; an innocent woman was lynched in Tennessee because her brother was accused of thievery; a man thought to be one Ed Claus was riddled with bullets by mobsters who, after they had killed him, discovered he was not Claus at all; a mob in Georgia, having announced its intention of clearing the jail, broke in and massacred seven of its inmates, only one of whom had been convicted of a crime. And in Tennessee a Negro farmer and his two daughters, taking a wagon full of cotton to a gin, were ambushed, all three were hanged from a tree, and the load of cotton was burned under their dangling bodies.

Western mobs went in for hanging, but southern mobs seemed to delight in burning. The *St. Louis Post-Dispatch* reported that Dan Davis, a Negro, screamed as the fire reached his body, " 'Lord, have mercy on my soul,' and that was the last word he spoke, though he was conscious for fully twenty minutes. . . . His black body hung nude in the gray dawn light. . . . Meanwhile the crowd jeered the dying man and uttered suggestive comments of a cannibalistic spirit. Some danced and sang to testify to their enjoyment." In a detailed report of the lynching of Ell Person in 1917, the *Memphis Press* stated that "15,000 men, women and children cheered as they poured the gasoline on the ax fiend and struck the match. They fought and screamed and crowded to get a glimpse of him, and the mob closed in as the flames flared high and the smoke rolled about their heads. . . . The Negro lay in flames, his hands crossed on his chest. If he spoke, no one heard him over the shouts of the crowd. He died quickly, though fifteen minutes later excitable persons still shouted that he lived when they saw the charred remains move as does meat on a hot frying pan."

A mob near Valdosta, Georgia, frustrated at not finding the man they sought for murdering a plantation owner, lynched three innocent Negroes instead; the pregnant wife of one of the three wailed at her husband's death so loudly that the mob seized her and burned her alive, too. As the flames enveloped Mary Turner's body, her unborn child fell to the ground and was trampled underfoot; white parents held their children up to watch.

These were the authenticated facts—with names, dates, and places— that were carried throughout the world in the NAACP booklet on thirty years of lynching. Were not these events documented by innumerable eyewitnesses and widely reported in the press, it would be hard indeed to believe them.

The gentle Mary White Ovington, then chairman of the Board of the NAACP, wrote, "I can think of no more nauseating work for a kindly set of people than this task of setting forth brutality. We felt that it was the only way to end a method of community life in which a dark-skinned group was denied education, economic opportunity, and a full cultural life, while another group, the poor whites, also ill-educated, penniless, were encouraged to consider themselves inherently superior to the blacks because their own skin was white—or, more accurately, sallow. This second group was never punished for violence against the first, and so it indulged in brutalities partly for the fun of it, as boys torture animals."

The NAACP held in Carnegie Hall a great anti-lynching meeting organized by John R. Shillady. Charles Evans Hughes, governor of New York, Emmet O'Neal, ex-governor of Alabama, and James Weldon Johnson were among the speakers. The meeting urged the passage of the Dyer Anti-Lynching Bill then before the Senate. In the *New York Times*, thanks to the money raised by a group of Negro clubwomen under the leadership of Mary B. Talbert, a full-page advertisement headed THE SHAME OF AMERICA dramatized the story of lynching.

War: Home or Abroad

When in April, 1917, the United States entered World War I against the Germans under the slogan, "Make the World Safe for Democracy," Negroes in the military services at home were entirely segregated. Whites and blacks neither trained nor fought together—but white officers commanded Negro troops. "Tote that barge, boy, lift that bale," might well have been the Negro slogan for service, since most Negroes were assigned to stevedore or labor battalions. In the Navy, Negroes could serve only as cooks or messmen. They were not enrolled in the Marines or in aviation units, for these were for whites only. The Army was the main branch of the services that utilized Negroes. But within a week after the declaration of war Negro quotas were filled, and recruiting centers stopped accepting Negro volunteers. Yet when draft calls were issued, southern draft boards called up Negroes wholesale, frequently granting no exemptions. The result was that although Negroes constituted scarcely 10 percent of the national population, they supplied 13 percent of the inductees. About 200,000 Negro soldiers served overseas.

At the onset of American participation in the war there were no provisions for training Negro officers. The NAACP immediately concerned itself with this problem, as did the students of Howard, Fisk, and Atlanta Universities. Joel Spingarn headed a delegation to Washington to see what could be done. He was told that if 200 Negroes of college grade could be secured, a training center would be established for them. Fifteen hundred names were collected. Mass meetings were held, and pressure was brought to bear on Congress. The South did not want any form of higher training for Negroes; therefore, although opposed to segregation in principle, the NAACP approved a proposal for a separate officers school on the grounds that such a school was in reality "intended to fight segregation, not encourage it." Classes were established at Fort Des Moines, Iowa, in the spring of 1917, and 1250 young Negroes enrolled. In October, 639 Negro officers were commissioned. A partial victory over military prejudice had been won.

Southerners not only opposed the training of Negro officers, but also objected to northern Negro Recruits being trained in southern camps. Since many Army officers came from the South, in all camps the months of military training for young Negroes were often especially difficult. Both within and outside the Army camps, the normal courtesies granted other soldiers were not given Negroes. At Camp Lee in Virginia guardsmen even prevented Negroes from attending white religious services. Not a single building in the five YMCA installations on the grounds at Camp Greene in North Carolina was open to Negroes. However, one military "Y" there did provide a table outdoors at which Negro soldiers could write letters.

When Negro service men at Fort Riley, Kansas, insisted on attending the post theater, General Ballou, in charge of the all-Negro 92nd Division, issued an official order commanding his men not to go where they were not wanted. When resentment against northern Negroes grew particularly bitter in the town of Spartanburg, South Carolina, where the 15th New York Infantry was in training, military authorities made no attempt to protect their soldiers from it. Drum Major Noble Sissle, who later became one of the outstanding talents in the Broadway theater, was kicked and beaten by a white news vendor because he did not remove his hat when he went to purchase a paper. So incensed were his fellow soldiers that a near-riot ensued, and for days the situation remained tense.

Emmett J. Scott, special Negro consultant to the Secretary of War, was sent to Spartanburg to report on the situation and, ironically, to plead with the Negro service men not to "dishonor" their regiment. But some of the soldiers were of the opinion that war at home might be of more value to them than war abroad; they preferred to fight the Klan in the South rather than the Germans in Europe. Their white officers feared that if the regiment was kept in South Carolina, violence might erupt. But if it was sent to another camp, the Southerners might think they could ever thereafter force the War Department to evacuate Negro soldiers whenever they wished. The Negroes themselves were afraid that the least incident might be grounds for court-martialing their troops and giving them severe sentences. What the War Department therefore did hurriedly was to order the whole unit overseas to face the German juggernaut. Thus because of southern prejudice the 15th New York Infantry became the first Negro combat group to face enemy fire on the European front.

Riots and Protests

The Negroes of the 24th Infantry in Houston, however, were not so lucky. Instead of being given such a fighting chance, 13 of its soldiers were sentenced to death by hanging and 41 to life imprisonment for the deaths of 18 whites. The Negro soldiers, desperate over the brutalities of the Houston police and the taunts and insults of white civilians, had used their weapons in retaliation during the riots of September, 1917, after a number of Negro soldiers had been beaten and disarmed. The military court-martial of these soldiers was the largest mass murder trial in the history of the United States. Negroes did not feel that these men had been given a fair chance. The *New York Age* cried, "So sure as there is a God in heaven, at some time and in some way full justice will be done." The NAACP sent Martha Gruening, a white writer, to the scene of the Houston riots; her findings were reported in *The Crisis*. The entire Negro press protested the trials. Just before Christmas, the 13 Negro soldiers were hanged. Many called this "a legal lynching." But that same year 47 other Negroes were lynched without even a pretense of a trial.

Although it lost its battle to save the 13 condemned Negro soldiers from death, the NAACP continued its defense of the other 41. The fight was kept up for years, and included the submission to Presidents Wilson, Harding, and Coolidge of petitions bearing respectively 12,000, 50,000, and 125,000 signatures. Some additional death sentences were commuted, and all the prison terms were reduced. Only the bureaucratic stubbornness of the War Department kept the remainder in jail. On April 19, 1938, Stewart W. Phillips, the last of the prisoners, was released.

Shortly before the Houston riots more than 100 Negro men and women had been killed and 6000 driven from their burning homes in East St. Louis by a white mob who objected to the employment of Negroes in a plant that held government contracts. Martha Gruening and Dr. Du Bois were sent to the scene to gather facts for the NAACP. A newspaper in Tennessee announced in advance that a Negro would be burned alive, and some 3000 spectators gathered to witness the spectacle. (Nor was this the only such instance.) Stirred by such events, 15,000 Negroes led by the NAACP marched one Sunday down New York's Fifth Avenue in a "Silent Protest Parade" against America's ever-spreading racial terror. When, early in 1918, John R. Shillady was appointed executive secretary of the NAACP to succeed Roy Nash (who resigned to join the 92nd Division as a captain), one of Shillady's first acts was to send the following telegram to President Wilson: "We beg of you to break your silence and to denounce properly these terrible mob acts which cover us with shame and humiliation at the moment when we as a nation would speak for justice and righteousness, for decency and humanity abroad."

Ten days later, James Weldon Johnson headed a delegation to the President bearing a petition containing 12,000 signatures that requested clemency for the accused Negro soldiers of the 24th Infantry who were still alive—but in prison or under indictment—after the Houston hangings. One result of this protest was that Wilson granted clemency to five of the men who had been sentenced to death at the second Houston court-martial. But Negro protests against injustices to both soldiers and civilians continued to mount throughout the winter and spring. Finally in July the President issued a long-delayed statement on lynching: "I therefore very earnestly and solemnly beg that the governors of all the states, the law officers of every community in the United States, all who revere America and wish to keep her name without stain or reproach, will co-operate, not passively merely, but actively and watchfully to make an end of this disgraceful evil. It cannot live where the community does not countenance it." How little attention the South paid to its President's words is indicated by the fact that there were 20 *more* lynchings in 1918 than in the preceding year. Of the 67 persons killed by mobs in 1918, two were women—one an expectant mother—and six were children.

They Seek a City

"I've heard of a city called Heaven, and I've started to make it my home," sang the slaves in the days of bondage. But in the first quarter of the 20th century the harassed Negroes of the South sought Chicago, Pittsburgh, Cleveland, Detroit. During and following World War I, the industrial cities of the North became focal points of the greatest mass migration in American history. Sizable numbers of southern whites migrated, too, but not in such numbers as Negroes. Both groups brought with them to the North many of the old ugly problems inherent in southern prejudice. Race hatred rode the buses and the trains along with the migrants. The NAACP and the National Urban League sought to cope with some of these new urban problems, of which housing was the most urgent.

As in most wars when industrial plants are running full blast, professional men who practiced among the masses made considerable money. Negro doctors, lawyers, and undertakers maintained offices in the ever-widening urban slum communities, but with prosperity they themselves could afford to move their families to less crowded middle-class neighborhoods with lawns and quiet streets. Such neighborhoods generally had all-white residents who resented the coming of Negro neighbors. Often, too, real estate firms would not sell homes to Negro families. If they did sell (and at sky-high prices), when the Negroes moved in rocks were thrown through windows and bombs exploded under front porches. Sometimes mobs gathered and threatened the lives of the new owners.

This is what happened in Detroit in 1926, when a Negro, Dr. O. H. Sweet, moved into his newly purchased corner house. Stones came crashing through his windows one night, hurled by a menacing mob of whites milling about in the street outside; then gunshots were heard. Those inside feared for their lives and someone in the house fired into the hate-filled crowd, killing a white mobster. Dr. Sweet, his wife, his two brothers—one of them, Henry, was a student at Wilberforce—and seven friends were all arrested and charged with first-degree murder. The NAACP secured Clarence Darrow to defend them.

Because of Darrow's great fame—he had just concluded the sensational Tennessee "monkey trial"—white newspapers gave the Sweet case wide coverage. The Negro press wrote extensively about it for another reason—the necessity of proving that a Negro had the right to defend his home against a mob. Thousands of dollars to help clear the Sweets poured into the national offices of the NAACP, mostly from Negro donors. The Fund for Public Service (the Garland Fund), of which Roger Baldwin was president, voted to match every two NAACP dollars with one of its own. Judge Frank Murphy, who later became a Supreme Court Justice, presided over the first trial of the eleven persons involved in the case; it resulted in a hung jury. All eleven were released on bail.

The six months before the second trial the NAACP and its lawyers used for intensive preparations. At this session only Dr. Sweet's younger brother Henry was put on trial. The courtroom was crowded every day. The prosecuting attorney was known to be sympathetic to the Ku Klux

Klan, which was then operating openly in Detroit, with representatives in the City Council. Streams of hostile white witnesses took the stand to testify that there had been *no* crowds milling about the Sweets' home on the night of the shooting, *no* threats, *no* stone throwing, *no* riotous actions. When cross-examined by the defense, most of these witnesses were suddenly afflicted with a woeful lapse of memory. Almost no one remembered being present at an overflow meeting in a school on the Sweets' block where plans were made to rid the neighborhood of the Negro newcomers. Some of the white witnesses even testified that they had welcomed the Sweets.

But there was one man of basic integrity who, though admitting that he did not like Negroes, told the truth. There *had* been threats and stone throwing, there *had* been shots from the outside. A white woman from across the alley corroborated this. A newspaper reporter stated on the witness stand that the crowd had become so riotous that he himself had grown fearful and had left the scene. John C. Dancy of the Urban League of Detroit informed the court about the difficulties Negroes had in finding decent housing in Detroit in the face of restrictive prejudice. Character witnesses testified to the solidity, uprightness, and culture of the Sweet family, and the excellent scholastic record of young Henry Sweet. Finally rugged old Clarence Darrow arose to begin his summation for the defense. His speech to the jury that day has been called one of the greatest in the history of American jurisprudence.

The gist of Darrow's argument was that the Sweet case involved race prejudice, not murder. He said that if "white men had shot and killed a black while protecting their home and lives against a mob of blacks, no one would have dreamed of having them indicted. . . . They would have been given medals instead." But he praised the jury by saying, "You are twelve white men trying a colored man. I want you to be on your guard. I want you to do all you can to be fair in this case—and I believe you will." But with shocking directness he asked, "How would you like, gentlemen, to wake up in the morning and find yourself colored?" He told them that, in this eventuality, whenever they went to a theater or a hotel or a restaurant they might find that their money was refused. They would never know when they would be met with insults or curt denials. He said that not since the first slave ship landed had Negroes been given a fair chance. He pointed out that some of the white neighbors who could scarcely speak English still wished to drive a decent and cultured Negro family from the block.

Near the close of his seven-hour address, Darrow again placed his trust in the jury. "I never saw twelve men in my life that, if you could get them to understand a human case, were not true or right." Then very softly, very quietly, he concluded, "I do not believe in the law of hate. . . . I would like to see the time when man loves his fellow man and forgets his color or his creed. We will never be civilized until that time comes. I know the Negro race has a long way to go. I believe the life of the Negro race has been a life of tragedy, of injustice, of oppression. The law has made him equal—but man has not. And after all, the last analysis is what man has done. Gentlemen, what do you think is your duty in this case? I ask you on behalf of the defendant, on behalf of this great state and this great city which must face this problem and face it squarely, I ask you in the name of progress and of the human race to return a verdict of not guilty." Clarence Darrow sat down.

The next day the jury went into seclusion. Late that afternoon the twelve white men informed the court that they were ready to report. In the tense silence of the crowded chambers Judge Murphy asked, "Have you in the course of your deliberations reached a verdict in the case of Henry Sweet, and if so who will answer for you?"

"We have and I will," said the foreman. "Not guilty."

The Sweet case set a precedent for the law in relation to Negroes. For every citizen it reaffirmed that "a man's home is his castle."

Returning Soldiers

The NAACP's legal victories were heartening, but the continuing daily incidents of violence and flagrant racial discrimination North and South were disheartening. While men were dying in Europe in defense of democracy, others were dying in America at the hands of prejudice. Yet Negro support of America's war efforts on both the military and civilian fronts was not lacking. An estimated $250,000,000 worth of war bonds and stamps were bought by Negro citizens. The National Association of Colored Women through its affiliated clubs reported the purchase of some $5,000,000 worth of Liberty Bonds. The North Carolina Mutual, a Negro insurance company, invested $300,000 in bonds.

"We'll fight or work. We'll fight and work," wrote Du Bois. "If we fight we'll learn the fighting game and cease to be so easily lynched." Later, because he concluded that it was better for Negroes to fight for a system where equality was at least an ideal, rather than even passively aid an imperialism which contemplated no such ideal, Du Bois in his celebrated "Close Ranks" editorial in *The Crisis* (July, 1917) urged: "Let us, while this war lasts, forget our special grievances and close our ranks shoulder to shoulder with our own white fellow citizens and the allied nations that are fighting for democracy." Many white members of the NAACP did not completely agree with this, and some Negroes went so far as to call Du Bois "a traitor to the race." Though his editorial may or may not have helped national unity at a crucial time, it in no way slowed down the Association's continuing fight for equal rights. And in succeeding editorials Du Bois himself returned to his old stinging criticism of the American scene.

At war's end, with thousands of Negro troops returning from France, *The Crisis* reviewed the injustices these soldiers had endured both in training and overseas. Du Bois reminded them of the inequalities they would continue to face at home. In an editorial entitled "Returning Soldiers" he wrote: "This country of ours, despite all its better souls have done and dreamed, is yet a shameful land. It lynches . . . it disfranchises its own citizens . . . it encourages ignorance . . . it steals from us . . . it insults us. . . . We return. We return from fighting. We return fighting." Since Negro soldiers had died on the battlefields for an American ideal, *The Crisis* editorial ended: "Make way for Democracy! We saved it in France and, by the Great Jehovah, we will save it in the U.S.A., or know the reason why!"

Intimidation and Censorship

The Department of Justice in Washington found this editorial, "Returning Soldiers," objectionable. It had previously warned Du Bois about the tenor of some of his *Crisis* articles. So seriously did the Board of Directors of the NAACP consider Washington's indirect censorship (possible prosecution was implied) that it requested a member of the Legal Committee to read each future issue of the magazine before it went to press. When agents of the Department of Justice called upon Du Bois at the offices of *The Crisis* and demanded to know just what the NAACP stood for, he answered, "For the enforcement of the Constitution of the United States."

Nevertheless, Congressman James F. Byrnes of South Carolina attacked *The Crisis* in the House and demanded that it be investigated. In his speech he also declared that the "incendiary utterances of would-be Negro leaders circulated through Negro newspapers in New York, Boston, and Chicago . . . are responsible for racial antagonism in the United States." In 1919 the Attorney General, Mitchell Palmer, labeled a number of Negro publications subversive, and A. Philip Randolph, editor of the *Messenger*, was arrested. In 1920 the Joint Committee Investigating Seditious Activity for the New York State Legislature listed *The Crisis* as contributing to "revolutionary radicalism." That year *The Crisis* had a circulation of 104,000 and many of its readers were in the South. Throughout the South, however, not only *The Crisis* but the entire Negro press was considered dangerous. In some southern communities the sale of Negro papers was made illegal, and in others vendors did not dare display them openly.

An intimidated member of the NAACP wrote Dr. Du Bois that he must cease taking subscriptions for *The Crisis* in his area and said: "I would be glad to continue to serve you as agent as willing, but you are aware of the fact that the crackers or the Ku Klux will beat a colored man for giving *The Crisis* away in some sections of this country. I wish to stop here a little longer as I make good wages in the railroad service."

Because of its ardent support of the NAACP, and also because of its editorials advising southern Negroes that "it is better to die of frostbite in the North than at the hands of a mob in the South," the *Chicago Defender* was frequently subjected to intense southern hostility.

"A colored man caught with a copy in his possession was suspected of 'Northern fever' and other so-called disloyalties," wrote Carl Sandburg in the *Chicago Daily News*. In some cities entire shipments of the *Defender* were confiscated as soon as they arrived by train. Yet when Negroes could get it, a Louisiana reader reported, "My people grab it like a mule grabs a mouthful of fine fodder." Even religious publications suffered censorship by intimidation. From Birmingham it was reported that "members of the local Ku Klux Klan invaded the office of the *Baptist Leader*, official organ of the Alabama Baptist denomination, and notified the editor, Rev. R. N. Hall, that unless the publication ceased making attacks on the notorious order, harm would be done." A minister in Mississippi was given much more than a warning. The Reverend E. R. Franklin, taking subscriptions for *The Crisis*, was beaten by a mob while on a train. He escaped, only to be arrested the next day and sentenced by a justice of the peace without trial to six months on the chain gang. Released on bail, fearful for his life, he fled north, sacrificing his $2500 bond.

About the same time, a news dispatch from Yazoo City, Mississippi, read as follows: "Threatening her with death unless she stopped acting as agent for newspapers published by her race, Miss Pauline Willis was compelled to leave town." The Mississippi legislature passed an act that made it "a misdemeanor to print or circulate or publish appeals or presentations or arguments or suggestions favoring equality . . . between the white and Negro race." This made selling *The Crisis* and most other Negro publications tantamount to a crime.

Governor Charles Brough of Arkansas appealed to the Postmaster General in Washington to bar the *Defender* from the mails. The mayor of Pine Bluff, Arkansas, secured an injunction "restraining John D. Young, Jr., Negro, and any other parties from circulating the *Chicago Defender,* a Negro publication, in Pine Bluff or Jefferson County." In Long View, Texas, a major riot was touched off when a mob raged through the Negro section of the town searching for a Negro teacher accused of writing for the *Defender.* The principal of the Negro school was publicly flogged, homes were burned, and a number of Negro citizens were forced to flee for their lives.

End of a Decade

In the first ten years of its existence the National Association for the Advancement of Colored People had already begun to make a considerable impact upon American liberalism. Its Tenth Anniversary Conference, held in Cleveland, was widely reported in the white press. The theme of the Conference was "Fight and Vote" and among the speakers who stirred its audience were Eugene Kinckle Jones of the National Urban League, AME Bishop John L. Hurst, Cora Findlay, Charles Edward Russell, and Major Joel Spingarn, only lately returned from France. Major Spingarn had for a time commanded a battalion in Europe composed largely of poor southern whites. In his speech at the Cleveland Conference he said that one day he asked one of these soldiers, "Where do you come from?"

"Tombs County, sir," the private replied.

"Where is that?" Major Spingarn inquired.

"Tombs County, sir?"

"In what state?" asked Spingarn.

"I never heard tell, sir," the man answered.

Spingarn remarked to the NAACP delegates, "It is in the hands of such ignorance as this that the destiny of the American Negro rests."

Mary White Ovington and John R. Shillady, who had worked for weeks preparing the organization and agenda for the working sessions of the Conference, were greatly pleased at the number of Negroes from all over the country who were now taking an active part in the deliberations. Miss Ovington later wrote that she herself and Shillady "were trying to direct and yet continually learning how little direction was needed. . . . We white delegates were working *with* the people we were trying to help . . . and were constantly learning from them. Time has shown that white direction was short lived. . . . The National Association for the Advancement of Colored People, started by whites, was being organized all over the United States by Negroes."

Concerning the Cleveland Conference, *The Crisis* observed that "in many ways it was the greatest assembly ever held by Negroes in the United States. Of the total of 310 branches, 175 were represented by delegates from 34 states." There was encouraging news to report. In the South, in spite of the ever-present shadow of violence, over 150 NAACP branches were active in carrying forward most of the phases of the national program. Among these were branches in Atlanta and Savannah, in Columbia, South Carolina, in Asheville, North Carolina, and in Birmingham, Montgomery, Austin, San Antonio, Chattanooga, and Nashville.

The register and vote drive of the Atlanta branch increased the number of Negro voters in that city from 700 to 3000, and they succeeded in defeating a school bond issue which made no provision for improvement of Negro schools. The special Moorfield Storey Membership Drive netted over 35,000 new members within the year. The Association now had an established press service which released news and information regularly to white and Negro papers across the nation. Over 400,000 pieces of literature relative to race relations were distributed that year, and the paid circulation of *The Crisis* amounted to more than 94,000. Contacts with organized workers were established and conferences held with the American Federation of Labor's executive council regarding the problems of Negro workers and the need for unsegregated participation in union activities.

Immediately after the signing of the Armistice at the end of the war the NAACP took part in the Conference of Demobilization and the Responsibilities of Social Agencies in New York City. And it sent Dr. Du Bois to Paris on the press ship *Orizaba* to cover the Peace Conference.

He remained in France to participate in the first Pan-African Congress which he had called "to focus the attention of the peace delegates and the civilized world on the just claims of the Negro everywhere." Delegates to the Congress included 12 Africans, 16 American Negroes, and 20 from the West Indies. As a result of the war, human beings everywhere were seeking freedom; and the American Negro, Du Bois felt, should help them and be helped in return. Blaise Diagne from Senegal, a member of the French Chamber of Deputies, was elected president of the Pan-African Congress, and Du Bois its secretary.

A few months before this Congress met in Paris, the NAACP had sponsored a Pan-African meeting in New York at which a resolution was adopted urging "upon the Senate of the United States the necessity for the creation at once of an international League of Free Nations which shall be charged, among other things, with the care and protection of the peoples of Middle Africa." Thus, toward the end of its first decade, the National Association's interest had extended to Africa and embraced such international concerns as those with which the destiny of all the colored peoples of the world, including those in America, could not help but be entangled.

2

Between Wars

A Shabby Bugaboo

In the early days of the NAACP one of the charges brought against it most often by those who opposed Negro progress was that it fostered social equality. What this usually boiled down to was the old question, "Would you want your daughter to marry a Negro?" The sex bugaboo raised its neurotic head in the North as well as the South. To Negroes in the South this seemed strangely one-sided, because from the days of slavery on, alliances between white men and black women had been common. Men who would not eat with Negroes or take a seat beside them in a public conveyance nevertheless slept with Negro women and fathered mulatto children with pleasure. Booker T. Washington was the child of such a union. Thomas Jefferson, signer of the Declaration of Independence, was reputed to have had a sizable mulatto family. There were 411,000 mulatto slaves at the outbreak of the Civil War. In addition, there were more than 150,000 free mulattoes because some slave owners freed their half-white children. Since Emancipation the proportion of persons of unmixed African ancestry in America has continued to decrease.

Marriage, however, has remained a privilege to be regulated by white people. Today there are states—including those of the entire South— that have laws prohibiting the marriage of whites with Negroes, Orientals, and Indians. Many whites maintain that any contact with Negroes— educational or otherwise—leads inevitably to intermarriage. Apparently it does not occur to them that all a woman needs to do if a Negro proposes marriage is to say "No."

The NAACP's position has always been that choice of a marital partner is a private affair. It opposes laws against racial intermarriage because such laws deprive a victimized Negro woman of a basic protection white women enjoy.

At the turn of the century Mary White Ovington belonged to the Cosmopolitan Club in Brooklyn; its president was a Frenchman and its membership included not only white ministers, physicians, and social workers, but several Negroes from old established families. One of their meetings, a dinner at which Oswald Garrison Villard and John Spargo spoke, was invaded by reporters and headlined in the papers the next day: Social equality—White and colored people dining together at a public restaurant!—White women sitting beside black men! As the news spread South, couched in utterly untrue terms, the occasion was described as "an orgy" despite the fact that it had been nothing more than a dinner and a cultural program. The *Richmond Leader* said, "We have bitter contempt for the whites that participated in it." And the *St. Louis Post-Dispatch* commented, "This miscegenation dinner was loathsome enough to consign the whole fraternity of persons who participated in it to undying infamy."

At that time there were many restaurants in New York and Brooklyn that would not serve Negroes or interracial groups. Arthur Spingarn recollected that during the early years of the NAACP, when male staff members left the office on a hot day and wanted to stop in at a café for a cool glass of beer, if the white bartender served them he might smash the glasses afterwards. In 1928, the Association wished to honor James Weldon Johnson with a large public dinner, but had difficulty in securing a place for it. Finally one of the big hotels agreed to accommodate the banquet provided the number of Negro guests was limited. For Negroes and whites to dine together was considered social equality. "The mere term," wrote James Weldon Johnson, "makes cowards of white people and puts Negroes in a dilemma. . . . In the South, policy exacts that any plea made by a Negro—or by a white man, for that matter— for fair treatment to the race, shall be predicated upon a disavowal of 'social equality.' . . . There should be nothing in law or public opinion to prohibit persons who find that they have congenial tastes and kindred interests in life from associating with each other, if they mutually desire to do so."

Du Bois was equally forthright. "*The Crisis* believes absolutely in the Social Equality of the Black, White and Yellow races, and it believes, too, that any attempt to deny this equality by law or custom is a blow at Humanity, Religion and Democracy. . . . Social equals, even in the narrowest sense of the term, do not have the right to be invited to or attend private receptions or to marry persons who do not wish to marry them. . . . On the other hand every self-respecting person does claim the right to mingle with his fellows if he is invited and to be free from insult and hindrance because of his presence." These statements seem to express the NAACP position over the years on what is often a touchy subject in discussions of American race relations.

Fists Against Facts

The sending of competent investigators into troubled regions to gather facts on racial difficulties early became an established part of NAACP activities. Information so recorded was used not only to acquaint Congress and the public with contemporary happenings, but also as a basis for court cases, legal petitions, and appeals. Just as the *Thirty Years of Lynching* booklet had been of immense value in propagandizing against that evil, so numerous other NAACP pamphlets and leaflets—all based on accurately compiled and carefully documented information—were of great value to its program, its fund raising, and its reputation for soundly based civil-rights efforts. But even for white investigators the collecting of racial data in the South was risky. The NAACP could not pay any of its courageous investigators adequately for the physical danger involved, nor did they expect to be paid. Roy Nash, its first secretary, then Martha Gruening, John R. Shillady, James Weldon Johnson, and later Walter White went south on fact-finding missions because of zeal and devotion to the cause they represented. Such devotion could not be reimbursed in terms of dollars.

The first NAACP official to suffer actual physical assault on a mission in the South was Executive Secretary Shillady, who was responsible for launching the study of three decades of lynching. (In 1918 he became the first executive secretary to be adequately paid; his salary was $6000 a year.) This attack happened in Austin, the capital of Texas—a state in which the NAACP had 29 branches. The Dallas and San Antonio branches each had over 1000 members, and *The Crisis* circulated widely in the state. It had aroused the ire of the white politicians, especially after the Longview riots during the war, when white civilians had clashed with Negro soldiers. These politicians were also incensed by NAACP agitation for the abolition of segregation in public carriers. State legislators at the capital demanded that the Austin branch be closed and asked the attorney general to impound its records. The secretary of the Austin branch wrote the national office of the NAACP for advice. It decided to send Shillady to Texas to confer with the governor and the attorney general and to inform them that the NAACP was a legally incorporated association that operated throughout the country. Once the attorney general realized its legality, it felt that he could not do otherwise than withdraw his demand for the books of the Austin branch.

It was summer and the train trip to Austin was long and hot. Upon his arrival at the Texas capital Shillady found that neither the governor nor the attorney general was in town. However, he was received by the acting attorney general who used the word *nigger* freely in his conversation and seemed under the impression that black Texans were organizing to attack whites. Shillady showed this man the hundreds of signatures on the NAACP anti-lynching petition, including those of several governors and the Attorney General of the United States. He contended that such eminent men would hardly sign their names to anything circulated by an organization that planned to arouse racial violence. The Texan listened unconvinced, but dismissed Shillady in a courteous manner.

Just outside the building, a constable stepped up to Shillady and served him with a subpoena. He was haled before a Court of Inquiry and subjected to severe questioning by a group of belligerent politicians. These men were armed with copies of the NAACP resolutions passed at the Cleveland Conference, some of which they claimed were in violation of the Texas segregation statutes. They taunted the tall distinguished middle-aged white man in their midst with the old question, "Would you want your daughter to marry a nigger?" When Shillady was finally permitted to leave the courthouse, he was attacked in the street by a group of white bullies. Without warning, one of them struck him full in the face. He was then kicked and slugged almost into unconsciousness.

After a doctor had stitched up his wounds, under the grudging protection of the mayor, the badly beaten Shillady managed to reach the railroad station, and fortunately secured a Pullman berth on the night train. The Associated Press wired the story of his beating across the country and it was headlined in New York. A few days later when Shillady arrived at the Pennsylvania Station in New York City the Negro redcaps there gave him an ovation; almost the whole office force of the NAACP was at the train to meet him. Shillady was still in a state of near-shock when his wife took him home. He never fully recovered from his encounter with southern brutality, and his faith in law and order was permanently shaken. A few months later he sent the NAACP a letter of resignation.

The NAACP attempted to have the identifiable members of the Texas mob arrested, but without success. None of Shillady's attackers were ever taken into custody, and no lawyer in the entire State of Texas could be found who was willing to bring charges against them. It was the old pattern all over again. Mobsters, not their victims, were protected. In answer to an NAACP appeal for the punishment of Shillady's assailants, Governor Hobby wired that its representative had gotten exactly the kind of treatment he deserved and that the same treatment awaited any other white man who dared interfere with the way Texas controlled its Negroes. No wonder, in submitting his resignation to the Board of Directors, that Shillady wrote, "I am less confident than heretofore of the speedy success of the Association's full program and of the probability of overcoming, within a reasonable period, the forces opposed to Negro equality by the means which are within the Association's power to employ."

A White Colored Man

In 1920, Shillady's work as an investigator was taken over by Walter White, and his position as executive secretary by James Weldon Johnson. Johnson's appointment marked the first time a Negro had headed the staff of the National Association. He remained secretary for nine years and was succeeded by Walter White. A graduate of Atlanta University, White had come to the NAACP as assistant secretary on the recommendation of James Weldon Johnson. Almost immediately he began his daring on-the-spot investigations of lynchings and race riots which were soon to make him famous. On such undercover missions he had an advantage over Johnson, Pickens, and other Negro staff members of the NAACP. Although a Negro, White *looked* white. He could "pass"—and in the South he often did. Southerners who usually contend they can always recognize a Negro no matter how light his complexion may be, were fooled by Walter White. Fair, blond-haired and blue-eyed, even in his native Georgia Walter White was never taken as colored except in his own neighborhood in Atlanta. He delighted in his powers of racial deception when mingling with southern mobsters, and, once back in New York, he would gleefully relate how the lynchers had confided to him just who lighted the match to touch off the flames that burned their latest victim to death.

Both of Walter White's parents were light-complexioned, and their home in Atlanta was the last house on the border between the white and Negro neighborhood. Young Walter was one of the few Negroes who could boast of having had a white "mammy," for when his own mother's breasts went dry he was suckled by a kindly white neighbor. As a child Walter discovered that he could sit at the counter and drink a soda at white soda fountains, but that brown-skinned youngsters the color of some of his own relatives could not. As a teen-ager he worked at jobs not open to obviously Negro boys. Thus, even in the South, he learned early to move in both the Negro and the white worlds. But white youngsters in the blocks adjacent to his home knew him as a Negro, and when in an unfriendly mood would call him *nigger.* At thirteen Walter experienced at first-hand the horrors of one of America's worst race riots.

His father drove a United States mail cart that made late afternoon and evening collections from the mailboxes. Sometimes his son rode with him. One sultry Saturday in 1906 on Peachtree Street, Atlanta's main thoroughfare, father and son heard the roar of an approaching mob pursuing a lame Negro shoe-shine boy whom they both knew from Herndon's Barber Shop. The crippled boy could not outrun the mob, and before Walter's eyes he was trampled and beaten to death on the pavement. A few moments later the two saw another terrified Negro knocked to the ground and hacked to death with knives. The mob did not bother the two on the mail cart, for they took them to be white. But the cart was caught in the midst of a raging crowd that howled, "Get the niggers! Get the niggers!" and chased every Negro man and woman it saw. Walter White's father, handing the horse's reins to his son, rescued a stout Negro cook who was fleeing from the mob and hastily pulled her up into the wagon where she hid among the mail bags.

When they got home, they found a friend who had come to offer the White family guns, for everyone expected the downtown mobs to invade the Negro sections of Atlanta under cover of darkness. Never having had a gun in the house before, the elder White did not want to accept the offer, but his wife said, "Take those guns. These crackers have gone crazy. No telling what they will do." White mobs did invade the Negro sections as the riots continued. On Sunday night there was an ominous roar from the adjacent white neighborhood as mobs poured down the street leading to the Negro homes. All the lights in the house were extinguished, and Walter's mother and the younger children were sent to the rear of the house. Father and son took their places at the darkened windows upstairs, the triggers of their guns cocked. Young Walter had never fired a gun before and did not want to kill. But through the shutters he could see the mob approaching, carrying torches. Then he heard the son of the white grocer with whom his father traded shout, "Here's where that nigger mailman lives. Burn the house down!"

Walter's father said, "Son, don't shoot until the first man puts his foot on our lawn—and then *don't miss!*"

But the Whites did not have to shoot. Before the mob reached their house, other Negroes in nearby houses began to fire volleys into the streets. The mob stopped, their astonished leaders backing away; then it fled in panic to seek another, less militant Negro neighborhood. Years later Walter White wrote in his autobiography that, as the mob approached, "I knew who I was. I was a Negro, a human being with an invisible pigmentation which marked me a person to be hunted, hanged, abused, discriminated against, kept in poverty and ignorance. . . . It made no difference how intelligent or talented my millions of brothers were, or how virtuously we lived . . . . There were white men who said Negroes had no souls and who proved it by the Bible. Some of these now were approaching us, intent upon burning our house."

The Whites' house was not burned, but during the three-day riot the homes of other Negroes in Atlanta were destroyed. That week end an old family friend, Dr. Bowen, president of Gammon Theological Seminary, was beaten almost to death—not by the mobs, but by members of the Atlanta police force whom he had asked to protect his campus. The number of casualties that tragic week end were never fully known, but officially 12 persons were listed as killed and 70 men and women seriously wounded. The mobs never penetrated deeper than the fringes of the most thickly populated Negro neighborhoods, once they learned that many Negro citizens were armed. The word had gotten around that the Negroes in Darktown, one of Atlanta's worst slums, had said, "Don't send us the militia—we want the mob!" The cowards who make up mobs have no desire to tangle with Negroes who are likely to fight back.

During Walter White's junior year in college he learned that not all violence was directed against Negroes. Leo Frank, a Jewish factory owner in Atlanta, was tried and convicted for the rape and murder of one of his white employees. Frank, a Northerner, had become president of the local B'nai B'rith, and as such was a man of prominence in Jewish circles. Because he was a "damn Yankee Jew," his trial generated waves of anti-Semitism in the Atlanta press. His conviction—obtained in a prejudicial atmosphere of religious animosity—was appealed all the way to the United States Supreme Court. That court ruled in essence that it had no authority to pass on the spirit which dominated a trial as long as legal procedures were not violated. It refused to reverse the death sentence the lower court had imposed. When the governor of Georgia commuted Frank's sentence to life imprisonment, the bigots in the state got busy and raised the cry, "Kill the Jew!" An armed rabble broke into the penitentiary, took Frank to the town of Marietta where the murdered girl was born, and lynched him.

To counterbalance the intense racial hatred and religious intolerance that infested his native Georgia, Walter White, as a student of many fine northern white men and women on the Atlanta University faculty, early realized that some whites were not "infected with delusions of racial superiority and opposed to progress for the Negro." He later wrote, "It was they who saved me from the defeatist belief that all whites are evil and bigoted in their attitude toward dark-skinned peoples."

Passing for White

Twelve days after he arrived in New York, Walter White's first investigation took him into the South to Estill Springs, Tennessee, to find out who had taken part in the torture-death of a Negro farmer. As White reported it in *The Crisis:*

> Jim McIlherron was prosperous in a small way. He was a Negro who resented the slights and insults of white men. He went armed and the sheriff feared him. On February 8, 1918, he got into a quarrel with three young white men who insulted him. Threats were made and McIlherron fired six shots, killing two of the men. He fled to the home of a colored clergyman who aided him to escape and was afterwards shot and killed by a mob. McIlherron was captured and full arrangements made for his lynching. Men, women and children started into the town of Estill Springs from a radius of fifty miles. A spot was chosen for the burning. McIlherron was chained to a hickory tree while the mob howled about him. A fire was built a few feet away and the torture began. Bars of iron were heated and the mob amused itself by putting them close to the victim, at first without touching him. One bar he grasped and as it was jerked from his grasp all the inside of his hand came with it. Then the real torturing began, lasting for twenty minutes. During that time, while his flesh was slowly roasting, the Negro never lost his nerve. He cursed those who tortured him and almost to the last breath derided the attempts of the mob to break his spirit.

These things Walter White discovered while passing as a white man in the country town of Estill Springs, so remote from outside contacts that only one resident, the mill owner, received a newspaper. Fortunately, White's own southern accent kept anyone from suspecting that he was fresh from the North. Pretending to be interested in purchasing farm land in the region, he moved freely about the countryside, joined the men around the stove in crossroads stores, and got acquainted with the natives. White claimed never to have heard of the recent lynching and acted as if it was of little interest to him. He asked no questions. He simply let the people talk of their own accord. The excitement of the lynching was still their favorite topic, and a number of men boasted of their role in it. Everybody agreed that the white ruffians who first provoked McIlherron into defending himself were "no good." But they concluded that any time a black man struck back at a white man, for no matter what reason, "he's gotta be handled or else all niggers will get out of hand." When White returned to New York, he knew the names of most of the mob members who had "handled" McIlherron.

A few months later, White was off to Arkansas, this time to investigate a reign of terror against the Negro sharecroppers of Phillips County. A meeting of the Progressive Farmers and Household Union, organized to keep the big landowners from cheating their cotton tenants and farm workers, had been fired upon. Through the windows of the meeting place, a little Negro church at Hoop Spur, there suddenly came out of the darkness volley after volley of shots. The assembled Negroes returned the fire. Several Negro men and women inside the church were killed and others were wounded; but as the mob outside fled, a white man lay dead in the road. The death of this white man set off anti-Negro massacres throughout the countryside. For days, roving gangs of whites beat or killed every Negro they could catch. Thousands of plantation Negroes fled through the woods and swamps, leaving their meager belongings behind. But the southern papers claimed that it was the Negroes who were "massacring" the whites, and federal troops were called. The troops put more than 1000 Negro farmers into stockades.

A kangaroo court of white plantation owners and commissary store-keepers was set up to sort out the "good niggers" from the bad—the bad being those who had joined the Progressive Farmers Union. When 79 Negroes refused to be intimidated into testifying against themselves, they were indicted for insurrection or murder. Within five days all had been tried at Elaine, Arkansas, and 12 were sentenced to die; 67 other cotton pickers received from twenty years to life in prison. These over-speedy trials were held in a courtroom filled with mobsters. The defendants did not have a chance; none were cleared.

The *Chicago Daily News* gave Walter White a press card which he presented, on arrival, to the governor of Arkansas. The governor was delighted that a white reporter with seemingly unbiased views had at last come to get the "truth," in distinction to the lies he said the *Chicago Defender* had printed about the trials at Elaine and the conditions of the Negroes in Phillips County. Northern agitators, the governor said, were the cause of all the trouble there. When Walter White left for the plantation country, he had a letter of commendation from the governor. Not until White sought to interview alone the Negro prisoners being held in the county jail at Helena were suspicions probably aroused. The sheriff would not commit himself, but told White to come to the jail later and he would see.

On the way to the prison that afternoon, a Negro passed White and without stopping whispered quickly, "Follow me." When he thought they were unwatched, he warned White of impending danger. There were only two trains a day out of Helena. One was due then; the other, late at night. Leaving bag and baggage behind, Walter White made the train due then, climbing aboard on the wrong side just as it pulled out of the station. He did not stop to buy a ticket. As the conductor was taking his money, he said to the still panting passenger, "Mister, you're leaving just as the fun is starting. There's a damn yellow nigger down here passing for white and the boys are going to get him now. When they get through with him, he won't pass for white no more." That night in Memphis, it was rumored that Walter White had been lynched in the cotton country. But he had gotten safely across the Mississippi River into Tennessee.

In Arkansas more Negroes were arrested and more trials were held. In the end, 92 men and women from the cotton fields, most of them illiterate, were under sentence. The NAACP, ably aided by Arkansas' courageous Negro lawyer Scipio Africanus Jones, argued their cases. Application for a writ of habeas corpus was made in the federal courts and dismissed. This ruling was appealed to the United States Supreme Court and argued there by Moorfield Storey. An opinion delivered by Mr. Justice Holmes reversed the lower court decision. Eventually, all the defendants were freed. But their freedom came only after six long years of costly legal battle. The cost of copying transcripts alone was staggering.

This case, *Moore v. Dempsey,* was of the utmost significance for American criminal law. The convictions were reversed by the United States Supreme Court because the biased atmosphere of the trial (including a courtroom ringed by armed mobsters) was held to be a denial of due process of law. Thus, in less than ten years, the principle which the courts had denied in the case of Leo Frank had become accepted as law through NAACP action.

The Ku Klux Klan

Not all of Walter White's investigations were concerned with violence to the poor and uneducated. In Ocoee, Florida, a town run by the Klan,

Moses Norman, the wealthy Negro owner of extensive orange groves, went to the polls to vote. For his audacity in wanting to exercise the basic right of the ballot he was set upon at the polls and beaten. The whites ordered him home. Instead, Norman went to the house of a friend, July Perry, another well-to-do Negro. Thereupon masked Klansmen surrounded Perry's home and burned it down; they fired nearby Negro houses as well, and shot men, women, and children as they ran from the flames. It was believed that many more than the 5 Negroes listed in the papers were burned to death that day in the 18 homes, two churches, and the Negro school and the lodge hall that went up in smoke. The names of participating Klansmen were easily gathered, as were eyewitness accounts. Although the NAACP submitted all the assembled data to the Department of Justice in Washington, no one in Ocoee was ever apprehended.

Klan power continued to grow, in the South and also in the North. By the end of World War I, this white-robed organization that had been formed in 1865 to keep the newly freed Negroes from voting or from organizing for civil rights had grown so bold that it had chapters as far north as New York and Boston. After his exposure of Ku Klux activities in Florida in the nation's press, Walter White was denounced at a Klavern meeting in the Bronx and an implied threat was made against his life and against members of his family. The New York City Bomb Squad assigned a guard to his home for a while, and Negro neighbors in Atlanta volunteered to protect his parents, who were also in danger. In Washington in 1925, the Ku Klux Klan in full regalia paraded down Pennsylvania Avenue and past the White House; the parade lasted for hours and took place with the government's permission. Masked terror had become respectable.

Of the millions of Negroes in the South, only a very small number dared attempt to register and vote, even in national elections. James Weldon Johnson, Walter White, and William Pickens of the NAACP's national office and Archibald Grimké of its Washington office had testified before legislative committees concerning these conditions and urged a Congressional investigation of presidential elections in southern states. They also urged a reduction in representation, as provided in the federal Constitution, in southern electoral districts where denial of votes to thousands of citizens was proved. Before his election to the Presidency, Warren G. Harding had been informed by the NAACP of the issues most vital at that time for the Negro—the right to vote, the right to protection from mob violence, the danger from the Ku Klux Klan, and the need for an interracial commission to study the entire field of civil rights. Upon becoming President, Harding approved the creation of such a commission. And in a message to both House and Senate he said, "Congress ought to wipe the stain of barbaric lynching from the banners of a free and orderly representative democracy." Fine words, but no federal legislation was forthcoming.

On the international front, NAACP activities included sending Dr. Du Bois, Walter White, and Jessie Fauset as delegates to the sessions of the Second Pan-African Congress that met in London, Brussels, and Paris in 1921. Dr. Du Bois remained in Europe to place before the League of Nations the resolutions passed by that Congress.

The Southern and the Yellow Dog

"He's gone where de Southern cross de Yellow Dog," says a famous old blues that the late great Bessie Smith used to sing. The Southern is a railroad that cuts through the South from Washington to New Orleans, across all the states where Klan robes have flapped in the breeze so openly and so long—the Carolinas, Georgia, Alabama, Mississippi, and Louisiana. Where the Southern crossed the now defunct Yazoo Delta Line (nicknamed the Yellow Dog) in Mississippi must have been the stone end of nowhere. But people lived there and trains ran, and some of the switch engines in the Mississippi railroad yards had Negro firemen. Gradually the white trainmen became jealous of these Negroes, especially after the NAACP won wage equalization for them, with large amounts of back pay. The whites stopped at nothing—even murder—to take these jobs from the Negroes.

Before World War I about eight out of ten firemen on any big southern railroad were Negroes. Ten years afterward only one in ten was Negro. In 1921 federal agents arrested two white men charged with ambushing Negro firemen in Mississippi. In 1923 seven Negro firemen were murdered, a number wounded by snipers, and one flogged severely in an effort to drive Negroes off their jobs. The lily-white Railroad Brotherhoods would not admit Negro workers, and white railway men contended that Negroes should not work if they were non-union. So went the vicious circle. The Atlanta terminal ruled that white firemen were always to be given preference over Negroes. The desire to halt all employment of Negroes on steam engines in the South resulted in the concerted killing of Negro firemen in 1932. Ten Negro trainmen died by unknown hands that year on the Illinois Central. In this case, the wanton murder for jobs ended when the Negro firemen armed themselves and retaliated and an NAACP-instigated investigation turned up five of the guilty parties. However, the overall situation worsened until finally the Association of Colored Railway Employees appealed to the NAACP. Despite the latter's efforts, the railroad unions have thus far prevailed, and with the supplanting of steam engines by diesels Negro firemen have all but disappeared. There are no more Negroes stoking engines where "de Southern cross de Yellow Dog." Today the Railway Brotherhoods are virtually as Nordic as Hitler's Bunds.

The Negro Renaissance

The Crisis and the NAACP in general played a considerable part in the cultural awakening, known as the Negro Renaissance, that centered in Harlem in the 1920's and early 1930's. On the National Association's staff there were four excellent writers—Dr. Du Bois, the essayist and editorialist; James Weldon Johnson, the poet and journalist; Walter White, recipient of a Guggenheim Fellowship for Creative Writing; and Jessie Fauset, whose novels, *There Is Confusion* and *The Chinaberry Tree,* were widely read fictional treatments of Negro intellectual life.

In 1924 the Amy Spingarn Prizes in Literature and Art were established by *The Crisis.* Sinclair Lewis, Edward Bok, Charles W. Chesnutt, and Robert Morss Lovett were among the judges. Recipients of awards included Arna Bontemps and Frank Horne in poetry, and Rudolph Fisher in the short story. During that period a short story by Anita Scott Coleman appeared in *The Crisis;* one of its lines—"You can stand anybody's dying but yourself"—has been much quoted. The poems of Claude McKay, Langston Hughes, Countee Cullen, Georgia Douglass Johnson, and Jessie Fauset appeared in *The Crisis.*

While he was executive secretary of the NAACP, James Weldon Johnson's famous "God's Trombones" was published in 1927; and he wrote "Saint Peter Relates an Incident of the Resurrection Day," as well as "Along This Way," one of the earlier portions of his autobiography. Both Johnson and Jessie Fauset held many cultural soirees at their apartments in Harlem. Celebrities of both races who often attended included the Carl Van Vechtens, the Clarence Darrows, and the young Paul Robesons; Miguel Covarrubias and Aaron Douglas, the artists; Charles S. Johnson, the sociologist; Rebecca West, the English novelist; and Salvador Madariaga, the Spanish philosopher. Walter White's parties too, on Edgecombe Avenue in what was then Harlem's most fashionable apartment building, brought together brilliant company—Sinclair Lewis, Willa Cather, Rudolph Fisher, Heywood Broun, George Gershwin—and perhaps included more stars of the theater than the other gatherings did. His stunning café-au-lait wife Gladys, one of Harlem's most beautiful women, had appeared briefly on the Broadway stage. White's genial personality and complete informality—he called everyone from Supreme Court judges down by their first name after their first meeting—made his parties extremely relaxing and usually just plain fun.

Upon receipt of his Guggenheim Fellowship, Walter White took a well-deserved leave of absence from NAACP duties and took his family to the Riviera in 1927 where he spent a year writing. He completed his study of lynching, *Rope and Faggot,* and a portion of a second novel. Articles by him and by Du Bois and Johnson had begun to appear in America's best magazines. The prose and poetry of these men did much to dispel the common delusion in the United States that all Negroes spoke and wrote in dialect. Until well after World War I, popular white writers such as Octavus Roy Cohen, Irvin Cobb, Julia Peterkin, and Roark Bradford depicted all their Negro characters as not being able to pronounce even "the" correctly. Motion pictures and the stage did little to ameliorate a mass impression of Negro illiteracy. Hollywood limited Negro actors almost entirely to the role of unlettered servants whose characterizations on the screen were usually further narrowed by directors to imbecilic clowning. Through writing, speaking, and by just being, the NAACP and its highly literate staff made a great contribution to helping change the general American impression that *all* Negroes had neither sense nor education.

The Spingarn Medal

To help counteract stereotyped thinking regarding Negroes, Joel Spingarn established the Spingarn Medal, "a gold medal to be awarded for the highest or noblest achievement by an American Negro during the preceding year or years. . . . The purpose of the medal is twofold—first, to call attention of the American people to the existence of distinguished merit and achievement among American Negroes, and secondly, to serve as a reward for such achievement, and as a stimulus to the ambition of colored youth." The first medal was awarded to Professor Ernest E. Just of the Howard University Medical School for distinguished research in biology, and was presented on Lincoln's Birthday, 1915, by Governor Charles S. Whitman of New York.

Since that time, each year, save one, the medal has been awarded by a special nine-member Committee of Award selected by but not exclusively from the Board of Directors of the NAACP. On this Committee over the years have served such distinguished persons as Theodore Roosevelt, William Howard Taft, Dr. John Haynes Holmes, Mary McLeod Bethune, Edwin R. Embree, the Honorable Frank Murphy, Sinclair Lewis, Dr. Buell Gallagher, A. Philip Randolph, and Dr. Allan Knight Chalmers. Since the award may be made "in any honorable field of human endeavor," the Committee "is bound by no burdensome restrictions, but may decide for itself each year what particular act or achievement deserves the highest acclaim." The recipients, therefore, have been in many and varied categories, with the arts and sciences predominating; to date, more than a quarter of the awards have been made in some field of the arts. Writers William Stanley Braithwaite, James Weldon Johnson, Charles W. Chesnutt, Richard Wright, and Langston Hughes have received the Spingarn Medal, as have such performing or creative musicians as Harry T. Burleigh, Roland Hayes, Marian Anderson, and Duke Ellington. In the theater, the award has gone to actors Paul Robeson; Charles S. Gilpin, the original Emperor Jones; and Richard B. Harrison, De Lawd of *The Green Pastures.*

The field of education ranks next to the arts. But in former years distinguished Negro educators were leaders in other areas of American life—civic, fraternal, or political—as well as the academic. Dr. Carter G. Woodson, teacher and historian; Mordecai Wyatt Johnson, president of Howard University; Henry A. Hunt, pioneer industrial educator of Fort Valley, Georgia; Robert Russa Moton, principal of Tuskegee; William Taylor Burwell Williams, dean of Tuskegee; and Mary McLeod Bethune, founder of Bethune-Cookman College, were awarded the Spingarn Medal. Most of those receiving the award for outstanding work in the physical sciences were teachers at some time—George Washington Carver, famous in agricultural chemistry; Dr. Charles R. Drew, who initiated the first blood banks; Percy L. Julian, biochemist who extracted hormones from soy beans and invented the foam method of extinguishing fires; Dr. Theodore K. Lawless, dermatologist; and Dr. Louis T. Wright, fellow of the American College of Surgeons and the first physician to use aureomycin on human beings.

The only year the medal was not presented was 1938, when the award was refused by Dr. William A. Hinton of the Harvard University faculty.

This distinguished bacteriologist, the originator of the Hinton test for syphilis, declined the honor on the grounds of not wishing his work to be identified with race.

There have been four Spingarn Medal awards to women individually. Other than Mrs. Bethune and Miss Anderson, these were Mary B. Talbert of the National Association of Colored Women, and Mabel Keaton Staupers, president of the National Association of Colored Graduate Nurses which under her leadership later became affiliated with the general national nurses organizations when it was felt that the separate organization had served its purpose. Women were also included in the only group award of the Spingarn Medal. In 1958 it went to Daisy Bates and the teen-agers of the Little Rock Nine for their courageous stand in the face of mobs when the schools were integrated.

Other recipients of the Spingarn Medal include Anthony Overton, insurance executive; A. Philip Randolph, labor leader; Judge William H. Hastie; Paul R. Williams, architect; Carl Murphy, publisher; Jackie Robinson, who broke the color line in big-league baseball; the Reverend Martin Luther King; Dr. Ralph J. Bunche; and Kenneth B. Clark, whose studies of the effects of segregated education upon children formed a vital part of the NAACP arguments before the United States Supreme Court in the epoch-making decision declaring public-school segregation illegal. The medal has thrice been awarded posthumously—to John Hope, educator and president of Atlanta University, in 1936; to Charles Hamilton Houston, the brilliant lawyer, in 1950; and to Harry T. Moore, the martyred Florida NAACP organizer, in 1952.

The annual awarding of the Spingarn Medal receives national press coverage, thus bringing to the attention of the public an aspect other than crime or deep-rooted problems regarding the Negro's place in the American scene. The year James Weldon Johnson received the medal for his poems and prose, Albert C. Barnes, a pharmaceutical magnate and founder of the Barnes Foundation for modern art, wrote in the *Survey Graphic:* "We are beginning to recognize that what the Negro singers and sages have said is only what the ordinary Negro feels and thinks, in his own measure, every day of his life. . . . When we take to heart the obvious fact that what our prosaic civilization needs most is precisely the poetry which the average Negro actually lives, it is incredible that we should not offer the consideration which we have consistently denied to him." Barnes concluded by saying that the Negro "may consent to form a working alliance with us for the development of a richer American civilization to which he will contribute his full share." Through the contributions of its own writers and its attention-attracting Spingarn Medal awards, the NAACP has aided in conditioning American thinking about accepting the Negro as a valuable contributor to the national culture.

James Weldon Johnson

"In the pitched battle between justice and wrong," one of the "fields on which causes may be won" is writing, according to James Weldon Johnson. Much of his writing concerned the Negro cause. The year after he joined the NAACP staff, "To America," a short poem addressed to his white fellow citizens, appeared on the back of the Association's 1917–1918 report:

> How would you have us, as we are
> Or sinking 'neath the load we bear?
> Our eyes fixed forward on a star
> Or gazing empty at despair?
> Rising or falling? Men or things?
> With dragging pace or footsteps fleet?
> Strong, willing sinews in your wings?
> Or tightening chains about your feet?

Later, in a speech at Carnegie Hall, Johnson said, "The race problem in the United States has resolved itself into a question of saving black men's bodies and white men's souls."

"There are more ways than one to kill a cat" and "The pen is mightier than the sword" are equally trite. But in contending with the "cat" of race prejudice, James Weldon Johnson used the "pen" to turn out writing in *all* its forms—polemic, poems, fiction, and fact presented in articles, journalistic pieces, pamphlets, leaflets, and speeches. During his years with the NAACP he made hundreds of speeches from one end of America to the other, and under his leadership the number of NAACP branches rose from 67 to 372, many of them in the South.

Tall, brown-skinned, Johnson made a striking platform figure. He wore glasses with a flowing ribbon to read, but removed them when he was speaking. His speeches—quiet, often scholarly, well-documented— lacked the rolling oratory of the old school. In her profile of Johnson, Mary White Ovington says, "The outstanding trait in this man of many talents is his charm. Charm is a hard thing to define. Friendliness must surely be there and a kindly spirit. But many *feel* friendliness and are unable to express it. An unconscious self-respect must also be present. The personality escapes in a gesture, an expression, a word, and meets its friend. So it is with this colored man. . . . One knows him to be one reared in gentle ways, endowed with graciousness." The same qualities well apply to his wife, Grace Nail Johnson.

Johnson's mother read the English classics to him when he was a child in Florida, and he studied the liberal arts at Atlanta University. After college he became principal of a Negro grammar school in Jacksonville. Without fanfare—without even informing the school board—he raised that institution to the status of a high school simply by keeping the eighth-grade class there a year longer and teaching it himself. Then he kept it another year, and another, until that group of students had had four years of high-school work. Since that time, Jacksonville has had a high school for Negro children.

Johnson usually found a practical way of getting around almost any problem without dramatics. He often illustrated this more-than-one-way-to-kill-a-cat by his story about the balky mule. It seems that one evening this stubborn animal refused to move forward on the way home from the cotton gin; instead, it backed up each time the driver tried to get it to go forward. The supper hour was near and the sun was setting. Finally, unable to get started for home, the driver got down from the cart, unharnessed the mule, turned it around facing the cart, and harnessed it up again. Now when he said, "Git up!" the mule still persisted in backing up but was headed toward home. So they got there just the same.

In 1900 James Weldon Johnson wrote a song for Florida school children called *Lift Ev'ry Voice and Sing,* with music by his brother J. Rosamond Johnson. It attained such popularity with Negroes everywhere that it came to be known widely as the Negro national anthem. After several years of teaching, Johnson came to New York from Jacksonville. There at the turn of the century, with his brother Rosamond, he wrote some of America's hit songs, among them Marie Cahill's success, *The Maiden with the Dreamy Eyes,* and the lyrically lovely *Since You Went Away,* introduced by John McCormack. Then came seven years in the United States consular service in Venezuela and Nicaragua, an admirable training ground for his future work with the NAACP. As consul he met and had dealings with all sorts of people—from distinguished diplomats to waterfront roughnecks, from prejudiced Southerners to world sophisticates who moored their yachts near his consulate. Johnson learned both Spanish and French, the latter standing him in good stead when the

NAACP sent him to Haiti in 1922 to investigate conditions there under the American occupation.

Johnson had a practical knowledge of politics. For half a century Negroes had said, "The Republican party is the ship, all else is the sea." But when, after more than two years of intensive efforts to achieve its passage in Congress, the Dyer Anti-Lynching Bill was defeated in the Senate in 1922 by the anti-civil-rights coalition of northern Republicans and southern Democrats, Negroes in ever-increasing numbers began to consider voting otherwise than Republican. Lincoln's Grand Old Party had become less and less concerned with Negro rights over the years. Borah, the Republican Senator from Idaho, had declared the Dyer Bill unconstitutional even before it went to a vote. Although the NAACP has always been non-partisan, Johnson was himself a Republican. When the Senate voted against the bill for whose passage he had spent two years lobbying in Washington, he himself was deeply disillusioned. "The Association had been working at high pressure," he wrote in his autobiography. "It had aroused the colored people of the country; it had secured the cooperation of the Negro press, and enlisted the aid of many influential agencies. A constant shower of communications urging the passage of the bill was being poured on members of Congress. The Dyer bill brought out the greatest concerted action I have yet seen the colored people take." When it passed the House, Negroes in the gallery cheered.

A committee from the NAACP then presented a memorial to the Senate urging the passage of the bill there. The petition was signed by the governors of 24 states, 39 mayors, 88 bishops and prominent churchmen, and many other outstanding citizens. Although on the very day it was presented, three Negroes were burned alive in Kirby, Texas, the Senate employed all sorts of delaying tactics against the bill. In the end, Johnson commented, "The Dyer Anti-Lynching Bill did not become a law, but it made of the floors of Congress a forum in which the facts were discussed and brought home to the American people as they had never been before." As a Congressional subcommittee reported later, agitation for the passage of the measure was probably the prime factor in reducing the number of lynchings in the decade that followed. It served to awaken the leaders in the southern states to the necessity of curbing the lynch habit in order to avoid the federal intervention that there certainly would have been otherwise. In the year 1928 when, for reasons of failing strength, James Weldon Johnson resigned from his position in the NAACP, the lynch total was down to 11.

Complete inactivity hardly suited a man like Johnson. He accepted the Chair of Creative Writing at Fisk University, where he remained until his death in an automobile accident in 1938. While at Fisk he wrote a little book called *Negro Americans, What Now?* Its closing pages relate how, in spite of a southern childhood and years of struggle with race problems, Johnson still maintained his inner assurance. "In the situation into which we are thrown," he advised the Negro people, "let each one of us, let the whole race, be ceaselessly on guard against the loss of spiritual integrity. So long as we maintain *that* integrity we cannot be beaten down, not in a thousand years. . . . I will not allow one prejudiced person or one million or one hundred million to blight my life. I will not let prejudice or any of its attendant humiliations and injustices bear me down to spiritual defeat. My inner life is mine, and I shall defend and maintain its integrity against all the powers of hell."

The NAACP and Judge Parker

As the nation and the world moved from the heights of the 1920's into the Deep Depression, the NAACP manifested in spectacular fashion the sheer power of organization and the volume of organized protest which it makes possible. Under Walter White's leadership it took on a challenge and enemies which, by any rational appraisal, its meager resources and personnel simply had no business being engaged with.

In March, 1930, President Hoover nominated for the United States Supreme Court John J. Parker of North Carolina, a United States Circuit Court judge, and sent his name to the Senate for confirmation. Ten years earlier Parker had referred to political participation by Negroes as "a source of evil and a danger to both races." The NAACP opposed his nomination and urged its withdrawal.

When President Hoover refused to withdraw Judge Parker's name, the NAACP launched a massive and dramatic six-week campaign to prevent his confirmation. An avalanche of wires, letters, and telephone calls descended on every Senator whom there was any hope of influencing. The NAACP branches in all parts of the country added the weight of their deeply affected members. The Negro press and important segments of the white press, as well as organized labor (which had its own anti-Parker ax to grind), joined in. In the showdown Parker failed of confirmation by a 41–39 vote.

The Association then carried out the "or else" part of the proposition it had made to recalcitrant Senators. In the next elections campaigns were waged against Senators who had voted for Parker and who could be affected by Negro voting power. In Kansas, Senator Henry Allen was defeated, the margin clearly furnished by Negro voters in response to the NAACP's appeal. The same fate befell Senators Shortbridge of California, Patterson of Missouri, Watson of Indiana, Fess and McCulloch of Ohio, Reed of Pennsylvania, Harfield of West Virginia, Kean and Baird of New Jersey, Walcott of Connecticut, and Herbert of Rhode Island. All these men had been retired by 1934.

Inching Along

When Walter White succeeded James Weldon Johnson as executive secretary of the NAACP, Harlem's Negro Renaissance and the exuberance of the Roaring Twenties were nearing their end. The Great Depression was about to set in. The crash of the stock market in 1929 and the ensuing bank failures wrought havoc inside and outside the Association. Always the last to be hired and the first to be fired, Negroes across the country began to feel the depression even before the mass of white workers realized what was happening. This was reflected immediately on the NAACP's books. For example, many subscribers could no longer pay their dollar a year for *The Crisis*. By mid-depression the magazine's paid circulation had dwindled to only about 10,000—a tenth of what it had been at its peak.

The long anti-lynching fight, not counting numerous legal cases, had drained the NAACP's finances. Even before the depression there were months when James Weldon Johnson and Walter White went without their pay checks. More than once an urgent message went out from New York to dedicated and tireless Field Secretary Daisy Lampkin. Almost always, Mrs. Lampkin was able by intensified campaigning to pull a rabbit out of the hat and forward precious dollars to the national office to meet a lagging payroll. For some years now, she has served with distinction on the Association's Board of Directors.

A mammoth fund-raising benefit for the NAACP was held in 1929, to which Duke Ellington, Libby Holman, Clifton Webb, and other stars of the theater donated their services. The following year William Rosenwald offered to match each $1000 donated to NAACP work by others. Edsel Ford, Herbert Lehman, Mr. and Mrs. Felix Warburg, and a few other people of means made the same offer. But it was from the American Fund for Public Service that the NAACP received the first large grant, $10,000, and at a most critical time.

Charles Garland, a young white man with idealistic views, inherited more than a million dollars from his father. But young Garland believed that no one had a right to enjoy wealth unless he had earned it. Accordingly he set up the Garland Fund for Public Service, with Roger Baldwin as president. Among its beneficiaries, besides the NAACP, were the National Urban League and the Brotherhood of Sleeping Car Porters. Even with its help, the NAACP was forced to make drastic economies. Robert Bagnall, its director of branches, and part of its secretarial staff had to be dropped. The printing of pamphlets and publicity material had to be curtailed, and the number of pages in *The Crisis* was reduced. But the work had to go on, for new appeals came every day for NAACP assistance, legal or otherwise. Lynchings were on the increase again, and the depression created new problems of discrimination.

With white middle-class income drastically reduced, almost half a million Negro women domestic workers found themselves without jobs. In some of the big industrial cities in the North, as many as 40 percent of the Negro men were soon unemployed. In the South, hungry whites began to clamor for traditionally "Negro" jobs. Bellhops and other Negro workers found themselves discharged so that whites might take their places. At the peak of the depression 65 percent of the Negro workers in Atlanta and 80 percent of those in Norfolk were on relief. The Works Projects Administration and other agencies set up to cope with the depression often discriminated against Negroes, particularly in the South. In some places wage differentials on public works were set up—one scale for whites, a lower one for Negroes. The same thing was true in various communities in the doling out of public assistance.

Thousands of complaints concerning the Federal Emergency Relief Administration poured into NAACP offices. Private charities—even a number of religious organizations—also found ways of favoring needy whites above needy Negroes. Some soup kitchens and bread lines shamelessly turned away Negro men and women. Angelo Herndon was sentenced to twenty years on the chain gang in Georgia for leading a hunger march that sought to petition the county commissioners for relief that was legally due Negroes. Negro applicants were frequently locked up for what white relief administrators labeled "impudence" or "disturbing the peace." Hunger and discrimination kept official company from coast to coast.

With thousands of former members forced by economic circumstances to drop their membership, the National Association for the Advancement of Colored People nevertheless kept inching along and managed to keep its head above water. The 26th Annual Convention in St. Louis in 1935 was attended by 200 delegates representing 38 branches. The economic aspects of civil rights were high on the agenda. A major topic was the failure of the New Deal to provide adequately for Negroes deprived of work by the depression. Harry L. Hopkins, Federal Emergency Relief Administrator, was asked to appoint a qualified Negro as deputy administrator in every state that had a large Negro population. And at this Convention Roscoe Dungee, the militant editor of the *Oklahoma Black Dispatch,* was awarded the NAACP Medal of Merit. Mary McLeod Bethune, president of the National Council of Negro Women and director of Negro affairs for the National Youth Administration, received the Spingarn Medal. A friend of the Roosevelts, she brought greetings from the White House, and words of encouragement from her own great heart for the lean years of the locusts.

Old Man River

> There was wind and water
> And there warn't nowhere to go,
> The levees all bustin'
> When the river overflow;
> Risin' water's done
> Washed my house away.
> So many poor peoples
> Is got nowhere to stay. . . .

That is how it was during the great Mississippi floods of 1927 when droves of poor whites and Negroes from Arkansas to the Gulf were washed off the land. The Negro press said the flood was a blessing in disguise because it rescued thousands of Negro field hands and their families from peonage, but the bedraggled refugees hardly found this to be so. Since the floods constituted a national emergency, the Red Cross set up in Baton Rouge a vast camp for flood refugees, and hundreds who had never been out of the plantation country were brought there. The treatment of the flood victims was based on race, a classic example of southern custom.

White refugees were brought down the Mississippi to Baton Rouge in steamers with cabins and covered decks that protected them from the elements; the Negroes were loaded on flatboats and freight barges that trailed behind the steamers and were open to wind and storm. In Baton Rouge the whites were housed in a group of tree-shaded buildings, the armory or former barracks. The Negroes—men, women, and children alike—were housed in small tents in an open field where the mud was ankle-deep when it rained. The whites had three hot meals a day; the Negroes, two. The whites were given regular rations of tobacco, snuff, and candy; the Negroes got what was left over, if there was anything.

Many Negro peons told horrifying tales of having to do forced labor at gunpoint on levees that finally gave way; of terrified whites fleeing in all the available boats, leaving their Negro sharecroppers to find their way to safety as best they could; of hair-raising nights on roofs or knolls or flood-surrounded portions of the levee, fighting off the snakes and small wild animals that sought refuge there too. Most of the refugees could not read or write; most of them had never seen a city before; some of them had never been off the plantations where they were born; some of the adults had never had ten dollars at one time in their whole life. What they would do or where they would go when the floods were over, they did not know. Most of them thought they would return to the plantations, because they had nowhere else to go.

However, the federal government decided to do something about flood control—to build bigger and better levees and try to rechannel the contrary old Mississippi that had had its way too long. Herbert Hoover was put in charge of flood relief. When he paid no attention to complaints from the Negro victims, Walter White went to Mississippi to investigate conditions for the NAACP. The data he brought back regarding numerous of these refugee compounds made the one at Baton Rouge seem like paradise in comparison. Some of them were almost like concentration camps. Some were surrounded by National Guardsmen. Negroes were not allowed outside the gates without permission of their landlords, who were waiting for the waters to subside so they could force these refugees back into semi-slavery. In some camps the inmates had to pay for Red Cross supplies that were supposed to be free. When presented with these findings, Walter White reported, "Mr. Hoover unequivocally and indignantly denied the charges." But public protests finally forced the appointment of a Negro committee of investigation headed by Dr. Robert R. Moton of Tuskegee. This group of conservative southern Negroes also confirmed the abuses, and eventually some of them were corrected.

The problems created by Old Man River continued to concern the NAACP well into the depression years, and much staff time and official funds were expended in an attempt to solve them. The federal government, through the War Department, had hardly set up its Mississippi River Flood Control Project extending from Minnesota to New Orleans, before reports of discrimination against Negro workers began to reach the NAACP offices. Government contracts for building levees and for other projects were allotted to private contractors, and most of the men employed in executing them were white Southerners. Wage differentials were established—less money for Negroes than for whites doing the same work—and separate camps and commissaries were set up, Negroes often being charged higher prices than whites for food and other commodities. Even before the NAACP sent a trio of investigators south, these facts had been confirmed by an American Federation of Labor report, but that body refused to allow the NAACP to use these findings. It was then that the Association decided to send its own investigators into the field.

The first to be sent south was Helen Boardman. On her return to New York she reported that all along the Mississippi she saw Negro workers crowded into floorless tents. They worked twelve hours a day seven days a week at an average wage of ten cents an hour, their pay coming from funds allotted contractors by the United States government. Private commissary owners were making fortunes overcharging illiterate Negro workers; some camps even charged them for the water they used. The NAACP sent Miss Boardman's report to the President, who turned it over to the Secretary of War. When conditions at the levee camps remained unchanged, Walter White sent out his young assistant secretary, Roy Wilkins, accompanied by George S. Schuyler of the *Pittsburgh Courier,* to gather additional facts that might not only be presented to the government but be used for an exposé in *The Crisis.*

Disguised as itinerant laborers in dirty overalls and tattered coats, Wilkins and Schuyler showed up on the levee near Memphis one bitter cold winter day. Together or separately for three weeks they talked with Negro workers in more than twenty camps on both banks of the Mississippi. They found that some of the men had been paid so poorly all their lives that even ten cents an hour seemed a good wage. But the Negroes had no protection from the bullying brutality of the southern levee camp bosses or the rapacious greed of the commissary owners.

In a Vicksburg rooming house one night, Schuyler had a narrow escape from possible violence. Two policemen, pistols drawn, burst into his room, pulled him out of bed, handcuffed him, and took him to jail. The police confiscated his money, his fountain pen, and the notebook in which he had jotted down his data. When he asked on what charge he was being detained, they cursed him and said that they would ask the questions. They questioned him all night long. Since the police had his notebook, Schuyler realized that it was useless to try to hide the purpose of his mission. He told them frankly he was investigating the wages and working conditions of flood control workers. He contended that any improvement in their lot would benefit the South. For example, a Negro who was paid more money could spend more money. The depression had closed many small white businesses. The money the Negroes spent would help to keep others open. Schuyler's calmness and logic seemed to cool the police wrath to some degree, although there was no doubt that they suspected him of being a troublemaker. After almost twenty-four hours, he was released and told to leave the state as fast as he could. Schuyler never did get back his fountain pen or his money; fortunately, however, he had hidden some bills in the toe of his shoe.

All that Wilkins and Schuyler saw confirmed Helen Boardman's earlier reports. The NAACP printed 10,000 copies of a leaflet, *Mississippi River Slavery—1932,* to inform Senators and the public of the deplorable conditions prevailing on the government's flood control project.

In the face of the War Department's indifference to the NAACP revelations, Senator Robert F. Wagner of New York was asked to introduce a resolution requesting a senatorial investigation. He waited for a time when the Senate was almost empty of Southerners, then brought the resolution up for a vote. Thus it was passed by a fluke. In the spring of 1933 official investigations began, and by September the government had set minimum standards of working conditions and wages for *all* unskilled labor engaged in flood control. The benefits thus were applicable to both Negroes and whites. As a matter of fact, most NAACP-sponsored legislation of benefit to Negroes has proved beneficial to whites as well.

At Boulder Dam, which had almost no Negro workers, and in the Tennessee Valley Authority projects where Negroes were used only as unskilled laborers, NAACP intervention resulted in improved conditions and better jobs. But it was not just in the hinterlands that Negroes faced employment difficulties. In New York City itself—even in Harlem, the Negro quarter—there was job discrimination. Therefore, in the 1930's many members of the NAACP's New York branch—among them, Adam Clayton Powell, Jr.—took their places on picket lines before white-owned shops on West 125th Street. The Negro Renaissance of the 1920's had turned into the Harlem Remonstrance of the 1930's.

Buy Black

DON'T BUY WHERE YOU CAN'T WORK read one of the slogans painted on the signs carried by Negro pickets marching in front of white stores. BUY BLACK read another. Today it is hard to believe that once there were hundreds of shops and businesses in Negro Harlem that catered to Negroes but refused to employ Negro workers. The owners were white, the clerks were white. The cashiers at the movies were white, the operators in the film projection booths were white. The stagehands in the theaters were white. The insurance collectors were white. The switchboard operators in the telephone exchanges were white. The drivers of delivery trucks were white. Most newspaper vendors were white. Harlem was beginning to be resentful of all this whiteness.

The few Negro-owned businesses that managed to survive the depression years were bolstered by the BUY BLACK slogan. But Negro businessmen found it extremely difficult to get good locations. It was almost impossible for Negro merchants to buy or rent on 125th Street. Banks would not grant them loans, insurance companies would not insure their stock. Supply dealers made it hard to obtain credit. In 1935, when Mussolini invaded Ethiopia, the Negroes were about ready to attack the white merchants in Harlem. This they did, on March 19. Violent riots destroyed more than $2,000,000 worth of property, hundreds of white store windows were smashed and shelves looted. James E. Allen, then president of the New York branch of the NAACP, testified before the mayor's commission investigating the causes of the riots, and Mayor La Guardia appointed an interracial Commission on Conditions in Harlem. All conclusions from every source indicated that a basic cause of community unrest was resentment at racial discrimination in employment.

On the national front, there continued to be numerous employment problems. For example, in many states Negro teachers were paid less than white teachers. In Maryland white teachers received almost twice as much money as Negroes who taught the same grades. Thurgood Marshall appeared before the Maryland State Board of Education to argue for equalization of public-school salaries. The NAACP also took up the cause of underpaid Negro teachers in Kentucky and other states, with eventually encouraging results. Obtaining employment for Negroes in chain stores and public utilities except as janitors and cleaning women occupied the attention of both the NAACP and the National Urban League. In many cities local branches of these organizations collaborated toward this end. The depression had caused some major labor unions to cling even more closely to their anti-Negro bias, thus making it almost impossible for Negro men to secure skilled jobs. The vocational training and special skills many young Negroes had acquired in National Youth Administration programs or the CCC Camps were going to waste. As the depression years drew to a close and most whites were once more gainfully employed, 3.5 million Negro workers were still unemployed. In 1941 a Wright aviation plant hired two unskilled Negro workers; all of its white workers went out on strike. Across the nation from Harlem to California the right to work was in jeopardy. Securing this right was one of the gravest problems facing Negro Americans on the eve of World War II. In a most dramatic fashion, the NAACP took part in effecting a partial solution.

The March on Washington

A. Philip Randolph, the dignified gray-haired patriarch of labor who headed the Brotherhood of Sleeping Car Porters and Maids, had not been in the news much since his union was recognized in 1925. But suddenly in 1941 he made front-page headlines in all the papers, for it was he who originated the idea of a March on Washington. From 50,000 to 100,000 Negroes were to converge on the nation's capital to support the demand for the right to work in defense industries. America was preparing to go to war. Aviation plants, munitions factories, steel mills, and numerous other industries had been awarded huge government contracts for war materials to be paid for by public funds derived from the pockets of Negro as well as white taxpayers. Many of these industrial plants employed no Negroes; in the few that did, Negroes were hired only for unskilled labor. Sometimes it was the unions, sometimes it was management that barred Negroes. Sometimes it was just plain cussedness—as long as a white man could be found to fill a job, the job would not go to a Negro.

An executive of North American Aviation said that "under no circumstances" would that company employ Negroes other than as janitors. Another aviation plant in Kansas advertised for "white American citizens" only. Numerous instances of racial bias on the part of industrialists were relayed by the NAACP to the National Advisory Committee in Washington. In 1941 the United States Employment Service itself reported difficulty in placing skilled Negro workers in "essential occupations" related to defense. In electrical equipment plants, out of 1066 applicants hired in a three-month period that year, only 5 were Negro. Of 8000 people added to the payroll in aviation plants, only 13 were Negroes. In machine and tool shops, only 245 out of 35,000 new employees were Negroes. The government report concluded that not only were Negroes denied skilled jobs in most defense plants, "but they are receiving very few jobs of any type, even unskilled." On the verge of another war for democracy, the deep roots of prejudice in American life were still effective in keeping the Negro poor, helpless, and hungry. Official action was either lacking or ineffectual. Finally A. Philip Randolph proposed organizing a great mass demonstration that would parade down Pennsylvania Avenue and pass in front of both Houses of Congress. The NAACP gave its whole-hearted support, including money, its staff, and the indispensable collaboration of its branches. The date was set for July 1, 1941.

Government disapproval was communicated almost immediately to the March-on-Washington Committee, which, besides Randolph, included Walter White, Frank Crosswaith of the Harlem Labor Union, Henry Craft of the Harlem YMCA, Lester Granger of the National Urban League, and Rayford Logan, the historian. Offices were set up in the Hotel Theresa in the heart of Harlem. The Negro press from coast to coast gave the movement editorial support. Pledges of participation and money came in from churches, lodges, schools, women's groups, and all types of racial associations, north and south. It looked as if Washington would be full of Negroes on July 1. The government began to worry.

As head of New York's Office of Civilian Defense, Mayor La Guardia called the March-on-Washington Committee into conference in an attempt to prevail upon it to cancel the pending demonstration. Eleanor Roosevelt, first lady in the hearts of the Negro people, admonished, "You know where I stand, but the attitude of the Washington police, most of them Southerners, and the general feeling in Washington itself are such that I fear there may be trouble if the march occurs." But, like a tree that is planted by the waters, Randolph could not be moved. "The administration leaders in Washington," he said, "will never give the Negro justice until they see masses—ten, twenty, fifty thousand Negroes on the White House lawn. July 1 is our March day."

Then President Roosevelt himself sent for Randolph and Walter White to come to Washington. They met with Assistant Secretary of War Patterson, Secretary of the Navy Knox, Anna Rosenberg of the Social Security Board, and other officials, but with no concrete results. The membership of the March-on-Washington Committee grew swiftly until it included thousands and thousands of Negroes throughout the United States who had begun to save their money for tickets to Washington. When Roosevelt inquired exactly what Randolph's committee wanted, the answer was that it was nothing less than "an unequivocal executive order to effectuate the speediest possible abolition of discrimination in war industries and the armed services." Roosevelt then asked that a tentative draft be drawn up for his guidance. This he gave careful consideration. On June 25, 1941, just a week before the March on Washington was to take place, the President issued Executive Order 8802, and the March on Washington was called off.

Executive Order 8802 decreed: "There shall be no discrimination in the employment of workers in defense industries and in Government because of race, creed, color, or national origin. . . . And it is the duty of employers and labor organizations . . . to provide for the full and equitable participation of all workers." Clauses were inserted in all government defense contracts forbidding racial discrimination and, as a follow-through, the Fair Employment Practices Committee was set up. In spite of having only investigative rather than enforcement powers, according to Walter White, "more progress was made by the FEPC toward employment on the basis of ability in the face of racial and religious discrimination than at any other period in American history."

However, when the FEPC went into action, its mild investigations were viciously attacked by die-hard racists. Before the FEPC hearings in Birmingham, the *Gadsden* (Alabama) *Times* dubbed the Committee "a bunch of snoopers" sent from Washington "to determine whether the South is doing right by Little Sambo." The League to Maintain White Supremacy immediately called for an organization to be formed that would be "so strong, so powerful, so efficient, that this menace to our national security and local way of life will rapidly disappear. . . . Alabama must lead the way."

Mark Ethridge, the distinguished Kentucky liberal editor of the *Louisville Courier-Journal,* and the most prominent southern member of the FEPC, resigned. Believing that Committee policies were going too far, he declared, "All the armies of the world, both of the United States and the Axis, could not force upon the South the abandonment of racial segregation." Nevertheless, even in the most backward areas some employers modified their Jim Crow hiring policies rather than face FEPC charges. A number of plants in the North, finding Negro labor as useful as any other, dropped the color bar entirely. In the end, the March on Washington—that never occurred—paid off in practical results for thousands of Negro workers.

The Fruits of Effort

Just as the NAACP was about to round out its first thirty years its president, Joel Spingarn, died. He was succeeded by his brother Arthur, the long-time chairman of the Legal Committee. In 1937 founder Henry Moskowitz had died. Charles Edward Russell, another of the charter members of the Association, passed away in 1941. William English Walling, too, had died. But still on the job on the eve of World War II, and almost as active as ever at the age of 75, Mary White Ovington was outlining her personal history of the NAACP, *When the Walls Come Tumbling Down.*

Miss Ovington had seen the Association grow from a handful of members and a paid staff of only three, to an organization that could get the ear of Congress and confer with the President of the United States. The anti-lynching fight which had taken up so much time over the years did not result in federal legislation, but it had shamed America into an ever-widening public condemnation of mob violence. The rope and fagot of Walter White's book were no longer so prominent a part of the paraphernalia of the "Arsenal of Democracy," now that the United States again prepared to defend democracy in Europe. Largely as the result of NAACP pressure, Washington had even taken some steps to defend democracy at home for Negroes.

In little ways and big, after thirty years the NAACP was beginning to realize the fruits of effort. Increasingly its influence was felt nationally—and even internationally. Du Bois attended the inauguration of President King in Liberia, and maintained close contact with outstanding African leaders. The NAACP was represented at the first Pan-African Congress. Field Secretary William Pickens represented the Association at the Second World Congress Against Imperialism in Germany. Throughout the fifteen years of our occupation of Haiti, the NAACP helped hold in check the arrogant racial abuses on the part of the Marines stationed there. Arthur Spingarn concerned himself with the color line in Panama, for discrimination against Negro workers in the Canal Zone was "substantially the same as that existing in the lower South."

On the home front the Association's interests ranged from such widely divergent activities as supporting a student strike at Fisk University to taking part in the defense of nine Negro itinerants, aged 14 to 20, who were charged at Scottsboro, Alabama, with raping two white prostitutes on a freight train. This became one of the famous criminal cases of the 1930's, the NAACP's initial efforts in behalf of the boys being nullified by the intervention of the Communists. The latter, seeking to exploit the matter for their own ideological purposes, misrepresented the NAACP as being in league with "the lyncher bosses" and persuaded the boys to abandon the NAACP-provided counsel, which included Clarence Darrow and Arthur Garfield Hays. Later, as a participant in the Scottsboro Defense Committee, the Association helped raise funds for strictly legal expenses. Death sentences were imposed, appealed, reversed, reimposed, and appealed once more. None of the boys were executed; eventually, as the result of NAACP negotiations, they were successively released.

Southern plans to close down relief projects at the height of the depression in order to force Negroes into picking cotton at starvation wages were successfully opposed by the NAACP. The Association was also successful in preventing the exclusion of Negro Boy Scouts from the Scout Jamboree held in Washington in 1937. Throughout the depression it continued its fight for the ballot, equal education, unrestricted housing, and the right to belong to trade unions. In the single year of 1939, it prepared for court action nine cases involving the right of Negro students to attend tax-supported universities in the states where they lived. That same year, when the Daughters of the American Revolution refused to allow Marian Anderson to sing in Constitution Hall in Washington because no Negroes were allowed to perform there, NAACP intervention helped to secure the open-air platform of the Lincoln Monument for her concert. There on Easter Sunday, before the statue of the Great Emancipator, Marian Anderson sang to an unsegregated audience of more than 75,000 people.

Some sections of organized labor began to take NAACP objectives into account, and to support increased unionization of Negroes. The International Executive Board of the CIO's United Auto Workers demanded an end to discrimination in all plants with which they held agreements. The Association interested itself in breaking down segregation in the musicians union in cities where segregated locals kept Negroes from better-paying jobs. Board member John Hammond conferred with the major radio networks and secured their cooperation in using Negro players in studio bands. Some Hollywood producers began to listen to NAACP protests regarding the stereotyping of Negroes in motion pictures. (In later years, both Walter White and Roy Wilkins conferred directly with leaders of the film industry on these matters—White in 1942 and Wilkins in 1957.) Carl Van Vechten announced the founding of the James Weldon Johnson Memorial Collection of Negro Art and Letters at Yale University. The Washington NAACP continued to condemn the barring of Negroes from the National Theatre and other theaters in the capital. Of greatest eventual significance was the formulation and adoption in 1934 of plans for a systematic coordinated legal assault on discrimination in the schools, which led finally to the 1954 decision outlawing enforced public-school segregation.

Thus, by the end of its first thirty years, the National Association for the Advancement of Colored People had made its influence felt in many areas of American life—from art to autos, lynching to law. And the five initial letters of its name—NAACP—had become known from Alabama to Africa.

3

World War II

Defective Arsenal

An article in *The Crisis* entitled "Old Jim Crow in Uniform" reported that as America prepared for war only two infantry regiments, one cavalry regiment, and the Navy mess corps admitted Negroes. Other branches of the armed services were barred to Negro citizens. Secretary of the Navy Knox stated that Negroes were acceptable aboard ship *only* as messmen. In this he was supported by the chief of the Bureau of Navigation, Admiral Chester W. Nimitz, who claimed that discrimination in the Navy was "in the interest of harmony and efficiency." Many draft boards in centers with large Negro populations had no Negro members. Less than 30 Negroes were admitted to the newly established officer candidate schools. *The Crisis* editorialized, "We are for the national defense program, but we feel the strongest defense of democracy lies in giving all the people a stake in it—not a stake measured by comparison with Hitlerism, but one measured by the professions of democracy itself."

In 1940, Walter White, A. Philip Randolph, T. Arnold Hill of the National Urban League, and other Negro leaders submitted to President Roosevelt a seven-point program for the abolition of segregation in the military services. Senators were petitioned by the NAACP urging that the Selective Service Act be amended to provide for the induction of Negroes without discrimination. A Howard University student, Yancy Williams, filed suit to compel the War Department to consider his application for the Army Air Corps, then a lily-white branch of the service. The NAACP threatened lawsuits against various local boards of education that provided vocational defense training programs for white youths but not for Negroes. In the spring of 1941, NAACP attorneys met in Washington to plan legal action against the various racial restrictions in both the civilian and military phases of the defense program. But immediately after the bombing of Pearl Harbor, the Association called upon all Negro citizens to give unstinted support to the fight for victory abroad, and at the same time it urged continuation of the fight for democratic treatment at home.

99

Military Desegregation

Judge William H. Hastie, dean of the Howard University Law School, was appointed civilian aide to the Secretary of War; Colonel Campbell C. Johnson became executive assistant to the Director of Selective Service; and Colonel Benjamin O. Davis became the first Negro brigadier general. Special facilities were set up at the Army Air Field at Tuskegee for training Negro pilots and technicians. By the end of 1941 the 99th Pursuit Squadron was ready for action, and eventually some 600 Negro pilots were graduated at Tuskegee. In contrast to World War I, training for Negro army officers was early instituted in various unsegregated camps. Nevertheless, as American forces moved into action overseas, the military services were still divided into white and Negro units.

In 1942 the Navy agreed to accept Negroes for general service, but established a separate compound, Camp Robert Smalls (named after the Negro hero of the Civil War), at the Great Lakes Naval Training Station for their training. Lester Granger of the National Urban League was called to Washington as a consultant to the Secretary of the Navy. The Marines began training Negroes in 1942 and had accepted some 16,000 by the end of the war; however, they were confined mostly to menial or construction work. Both the WAC and the WAVES accepted limited numbers of Negro women, some for officer training in unsegregated units. Harriet Pickens, daughter of the NAACP's William Pickens, became the Navy's first Negro woman lieutenant, and Frances Wills its first ensign. Some 4000 Negro women served in the WAC and over 100 were commissioned as officers in all-Negro units. Both the Army and the Navy had restricted quotas for Negro nurses, but eventually about 500 were commissioned.

Many more Negroes served on local draft boards and in civilian advisory capacities in Washington than during World War I. Nevertheless, the NAACP was called upon thousands of times regarding discrimination in recruitment, mistreatment because of race during military training, and failure to upgrade Negro service men because of color. That a score of 39 was required of Negroes on army qualification tests whereas whites needed to score only 15 caused the NAACP to protest to the Secretary of War, but the ruling was not changed. A survey by the Negro Newspaper Publishers Association in 1946 showed that most Negro military units were largely officered by whites. Of 22,672 second lieutenants in the Army, only 818 were Negro. As the rank increased, the number of Negroes decreased proportionally. Thus only 7 of 5220 colonels were

Negro. Of 776 generals, Benjamin O. Davis was the only Negro general. In 1943 William H. Hastie resigned as civilian aide to the Secretary of War in protest against the continuing discrimination, particularly in the Air Force. His criticisms of official policy were given wide press coverage, and his carefully documented charges were published later in pamphlet form by the NAACP. They were helpful in eventually effecting reforms that in postwar years led to the almost complete abolition of discrimination at the lower levels of our military forces.

In the winter of 1944–1945 platoons of Negro riflemen were incorporated into some of the formerly all-white divisions of the First and Seventh Armies and fought through the Battle of the Bulge and across Germany. General Patton gave high praise to these Negro warriors, all of whom had volunteered for this combat duty. General Eisenhower stated, "All my commanders reported these volunteers did excellent work." Eleven members of the 104th Infantry received combat medals. In complimenting the entire battalion, Major General Lathan declared, "I have never seen any soldiers who performed better in combat than you."

Trouble on the Home Front

On the whole, the South treated Negroes in uniform encamped below the Mason-Dixon line as badly during World War II as it had a quarter of a century earlier during World War I. Historians of the period and NAACP files from 1940 to 1946 record incredible instances of disrespect and violence on the part of whites toward Negro service men and women. *The Crisis* reported, "There were beatings, shootings, riots and killings all over the South where most of the Negro troops were in training." And Mary White Ovington wrote: "The Army did not intend to break with the past. It trained Negro soldiers in separate camps, and failed to protect the uniform if worn by a man whose face was black. . . . Negro soldiers were segregated in buses, at motion pictures, in shops, at counters at drugstores. One would suppose that the Negro did not belong to the classification *homo.* The height of stupidity was reached when the Red Cross refused blood from Negro donors, but later accepted it and segregated it. . . . The too frequent treatment of the newly drafted Negro as inferior simply because of his color was unfortunate and cruel and affected Negro morale. These young soldiers . . . went to their various camps to be set apart as Hitler set apart the Jews."

A Negro soldier who entered a white USO or service club on a post might be arrested and court-martialed. The same thing might happen if he entered a white latrine because the call of nature was urgent. Buses might refuse to carry Negro soldiers who were on furlough and awaiting transportation at the camp gates. Trains arrived at southern stations with only a single Jim Crow coach that was usually so crowded that no other Negroes could board the train, but there would be a dozen cars for whites. At the Union Station in Washington, taxicabs often refused to carry Negro fares, soldier or civilian. But worst of all was the unpunished brutality that southern police, MP's, and civilians were permitted to inflict upon Negro soldiers, and the fact that their commanding officers ordered the Negroes not to retaliate.

America's participation in the war had hardly begun before 28 Negro soldiers were shot down by white civilian and military officers in Alexandria, Louisiana. Three Negro WAC's were beaten by civilian police in a Kentucky railroad station because the women did not move as rapidly from a WHITE ONLY waiting room as the officers wished. In North Carolina a white bus driver was cleared of murder, although he had shot a Negro soldier without warning in an argument over segregation. Service man Isaac Woodward had his eyes gouged out by a South Carolina sheriff while on his way home from overseas duty. In Vallejo, California, there were three riotous clashes between Negro military personnel and white service men and civilians. Race riots took place at the Mobile naval yard and at Fort Bragg, Camp Davis, Camp Lee, and several other military posts. More than 100 Negro officers were locked in the stockade at Freeman Field, Indiana, for entering a FOR WHITE ONLY officers' club. NAACP intervention freed three Negro WAC's in Kentucky who were accused of violating the Articles of War when they protested against being beaten by whites on a bus. These are only a few of the hundreds of such incidents reported to the NAACP.

In the South, German prisoners of war were served promptly in railway station restaurants, whereas the Negro soldiers guarding them often had to go hungry. Two of the major southern railway lines graciously provided a single table in their dining cars where Negroes might eat behind a curtain. But many railroads did not do this; hence Negro travelers, soldier and civilian, had to go without food. One case that was widely written up—many northern newspapers editorialized on the irony of it—concerned a group of Nazi captives who were being shipped under Negro guard to a west coast prisoner-of-war camp. The diner could serve only four Negro American soldiers at its segregated table, but the German prisoners ate without delay with other passengers in the main part of the diner. Witter Bynner's poem "Defeat" dramatized this well:

> On a train in Texas German prisoners eat
> With white American soldiers, seat by seat
> While black American soldiers sit apart—
> The white men eating meat, the black men heart.
> Now, with that other war a century done,
> Not the live North but the dead South has won:
> Not yet a riven nation comes awake.
> Whom are we fighting this time, for God's sake?
> Mark well the token of the separate seat—
> It is again ourselves that we defeat.

Civilian Explosions

Because the Negro newspapers continually headlined stories of racial insult and violence against Negro soldiers, the Department of Justice at one period during the war considered bringing charges of "sedition" against them. When this did not seem feasible, some of the papers found it difficult to obtain their quota of newsprint or paper. The NAACP called a conference of the editors of twenty-four of the largest Negro papers, with a circulation of several million copies. The conference reached agreement on procedures for presenting effective criticism but at the same time reducing the likelihood of suppression by the government. The NAACP was also instrumental in securing needed quotas of newsprint for some of these papers.

But it did not take the Negro press to keep relatives and friends informed of what Negro soldiers were facing in many parts of the country. Almost every letter from any southern camp contained this information. Negro parents became more and more enraged. The chip on many civilian shoulders became a stone. On the other hand, southern whites transplanted to the urban North resented what they called Negro "intrusion" into industry. To some whites the sight of a Negro in uniform anywhere was infuriating. It did not take much to set off race riots from Los Angeles to Philadelphia, from Beaumont and Houston to Detroit.

The worst of these riots occurred in Detroit. (Incidentally, the NAACP branch there was the largest in the country, with almost 12,000 members.) Early in 1942 there had been a minor riot at the Sojourner Truth

Housing Project when Negroes attempted to move into federally financed housing. Detroit police arrested 107 Negro tenants, but only two of the attacking mob of several hundred whites. The following spring 26,000 white workers making bomber engines at the Packard motor plant struck in protest against the employment of Negroes. Members of the Ku Klux Klan and followers of Gerald L. K. Smith were thought to be the chief agitators. Walter White reported hearing an orator in front of the plant scream, "I'd rather see Hitler and Hirohito win the war than work beside a nigger on the assembly line." Before the end of June, whites and Negroes were killing each other on the Detroit streets. It was America's worst race riot, and it brought war production to an almost complete stop for two days.

The rioting began on a hot Sunday night on the bridge leading from Belle Isle Park to the city. A fist fight was said to have broken out between a Negro and a white man, and the whole bridge was soon in turmoil. Rumor had it that in the mass fracas whites threw a Negro baby into the river, or—depending on which side was telling the story—a Negro threw a white baby into the river. Even wilder rumors were circulated throughout Detroit that night by both whites and Negroes. Before dawn crowds began to overturn cars driven by Negroes and to beat the fleeing occupants. Negro passengers, unaware of rioting, were dragged from street cars and mobbed in Cadillac Square. The Negroes in turn began to retaliate against the whites. However, the whites had the police on their side, for many policemen were former Southerners. Sam Mitchell, well-known Negro veteran of World War I, claimed that two police officers to whom he appealed for protection held his arms while white hoodlums slugged him at will. Whites invaded motion-picture theaters and beat up the Negro patrons in the aisles. Negroes began wrecking white-owned shops in Paradise Valley, the Harlem of Detroit. Within twenty-four hours, 34 persons were officially listed as dead; 25 of them were Negroes, of whom 17 had been slain by the police. Unofficial estimates of the dead were higher. Hundreds of persons were maimed, some for life. Property damage ran to about a million dollars.

The second day of the rioting, Walter White asked the governor of Michigan to call up troops, and he also telephoned the War Department at Washington. By nightfall 6000 federal and state troopers began to patrol the city in trucks and jeeps. But on Tuesday it looked as if trouble might start all over again, for city police and state troopers invaded the Negro St. Antoine YMCA, lined everyone inside the lobby up against the wall, beat some, and shot down one man who they claimed "reached for his pocket." The Detroit branch of the NAACP, aided by Thurgood Marshall, Lucille Black, and Daisy Lampkin of the national staff who had flown out from New York, set up relief and counseling headquarters in the basement of the Negro YMCA. Streams of bruised, battered, angry Negroes poured in for help; according to Walter White, they looked like the "bombed-out victims of Nazi terror in Europe. . . . Men, women and even children told their stories of violence inflicted upon them not only by members of the mob but also by Michigan state troopers and the Detroit police."

Thurgood Marshall visited the Vernor Apartments after the police had riddled the building with bullets and forced the occupants out with tear gas. As the terrified people ran into the street, the police entered, breaking down doors, smashing furniture, and looting. Many of the occupants never recovered their money and other valuables. Marshall reported that the interior of the apartment house "resembled a battlefield." Although the NAACP sought to have the worst of the police offenders punished for their brutality and hostility toward Negro citizens, no Detroit policeman was ever so much as reprimanded.

About a month after the Detroit explosion, Harlem blew up. The riots there began on a hot summer Sunday night, too. Walter White himself was almost mobbed in Harlem, because of his light skin. Shortly after the excitement began on the evening of August 1, White received a telephone call from Mayor La Guardia requesting him to meet him immediately at the West 123rd Street precinct station. If brown-skinned Roy Wilkins had not been sitting beside him, White might have been attacked as his cab went through the milling crowds on Harlem's Seventh Avenue, for the Negroes had begun to stone whites in passing cars. But the Harlem rioting was not primarily an attack on people; rather it involved destruction of white property. The riots were not city-wide. Few white people were involved, and the police acted decently. The Negroes simply went on a rampage—the cause being a rumor that a white policeman had killed a Negro soldier in the Braddock Hotel.

Harlem at that time was somewhat fed up with policemen. Ever since Negroes had picketed white shops in protest at racial discrimination in employment, Harlem had been flooded with white police. Groups of them stood on almost every corner, swinging their nightsticks; they walked in pairs. They rode on horseback down the streets, Harlem being the only section of New York City that was patrolled by mounted officers. They came suddenly around corners on speeding motorcycles. They stopped suspicious-looking Negroes and frisked them. They warned whites to stay out of Harlem. Downtowners who visited Negro friends at night sometimes had to convince the police that they really were in Harlem to see their friends and that they had no fear of the terrors the police seemed to feel existed. Harlem felt, too, that in handling suspected Negro culprits the officers were often rougher than was necessary. So when the word spread that a white cop had killed a Negro boy in uniform, Harlemites went mad.

What really happened was that a young Negro woman, Margie Polite, had gotten into some sort of name-calling bout with a white policeman in the lobby of the Braddock, a hotel near the stage entrance of the Apollo Theatre. A Negro lad in uniform objected to the way the officer addressed Miss Polite, and an argument followed. For what reason no one ever knew, the white policeman shot the Negro boy in the back. He fell. Margie Polite ran into the street, screaming about the soldier's death. The lad, however, did not die; he was only slightly wounded. But race hysteria carried Margie's screams all over Harlem. Anger and frustration did the rest.

In an attempt to solve some of the problems that had caused the Harlem outburst, the city-wide Citizens Committee on Harlem was formed. Algernon Black and Walter White were co-chairmen. It functioned for several years and, with the NAACP and the National Urban League, brought about some vitally needed improvements in the world's largest Negro ghetto.

Cash Gratitude

From the NAACP records come the following statements made by a young Negro soldier before the Navy Board of Inquiry on the island of Guam:

> "For what were you court-martialed the first time?"
> "I sat down in a bus on a seat that wasn't for colored."
> "What happened then?"
> "They arrested me and put me in solitary confinement for five days on bread and water."
> "And what was the charge the second time?"
> "I went into a white restaurant and asked to be served food."
> "What happened then?"
> "The same sentence, sir. Solitary confinement on bread and water for five days."

These things happened to a northern-born lad during his training period in the South before he was sent overseas. They were revealed in
Guam when 44 Negroes were sentenced to long prison terms for defending themselves against similar restrictions on that remote Pacific island.
After taunts, physical attacks, and hand grenades that prejudiced white
sailors tossed into their quarters, matters came to a climax for the Negroes on Christmas Eve, 1944, when a group of Negro sailors on liberty
passes were driven out of a recreation area by the gunfire of the whites.
On Christmas Day a Negro was killed, another wounded. That night
shooting broke out between white and Negro service men, but no one
was killed. Only Negroes were arrested, in accordance with the military
theory that when racial trouble developed, the Negroes were always at
fault. The MP's made mass arrests in the Negro barracks. Strong appeals
to the President and the War Department by the NAACP secured the
freedom of the Negro service men in this particular case. At Yerba Buena
52 Negro sailors were returned to duty after NAACP intervention when
they were charged with mutiny. But from every combat area all over the
world came appeals from service men for help. NAACP representatives
went to the European, Pacific, and African theaters of war to make investigations, talk with military commanders, and see what they could do
to ameliorate the ugly racial situations in which the Negro, nine times
out of ten, got the worst of things.

As a result of the NAACP's interest and help, grateful Negro service
men and women everywhere expressed their support of the Association
by individual and group contributions to the national office, as indicated
by random examples from the treasurer's books: August 24, 1944—
Unit of colored soldiers in an undisclosed Pacific area, $3920; October
14, 1944—Men of the 823rd Engineering Battalion on the Ledo Road
between China and India, $2000; January 21, 1945–1887th Engineer
Aviation Battalion, $2063; March 26, 1945—Southwest Pacific Seebees,
$1222; May 24, 1945—India-Burma 382nd Seebees, $4331. Sometimes
contributions came by cable, sometimes from a hardened service man
on furlough who had been chosen to represent his squad or company,
sometimes in a letter sent directly from the trenches on the eve of battle.

"It was then that the NAACP became an international organization,"
wrote Mary White Ovington. "At the January annual meeting, I listened
as the Treasurer's report was read for the year 1945. Money was coming
from all over the world: from Guam to India, from India to England,
from England to California. It was coming from the returned soldier
and from the soldier left to sweat it out more months. From the war

worker at home as well as abroad. The report ended, 'From all sources, memberships, contributions, subscriptions, $400,000.' "

Disillusion Back Home

There were a million Negroes in uniform before the war ended—700,000 in the Army, 170,000 in the Navy, 25,000 in the Marines and the Coast Guard, still others in the Air Force. After V-J Day, Roy Wilkins wrote in *The Crisis:*

> The Negro soldier proved what his people back home knew all along—that he could fight with all the weapons against the best the enemy had to offer. He flew fighter planes escorting bombers, and fighter-bombers against enemy communications; he fought light, medium and heavy artillery, one unit winning a Presidential citation; he fought tanks and tank destroyers; he fought anti-aircraft guns; he fought mortars, machine guns, bazookas, carbines, automatic rifles. In the closing weeks of the war in Germany he was finally given the chance for which he had been begging, the chance to fight side by side with his white fellow Americans in the same units. . . . It is to be hoped that the performance of our soldiers in Europe will move the War Department to abolish the color line in the Army.

The 332nd Fighter Group composed entirely of Negroes flew 3500 missions before D-Day. Eighty-eight Negro pilots received the Distinguished Flying Cross. For "outstanding courage and resourcefulness" at Bastogne, the 969th Field Artillery Battalion was awarded the Distinguished Unit Citation. Members of the 92nd Division, which lost more than 3000 men, won 65 Silver Stars, 162 Bronze Star Medals, and 1300 Purple Hearts. Some 10,000 Negro troops built the Ledo Road in Asia. In France Negroes manned the famous "Red Ball Express" that sped supplies to the front. Negro members of the Coast Guard were among the first to land at Okinawa. About 24,000 Negroes were in the Merchant Marine; they served largely on an unsegregated basis, thanks to the National Maritime Union. There were four Negro captains, the first one being Hugh Mulzac. Eighteen Liberty Ships were named after Afro-Americans; among them was the *James Weldon Johnson.*

In civilian activities related to the war a great many Negro citizens gave service, a considerable number in executive positions. USO centers in the North had interracial staffs, but those for Negro troops in the South were staffed entirely by Negroes. Several all-Negro USO shows were sent overseas. The various Stage Door Canteens never countenanced discrimination, and Negro stars of the theater waited on table or sang nightly. The leading government agencies all utilized Negro workers. The Office of Civilian Defense had Negro executives and typists. The Office of Price Administration employed numerous economists, statisticians, checkers, and clerical helpers who were Negro. There were undercover Negro operatives in the Federal Bureau of Investigation, as well as in Army Intelligence. Negro journalists were accredited as war correspondents. Walter White traveled to all the fronts writing magazine articles and gathering facts which he later incorporated in his book, *The Rising Wind.*

"We know that our battle for democracy will begin when we reach San Francisco on our way home," White reported hearing various Negro service men say in Asia. "White folks talking about the Four Freedoms—and we ain't got none," was a not uncommon saying. Another indication of the feelings of Negro combatants was expressed in one soldier's boast, "That Hitler! Think he can whip anybody! I'm gonna capture Hitler. I'm gonna deliver him to President Roosevelt, at the front door of the White House." The soldier added that he was "gonna fight for some rights" at home, too. "I pick up a paper and see where a Negro soldier was lynched and it makes me feel like, 'What am I doing here?'" This soldier had probably observed that, as Roi Ottley reported, within a period of only a few weeks, "while Nazi spies and saboteurs went to trial one after another in an atmosphere of judicial fairness and public calm—six Negroes were lynched! One of these, Cleo Wright, was burned, his body mutilated, tied to an automobile and dragged through the streets of Sikeston, Missouri." A short time later, two 14-year-old Negro boys were found hanging from a bridge in Mississippi. The war years brought a revival of lynchings at home. And race riots did not cease. No wonder many Negro service men thought that the battle for democracy would of necessity continue on native soil. Hardly had the war in Japan ended when an ugly battle did take place on home grounds.

Terror in Tennessee

The foreword of *Terror in Tennessee,* an NAACP pamphlet about this battle, stated, "It is in the interest of all freedom-loving Americans that the Association publishes this booklet based on the findings of Maurice Weaver, a white Chattanooga attorney, Z. Alexander Looby,

Nashville, Tennessee, member of the National Legal Committee of the NAACP, and Walter White." Here, condensed from this pamphlet, are the facts:

On Monday, February 24, 1946, at about 10:00 A.M., Mrs. Gladys Stephenson went to the Castner-Knot Electric Appliance store in Columbia, Tennessee, to see about a radio which was being repaired. With her went her 19-year-old son James, who, in spite of his youth, was a naval veteran with three years' service in the Atlantic and the Pacific. Mrs. Stephenson was anxious to have the radio back in their neat little home, now that James had come back safely.

Mrs. Stephenson was disappointed to find that the repair work was faulty and she told the repairman so. This man, William Fleming, whose brother was a highway patrolman, became abusive; and when she objected to his abuse he slapped and kicked her. James, seeing his mother assaulted, rushed to her defense and hit Fleming, who fell through the plate-glass store window. Although Fleming was not injured, people in the street immediately surrounded Mrs. Stephenson and her son. The two were slapped and punched; policeman Frazier rushed into the milling crowd and clubbed the boy. The mother remonstrated with the policeman, telling him that he should first investigate the facts; thereupon she was hit in the face. Mother and son were then hustled off to jail.

News of the disturbance spread quickly through the town. Rumors of impending mob violence assumed ominous proportions as reports of the development of mass feelings against the Negro community were discussed openly in the streets. Sheriff J. J. Underwood called in Saul Blair, an elderly Negro businessman, and other Negro citizens and asked their cooperation in spiriting the Stephensons out of town. In the courthouse square, which is less than one block from the Negro section of Columbia, groups of white men had been congregating all day. (It was from the windows of this same courthouse that a howling, liquor-reeking mob had hanged 14-year-old Cordie Cheek.) By six o'clock that evening approximately 75 people were milling around the square.

Men pounded and kicked on the doors of the jail, and muffled voices demanded that the doors be opened. The leaders of the mob, demanding that the Stephensons be turned over to them, refused to leave until they had been assured that the boy and his mother were not in the building. Two of the mobsters, so drunk that they were unable to leave with the others, were put in the jail to sleep it off; they were released the next morning.

The Negro population of Columbia, certain that their part of town would be invaded that night, locked their doors and drew their window shades. The children were herded swiftly into the back of the houses or up to the attic. The area was silent and blacked out except for one feeble street lamp. Families huddled together in their tiny houses and waited. Members of the mob fired shots into the Negro community. Bands of white men, fully armed, roamed the adjoining streets. Several cars tore through the darkened area pumping shots into the houses. Then a car, carrying some city policemen and showing no lights, drove slowly into the tense, blacked-out section. Certain that the mob was finally moving in against them, the Negroes waited. Then someone shouted hysterically, "Here they come!" Scattered shots rang out. No one knows who fired the shots, but they were aimed at the dark car moving through the dark street. There were no serious wounds, but four of the policemen were hit with buckshot. According to the sheriff, a cordon of state patrolmen and helmeted state guardsmen was thrown around the section so that no one could enter or leave.

Zero hour was at dawn on Tuesday morning. In the business section, the police and guardsmen, in full battle dress and armed with Tommy guns, automatic rifles, and machine guns, worked in platoons, smashing the shop windows and chopping down the doors. The streets were soon littered with furniture hurled out of the windows. The cloth was slashed on all the tables in a poolroom. A doctor's office was wrecked, the furniture and equipment shattered beyond repair, surgical instruments, drugs, and valuable clinical apparatus wantonly destroyed or stolen. The uniformed vandals left the offices of the Atlanta Life Insurance Company a hopeless shambles after carefully destroying all files and records. The law enforcement officers and troopers broke into a funeral parlor and stormed through the chapel. Draperies were slashed, lighting fixtures ripped from their sockets. The pulpit with its well-thumbed Bible was hacked to pieces, the light over the Bible smashed. The hate-ridden orgy was topped off with a huge KKK scrawled in white chalk across one of the caskets. Cash registers in all these establishments received special treatment as the officers stuffed their pockets with the hard-earned money of Negro businessmen. With this part of the "riot" operation successfully terminated, the armored patrols swung into the residential streets.

Employing the same tactics, the guardsmen and police first subjected the house fronts to a barrage from their machine and Tommy guns. After a few minutes during which volley after volley crashed into the pitiful wooden walls of the beleaguered houses, the small army began to advance into the smoke-filled area. Machine-gun bullets whipped into the windows and doors of the silent buildings, and walls disintegrated in the face of these blasts. Inside their homes Negro citizens—men, women, and children—lay flattened against the floors. Then the houses were rushed. The frightened Negroes were clubbed and jabbed, and screaming children searching wildly for their mothers were sent sprawling. The people, dazed and covered with blood, were pushed and thrown into the streets. Hot guns were jabbed into their stomachs and they were ordered to keep their hands raised high. Terror-stricken mothers yanked up the arms of children who were too young to understand. Finally all the Negroes had been forced into the streets. The unconscious and the injured were dragged out. Through streets teeming with uniformed men, the bloody Negroes were marched off to the jail. Press and radio announced triumphantly: RIOTING NEGROES UNDER CONTROL!

About 70 men were being held, although they had not been charged with any exact offense, and no list of their names was available. The prisoners—more than half of them just recently returned from fighting in Europe and the Pacific—were slated to appear before a Board of Investigation. The room in which these bruised and battered men were to be arraigned before the "board" was filled with the clamor of the troopers' hard-heeled boots and the metallic noise of Tommy guns and rifles. Helmeted troopers stood in groups along the walls and in the corridors. The NAACP representative informed State Attorney General Bumpus that in his opinion statements made by any of the men in a room bristling with white deputies armed to the teeth, as that one was, would be made under coercion and intimidation. He requested the right to advise them, as a lawyer, of their rights to refuse to make a statement. Mr. Bumpus joined the sheriff in refusing this request. At least 75 citizens were brought before the Board of Investigation and questioned concerning their involvement in what that body was obviously trying to label an insurrection. The group included all the town's Negro businessmen, the aged Mr. Blair among them.

A few minutes later, several volleys were heard in the anteroom where the men were being prepared for questioning, and the thoroughly riddled bodies of two Negroes were dragged from the room. The NAACP called upon United States Attorney General Tom Clark to investigate the situation. In the meantime a total of 28 Negroes were charged with attempted murder in the first degree, and three others with attempt to commit a felony. Thurgood Marshall filed pleas of abatement in the "attempt to murder" indictments on the grounds that Negroes were excluded from the grand jury. Meanwhile, Oliver Harrington, publicity director for the NAACP, was threatened with grand jury action for having released the facts about the riot.

On his return trip to Columbia for the trials, attorney Thurgood Marshall was arrested on trumped-up charges of drunken driving. White newspapermen covering the court sessions were harassed. The distinguished writer, Vincent Sheean, who was representing the *New York Herald Tribune,* was threatened with arrest. Officials made it difficult for Negro journalists and lawyers at the trials to find food and lodging. Every possible obstacle was placed in the way of NAACP attorneys who were defending the riot victims. Eventually, however, after many months of litigation the Association won freedom for all of them. But it was a dangerous, costly, and heartbreaking process—one hardly calculated to bolster a returning veteran's faith in democracy.

The United Nations

No wonder many Negroes both in and outside the NAACP looked to the newly formed United Nations as a possible source of help—a source that might bring world opinion into action concerning their plight. The United States Department of State sent Dr. Ralph Bunche to the organizational conference in San Francisco in 1945 as one of its official staff. Also accredited as observers were a number of other Negro leaders, including Mary McLeod Bethune, Mordecai Johnson, Dr. Du Bois, and Walter White, with Roy Wilkins as alternate. At the first meeting of the UN's Educational, Scientific and Cultural Organization in Paris in 1946, Dr. Charles S. Johnson was one of the members of the United States National Commission. "Universal respect for, and observance of, human rights and fundamental freedom for all without distinction to race, sex, language or religion" was stated in its charter as one of the aims of the United Nations.

When in 1946 the National Negro Congress filed a petition with the Economic and Social Council of the UN, seeking its influence in eliminating discrimination in the United States, those opposing the petition argued that discrimination was a purely domestic problem. However, Attorney Charles Houston of the NAACP contended that "a national policy of the United States which permits disfranchisement in the South is just as much an international issue as elections in Poland or the denial of democratic rights in Franco Spain." Because Negroes were denied the basic right of citizenship, the ballot, and because of the widespread discrimination against them in America, the NAACP made plans to petition the United Nations.

Accordingly in 1947 there was drawn up a carefully annotated document that had a very long and explicit title: "A Statement on the Denial of Human Rights to Minorities in the Case of Citizens of Negro Descent in the United States of America and an Appeal to the United Nations for Redress Prepared for the National Association for the Advancement of Colored People Under the Editorial Supervision of W. E. B. Du Bois, with Contributions by Earl B. Dickerson, Milton R. Konvitz, William R. Ming, Jr., Leslie S. Perry and Rayford W. Logan." In addition to a general introduction, the document had five sections: The Denial of Legal Rights of American Negroes, 1787–1914; The Present Legal and Social Status of the American Negro; Patterns of Social Discrimination Against Negroes; The Charter of the United Nations and Its Provisions for Human Rights; and The Rights of Minorities and Decisions Already Taken Under This Charter. The document itself had 154 pages.

In his introduction, Dr. Du Bois defined the composition of the "so-called" American Negro population, its history, and its relations with the rest of the country's population. He traced the effects of slavery upon both whites and Negroes, and showed how prolonged segregation and discrimination involuntarily brought the Negroes together so that they almost constituted a nation within a nation. "If, however," Du Bois wrote, "the effect of the color caste system on the North American Negro has been both good and bad, its effect on white America has been disastrous. It has repeatedly led the greatest modern attempt at democratic government to deny its political ideals, to falsify its philanthropic assertions and to make its religion to a great extent hypocritical."

Du Bois touched briefly upon a problem that plagues the United Nations even today:

> Since the United Nations has made its headquarters in New York, the United States is in honor bound to guard and respect the various peoples of the world who are its guests and allies. Most people of the world are more or less colored in skin; their presence at the meetings of the United Nations as participants and as visitors, renders them always liable to insult and to discrimination because they may be mistaken for Americans of Negro descent. Not very long ago the nephew of the ruler of a neighboring American state was killed by policemen in Florida, because he was mistaken for a Negro and thought to be demanding rights which a Negro in Florida is not legally permitted to demand. Again and more

recently in Illinois, the personal physician of Mahatma Gandhi was with his friends refused food in a restaurant, again because they were mistaken for Negroes. . . . A discrimination practiced in the United States against her own citizens and to a large extent a contravention of her own laws, cannot be persisted in without infringing upon the rights of the peoples of the world and especially upon the ideals and the work of the United Nations.

In concluding, Du Bois said of the American Negro:

The United Nations surely will not forget that the population of this group makes it in size one of the considerable nations of the world. We number as many as the inhabitants of the Argentine or Czechoslovakia, or the whole of Scandinavia. . . . We are larger than Canada, Saudi Arabia, Ethiopia, Hungary or the Netherlands. . . . We have more people than Portugal or Peru; twice as many as Greece. . . . In sheer numbers then we are a group which has a right to be heard.

It was, of course, not expected that this petition, presented by Dr. Du Bois and Walter White on October 23, 1947, to the Department of Social Affairs of the United Nations, would have immediate concrete results. But it did inform the world of the plight of millions of Negroes in the United States. It did influence public opinion on a national and international scale. And it did put down simply and clearly in black and white some of the problems of American Negroes so that all who read might know.

Several months after the presentation of the petition, Dr. Du Bois ceased working for the Association at the age of 79. In *The Crisis* the following year, Bette Darcie Latimer published a poem, "For William Edward Burghardt Du Bois—on His Eightieth Birthday."

"I have awakened from the unknowing to the knowing," the poem began. "The brown one, smiling, led me on with wisdom as a sturdy cane . . ."

This was the second time that Dr. Du Bois had left the NAACP because of basic policy differences. He had resigned as editor after an extended discussion of the segregation issue in the columns of *The Crisis* during the first six months of 1934, in disagreement with the Board's policy of unequivocal opposition to segregation under all circumstances.

He returned to the Association as director of special research in 1944 after serving during the intervening years as a professor at Atlanta University. His final departure from the NAACP came in 1948 when he found himself again sharply at odds with its policy. His public endorsement of Henry A. Wallace as a candidate for the Presidency that year violated the NAACP's longstanding ban on partisan political activity by its staff. In addition, Dr. Du Bois strongly disagreed with the Association's support of the Marshall Plan and other elements of this country's foreign policy.

4

Pinning Down the Law

Battle of the Ballot

Ballot: A method of voting, usually secret.

Democracy: A form or state of social organization in which people at large, possessing the whole sovereignty, are each entitled to an equal interest in the state.

Declaration of Independence, 1776: "We hold these Truths to be self-evident, that all Men are created equal, that they are endowed by their Creator with certain unalienable Rights, that among these are Life, Liberty, and the Pursuit of Happiness. That to secure these Rights, Governments are instituted among Men, deriving their just powers from the Consent of the Governed."

Fifteenth Amendment, 1870: "The right of the citizens of the United States to vote shall not be denied or abridged by the United States or by any State on account of race, color, or previous condition of servitude."

Archives of the Library of Congress, Reconstruction Period: "I was right smart size when I saw the Ku Klux. They would whip men and women that weren't married and were living together. On the first day of January, they would whip men and boys that didn't have a job. They kept the Negroes from voting. They would whip them. They put up notices: NO NIGGERS TO COME OUT TO THE POLLS TOMORROW. . . . Sometimes they would just persuade them not to vote. A Negro like my father, they would say to him, 'Now, Brown, you are too good to get messed up . . . we don't want to see you get hurt . . . stay 'way from the polls tomorrow.' And my father would stay away."

Memorial from Alabama Negroes to His Excellency the President of the United States, 1874: "The investigation made in the years 1870–71 by a committee of Congress known as the Ku Klux Committee, developed and established the fact of the organized existence in many parts of this State since the year 1868 of a secret, powerful, vindictive, and dangerous organization composed exclusively of white men . . . whose objects were to control the labor and repress or control the votes of the colored citizens of this State. . . . Before the State laws and State courts we are utterly helpless. If the laws of the United States . . . are not enforced, we hold all of our rights at the mere mercy of wrongdoers and criminals."

Library of Congress: "Union County had an insurrection over the polls about the year 1888. . . . They went around and commanded the Negroes not to go to the polls. . . . On Sunday before the election on Monday, they went around through that county in gangs. They shot some few of the Negroes. As the Negroes didn't have no weapons to protect themselves, they didn't have no chance."

Archives of the NAACP: June, 1915. The first Supreme Court case in which the NAACP participated resulted in an opinion that invalidated the "grandfather clause" in the Oklahoma State Constitution. The clause barred illiterate Negroes from voting but permitted illiterate whites to vote because of their ancestry. *The Crisis* hailed the ruling as "the most important decision affecting colored people rendered by the Supreme Court in twenty-five years."

March, 1927. The first Texas "white" primary case before the Supreme Court was won by the NAACP. Dr. L. A. Nixon of El Paso was refused the right to vote in a Texas primary election by reason of a Texas statute which provided that "in no event shall a Negro be eligible to participate in a Democratic party election held in the State of Texas."

May, 1932. The State Executive Committee of the Texas Democratic party, under authorization by a state law, adopted a resolution "that all white Democrats . . . and none others be allowed to participate in primary elections." Dr. Nixon, again refused the right to vote in the primary, brought an action for damages in the federal courts. When the case was dismissed, it was carried to the United States Supreme Court, which reversed the lower court.

May, 1939. In Miami, Florida, on the night before the city primaries, a 50-car motorcade of hooded Klansmen with lynch ropes dangling from car windows drove through the Negro sections of the city. Dozens of fiery crosses were lighted. Nevertheless, more than 1000 Negroes led by Samuel B. Solomon went to the polls the next day and voted.

July 24, 1939. William Anderson, president of the Greenville, South Carolina, NAACP Youth Council, was arrested for breach of the peace. He had been active in a voter registration drive. The KKK issued a statement saying, "The Klan will ride again if Greenville Negroes continue to register and vote."

June, 1940. Brownsville, Tennessee, NAACP leaders who were active in the voting drive were terrorized. The body of Elbert Williams was found in the river; and the president of the local branch, the Reverend

Buster Walker, was run out of town with seven other leading Negroes. The NAACP sent the Department of Justice at Washington the names of 60 white mob members.

March, 1942. Columbia, South Carolina, passed a ruling the effect of which was that Negroes had to be 87 years old in order to vote.

September, 1942. Thurgood Marshall presented to the United States Department of Justice more than 20 sworn statements from Negroes in the South who had paid their poll tax but had not been permitted to vote.

April, 1944. In ruling favorably on the third Texas primary case, the United States Supreme Court affirmed that the right to vote "is not to be nullified by a state through casting its electoral process in a form that permits a private organization to practice racial discrimination in election." For the first time in history Texas Negroes voted freely.

July 16, 1946. Notices tacked on the doors of Negro churches in Fitzgerald, Georgia, read: THE FIRST NIGGER WHO VOTES IN GEORGIA WILL BE A DEAD NIGGER.

July 20, 1946. Maceo Snipes, a veteran of World War II who voted in the July 17 primary, was dragged from his home in Taylor County, Georgia, and shot to death by four whites. A sign was posted on a nearby Negro church: THE FIRST NIGGER TO VOTE WILL NEVER VOTE AGAIN.

July, 1947. Southern-born Federal District Judge J. Waties Waring, whose home in Charleston was later stoned by racists, upheld the right of George Elmore and other South Carolina Negroes to take part in the Democratic primaries, for "under the law of our land all citizens are entitled to a voice in such elections . . . and if the only material and realistic elections are clothed with the name 'primary,' they are equally entitled to vote there. . . . It is time for South Carolina to rejoin the Union." NAACP lawyers headed by Thurgood Marshall presented this case.

November, 1948. NAACP president D. V. Carter of Montgomery County, Georgia, was brutally beaten by whites for escorting Negroes to the polls. And in nearby Vidalia, Robert Mallard, who had been warned not to vote, was lynched by a band of hooded men. At the same time in Mississippi, the Reverend William Bender, instructor at Tougaloo College and president of a branch of the NAACP, was kept from the polls by three whites, one of whom brandished a pistol. Walter White stated: "Either the Negro must attain full citizenship status with all the rights and obligations thereby involved, even in the most remote sections of Mississippi, or the democratic process for all America will be made meaningless."

December, 1951. On Christmas night Harry T. Moore, executive secretary of the NAACP's Florida branches, and his wife were killed by a bomb placed beneath their home. Both had been active in state-wide voter registration.

February, 1952. G. L. C. Glymph, 60-year-old Negro grocer of Gaffney, South Carolina, withdrew his candidacy for City Council after receiving a threatening communication signed KKK and written on the letterhead of the Invisible Empire Association of Carolina Klans of the Ku Klux Klan. It read: "It is not customary, as you know, for the colored race of South Carolina to hold public office or either [to] offer for same. We do not believe you are fully aware of the position in which you have placed yourself, but in the meantime we are asking you to stop and think . . . and let your withdrawal before February 12 be your protection for now and hereafter."

May, 1952. A crudely made bomb was thrown into a Negro polling place in Jacksonville, Florida, several hours before voting began, tearing a hole in the roof. Later a bomb was found in front of the home of David H. Dwight who had been influential in getting Negroes to register.

September, 1954. Several NAACP branches in Mississippi were threatened with violence because of their activity in voting drives.

May, 1955. The Reverend George W. Lee, the first Negro to register in Belzoni, Mississippi, since Reconstruction, was shot from ambush when he refused to remove his name from the voting rolls voluntarily. At his memorial service in Belzoni, Roy Wilkins said, "Reverend Lee was shot because he thought he should vote like other Americans." Also in Belzoni, Gus Courts signed a federal complaint against Sheriff Isaac Shelton for refusing to accept poll tax payments from Negroes. Courts was severely injured by a hail of bullets fired into his grocery store from a passing car, and he was forced to leave the state. At NAACP insistence, the FBI agreed to conduct an investigation.

November, 1955. Wilkins reported that the number of Negro voters in Mississippi had dropped from 22,000 in 1952 to only 8000 in 1955 because of terror.

February, 1956. James C. Evers, veteran of World War II and the Korean War, started an NAACP chapter in Philadelphia, Mississippi, where no Negroes could register or vote. Numerous threats forced him to flee with his wife and family after his credit had been cut off. Local

Negroes were threatened if they patronized his funeral parlor for burials or bought insurance through his agency.

October, 1956. When Senator Eastland announced that he would work for free elections in Poland, Roy Wilkins sent him a telegram asking that he "join us in urging free elections in Mississippi." There was no answer.

June, 1957. Negro residents of Tuskegee, Alabama, and teachers at Tuskegee Institute refused to continue to trade with white merchants in Tuskegee because of the gerrymandering of the town in order to eliminate Negro voters. Many white businesses failed. The boycott still continues. "If we can't vote," the Negroes maintain, "the white man will no longer slap us in the face with one hand while we give him our money in the other. No, Sir!"

This Is the NAACP (Pamphlet): In 1958 the Association launched an intensified campaign to increase the number of Negro voters in the southern states. Meanwhile the drive continues to expand the Negro vote in areas outside the South where, in some states, it is already an important balance-of-trade factor.

New York Post, December 7, 1959: According to Dr. John A. Hannah, chairman of the Federal Civil Rights Commission, "There are at least 16 counties in the United States in which one-third or more of the population is non-white, in which not a single non-white is permitted to register to vote."

NAACP Report, 1960: Major voter registration campaigns were conducted in sixteen southern cities—among them, Jacksonville, Tampa, Tallahassee, Savannah, Nashville, Knoxville, Memphis, Little Rock, and Pine Bluff.

An Atlanta Negro Lawyer, 1960: "If the Federal Government opens the way to vote, it will be up to the Negroes to use that right. There may be violent resistance in the rural areas; the burden will be heavy. A few will have to suffer. But that is the history of the struggle for civil liberties."

Archives of the NAACP: May, 1960. Negroes registered in Haywood County, Tennessee, for the first time since Reconstruction. The planters immediately began to intimidate them. The Memphis NAACP asked the Department of Justice to take action. A complaint was also filed with the Civil Rights Commission.

July, 1960. NAACP units across the country were asked to withhold patronage from national oil companies because local dealers refused service to Negroes in Fayette County, Tennessee.

August, 1960. The embargo on the sale of gasoline and oil to registered Negro voters in Fayette County was lifted following NAACP negotiations with representatives of the major oil companies. Many Negro tenant farmers and sharecroppers in Fayette and Haywood Counties
were forced to evacuate their cabins by their landlords; they had to live
like refugees in a hastily set up tent city, and were refused credit at commissary stores.

September, 1960. The Justice Department filed a civil complaint with
the Federal District Court at Memphis in behalf of the Negroes being
intimidated in Haywood and Fayette Counties; 27 merchants and two
banks were named.

November, 1960. The NAACP announced that more than $7500 had
been spent for food for these beleaguered vote victims since July.

December, 1960. James Farmer, NAACP program director, represented the Association at a Christmas party in Memphis for the evicted
residents of Fayette and Haywood Counties.

February 17, 1961. The Federal District Court held that the Tuskegee
gerrymander unconstitutionally deprived the affected Negroes of their
rights under the Fifteenth Amendment.

United Press International, August 4, 1961: The federal government on
August 4 filed three suits charging that Negroes were denied their legal
voting rights in Montgomery County, Alabama, and in two Mississippi
counties, Walthall and Jefferson Davis. All three complaints asserted
that voting officials applied "different and more stringent standards" to
Negro applicants for registration than to whites.

NAACP Pamphlet: The right to vote is the No. 1 right of the American
people. To secure this right for Negro Americans, regardless of the state
they live in, is the No. 1 project of the National Association for the
Advancement of Colored People.

Houses and Lands

Housing is not a recent problem for Negroes. More than half a century
ago many midwestern towns refused to allow Negroes to live within the
city limits. Some even put up signs such as: NIGGERS, READ AND RUN;
or, as in Elmwood, Indiana: NO NEGROES ADMITTED HERE. Others,
like Granite City, Illinois, and Owosso, Michigan, posted no signs, but
Negroes could not purchase land or houses. In cities that permitted
them, local customs or poverty kept them in slum sections, usually near

the railroad tracks or along a river. Eventually, however, some Negroes were able to buy or build decent homes in urban centers. Thereupon municipal segregation ordinances of various kinds began to appear, as well as costly building standards which were enforced loosely in the case of whites, but rigorously for Negroes.

Racially restrictive housing ordinances were enforced before the outbreak of World War I in Dallas, Atlanta, St. Louis, Louisville, Richmond, and Baltimore. When Negroes flocked north during and after that war, the big urban industrial centers began to try to preserve all-white areas, and restrictive covenants between property owners were made. The great black belts of New York, Cleveland, Detroit, and Chicago were hemmed in. "The kitchenette is our prison," wrote Richard Wright of Chicago's South Side, "our death sentence without trial." People were crowded into tenements to the window sills; perhaps there was one toilet—if that—for twenty or thirty people. As Pulitzer Prize winner poet Gwendolyn Brooks described it:

> Since Number Five is out of the bathroom now,
> We think of lukewarm water, hope to get in it.

The NAACP's first housing case, in 1911, resulted from an appeal for help from a group of Kansas City Negroes whose homes in a previously all-white neighborhood had been bombed. The first case before the United States Supreme Court that was initiated and carried through completely by NAACP attorneys also involved housing. A Louisville residential segregation ordinance was in question. The case was argued by Moorfield Storey and his associates. On November 5, 1917, the Louisville ordinance was declared unconstitutional by unanimous decision. There was also the famous Sweet case in Detroit in 1925, already discussed. In 1926 the NAACP carried to the Supreme Court a case involving two white property owners in Washington who were parties to a restrictive covenant not to sell to Negroes. One party broke the covenant, and the other sued in the lower courts to have the agreement upheld. He won. The case was appealed to the United States Supreme Court and dismissed for lack of jurisdiction.

At first, the United States Supreme Court was evasive in pronouncing direct judgments in cases concerning restrictive covenants between white property owners, or the inclusion of restraining clauses in deeds prohibiting the sale, leasing, or rental of property to Negroes, Jews, Orientals, or "other undesirables." The use of such covenants therefore became widespread throughout the country. The NAACP held that the courts should not be a party to enforcing discriminatory agreements of a private character. But it was not easy to pin down the law, state or federal, in this regard. White property owners' "protective associations" and even the University of Chicago took advantage of racially restrictive covenants. Everywhere the Negro urban ghettoes became more and more crowded; every city had its Harlem.

In 1929, when two professional men of means, Dr. A. M. Williams and Dr. E. D. Collymore, purchased homes in a white neighborhood in White Plains, New York, the Highland Property Owners Association tried to frighten them into selling, using "extra-legal" means if need be. The Westchester County Ku Klux Klan lighted a fiery cross on Dr. Collymore's lawn. When banks and real estate interests threatened to withdraw donations to the Community Chest, the YMCA removed both men from its Board of Management and fired S. R. Morsell, executive secretary of its Negro branch, who was living with the Collymores and refused to move from their home or to disavow their action. But at a stormy public meeting, Herbert J. Seligmann, then publicity director of the NAACP, succeeded in restoring reason to some members of the community. That week end Rabbi V. Goldman and the Reverend James I. Fairley preached sermons against race hatred. The neighborhood calmed down and the two Negroes remained in their homes. But in other cities where ministers were silent and rocks crashed through windows, mob will prevailed.

One of the most celebrated housing cases in which the NAACP participated was *Hansberry v. Lee* (311 U.S. 32). The case originated in Chicago, where by 1930 all but one-fourth of the city's residential property had been restricted to white occupancy. Negroes could not even walk safely in some neighborhoods, let alone live in them. Over 95 percent of the area surrounding the University of Chicago, including property belonging to it, was protected by white covenants.

Mr. and Mrs. Carl Hansberry—their daughter Lorraine later became a distinguished playwright—wanted to move into a pleasant middle-class area only a few blocks from the teeming Negro South Side. The Illinois Supreme Court had upheld the right of whites to bar them. The NAACP and other interested parties engaged a brilliant group of attorneys to carry the Hansberry appeal to the highest court in the land. Among them were the Chicagoans Earl B. Dickerson, Truman Gibson, and Irvin Mollison, and the outstanding California lawyer, Loren Miller. The expert services of sociologist Dr. Louis Wirth of the University of

Chicago and of Dr. Robert C. Weaver, housing authority, were also engaged in preparing the brief. In an opinion handed down by Mr. Justice Stone on November 12, 1940, the United States Supreme Court reversed the judgment of the lower court, and the Hansberrys were permitted to occupy their property.

Although in the Hansberry case the Supreme Court did not comment on the constitutionality of restrictive covenants as such, it did so in another NAACP housing case, *Shelley v. Kraemer,* decided on May 3, 1948. In this case Chief Justice Vinson handed down the opinion that restrictive covenants cannot be enforced by state courts. In a companion case decided the same day, it was agreed that such covenants could not be enforced in federal courts. Little by little, the supposedly legal props of residential segregation were being whittled away.

But the collusion of real estate interests with mass prejudices and the connivance of politicians in continually thinking up new kinds of zoning regulations still prevent Negroes from living freely wherever they wish. Mobs still attempt to control housing in some areas and even to keep Negroes out of projects built with public funds. In 1953, when seven families of Negro veterans moved into Chicago's Trumball Park housing projects, 3000 whites stoned the windows of their apartments. For weeks Negroes were beaten and chased by name-calling crowds, but finally law and order were restored, and a large police guard was maintained at the housing project for months. In San Pablo, California, the west coast regional office of the NAACP hired a special guard to protect the home of a Negro family who had been threatened; this was the only Negro family in a white neighborhood.

In Cicero, a Chicago suburb, one Negro family caused such a commotion a couple of years earlier that the Illinois National Guard had to be ordered in to keep the peace. Harvey Clark, a veteran, and his wife, both college graduates, and their young children were prevented from moving into an apartment they had rented by Cicero Chief of Police Ervin Konovsky. With the aid of the Legal Committee of the Chicago NAACP, a federal injunction was secured in 1951 ordering the police to protect the Clarks in occupying their new home. The Clarks moved in, but the police only looked on when a mob made a shambles of the apartment building; they made no arrests. They even permitted the mob to throw the Clarks' piano into the bonfire made from their furniture and personal effects that had been thrown into the street. Everything the Clarks possessed was burned up. A special grand jury indicted not the rioters, but the Clarks and their lawyer! The NAACP succeeded in having these indictments dismissed, but the Clarks never occupied this apartment. In some communities mobs, bomb throwers, and arsonists continue to be dangerous to Negroes who dare move beyond prescribed areas.

In Baltimore at the end of World War II, the Negro 20 percent of the city's population occupied 7 percent of its housing space. In Harlem, Negroes averaged 3871 per block. In Chicago's South Side, the density was 90,000 per square mile. In the Negro section of Cleveland there had been no appreciable construction of new housing, other than public projects, for forty years. The story in Detroit and other cities was the same, although public housing began to improve conditions to some extent. The federal court, called upon to order the Detroit Housing Commission to cease its segregated policies, ruled that the "separate but equal doctrine has no place in public housing." By 1959 five states— Massachusetts, Connecticut, Colorado, California, and Oregon—had enacted fair housing bills. But enormous private developments like Levittown in New Jersey accepted no Negro residents. And some communities like Atlanta still use federal funds for housing that is intended for whites only. NAACP protests continually call attention to these undemocratic conditions.

Since its financing of vast new residential projects has made the federal government the most important factor in the national housing picture, the NAACP seeks, as its current *Program for Civil Rights* states, "an Executive Order forbidding segregation or other forms of discrimination based on race, religion or national origin in all federal or federally-aided housing programs. The order should include slum clearance, urban renewal, relocation, public housing, and the insuring and lending functions related to housing. It should provide for the establishment of an executive commission to implement this order."

In its early days in New York, the NAACP itself had difficulty in finding housing—office space, to be exact—after it outgrew the rent-free quarters generously provided by Villard in the *Evening Post* building. No downtown office building was eager to lease space to an organization even partially staffed by Negroes—and with the word *Colored* in its name. Finally, one of the major textbook publishers, sympathetic to its aims, offered the national office of the Association room in his building. Thereupon the NAACP and *The Crisis* moved from Vesey Street farther uptown to an excellent location. But soon complaints began to reach the publisher about having Negroes in his building, and some of his salesmen reported that southern school boards which purchased large numbers of his textbooks intended to take their trade elsewhere if this "equal-rights" organization were not ousted. With great regret the liberal-minded publisher was forced to ask that the NAACP move; he himself offered to pay all the expenses of moving. The NAACP accepted—and moved.

A location was found at the corner of 14th Street and Fifth Avenue. There the national office had its headquarters for many years. Although it had a whole floor to itself, it was always in need of more space. When Freedom House proposed that its group join with the NAACP and other social-minded agencies and purchase a building to be dedicated as a memorial to the late Wendell Willkie, the Association's Board of Directors approved the idea. Now the National Association for the Advancement of Colored People is housed on West 40th Street opposite the New York Public Library in the very heart of Manhattan; *The Crisis* is near by, as is the Legal Defense and Educational Fund. At Freedom House the NAACP is among friends. But as its work continues to expand, so it continues to feel a need for more space.

Knights of the Bar

The NAACP has been called "the world's biggest law firm." Certainly it has legal representatives in most of our largest cities and in many small communities as well, and it represents America's 20,000,000 Negroes in court. But it operates for principle, not for profit. Its legal work is a major part of its activities—and currently the most celebrated. Thurgood Marshall, director of the Legal Defense and Educational Fund for over twenty years, is one of the few attorneys known all over the world.

Late one afternoon Executive Secretary Roy Wilkins remained in his office after the switchboard operator and everyone else but Jesse DeVore, his public relations assistant, had left. Both men were working overtime to mimeograph an urgent press release. The phone buzzed insistently, and finally DeVore picked up the receiver. It was a long-distance call and the caller would speak with no one but Roy Wilkins. Reluctantly Wilkins took the receiver.

"NAACP? NAACP?" cried a distraught voice over the miles. "Mr. Wilkins, my husband has quit me and I want the NAACP to take the case. I tell you, he was no good anyhow and I want to get him out of my life. He—he—I—I—He did—I said . . . that man, oh . . ."

When Wilkins finally managed to get a word in edgewise, he patiently explained to the excited woman that the NAACP did not take cases of a personal and domestic nature, only civil-rights cases that relate to Negroes—and usually only if they are test cases.

"This Negro has tested me!" cried the woman. "What this man has done to a Negro woman *is* a case for the NAACP—and I want you to take it."

With regret, the Association turned her case down. The NAACP has to refuse hundreds of cases every year, even some that come within the scope of its activities; otherwise its legal staff would be swamped with work beyond its human or financial capacity.

"The Association makes two conditions upon which it enters a case: (1) Does the case involve a color discrimination? (2) Is some fundamental right of citizenship involved?" wrote Mary White Ovington in *The Walls Come Tumbling Down*. "All of our cases involve the right of the individual as a citizen. Sometimes they concern his protection when accused. Thus in 1936 in Mississippi, and in 1940 in Florida, decisions of the lower courts were reversed since the convictions were obtained under physical torture. Chief Justice Hughes declared, 'The rack and torture chamber may not be substituted for the witness stand.'"

To secure equal enforcement of the laws for all, to clarify the laws when muddied by false interpretations or distorted for purposes of discrimination, to change the laws when they promote segregation, and to obtain the enactment of new laws as needed to make democracy a reality for Negroes have been the basic legal objectives of the NAACP since its inception. In seeking to fulfill these objectives, the Association has been aided from the beginning by some of the greatest legal minds of the 20th century, white and Negro, northern and southern. Many have given their services without charge; others have accepted lower fees from the Association than they would receive for handling private cases. As a result of their court activities on behalf of NAACP causes, the lives of some have been endangered.

David Lansden, a white attorney in Cairo, Illinois, was active in school desegregation there in 1952. For weeks stones came crashing into his living room windows, endangering his family. So that the cars of hate-mongers would not fail to find his house, a next-door neighbor put on his own garage a flashing red electric arrow that pointed to the lawyer's home. The arrow was kept on all night so that all would know where the despised white man lived who dared to defend Negro rights. In Greenville, South Carolina, attorney John Bolt Culbertson, whom local Negroes call "the South's bravest white man," has seen fiery crosses burn on his lawn and in front of his office. In Nashville, Tennessee, Z. Alexander Looby, Negro member of the NAACP's National Legal Committee, was bombed from his bed during the school desegregation and sit-in crises, and his home was partially destroyed by dynamite. Minor incidents like receiving obscenely threatening telephone calls or KKK letters, and finding one's tires slashed on emerging from court, are commonplace happenings to NAACP attorneys in southern and border cities. These men are true knights of the bar jousting in a noble cause—for in many communities a man has to have both moral and physical courage to go to court on behalf of civil rights. Death may be lurking in ambush.

Said the Reverend Martin Luther King at the height of the Montgomery bus boycott when he himself was arrested, "We must continue our struggle in the courts. Above all, we must continue to support the NAACP. Our major victories have come through the work of this organization. One thing the gradualists don't seem to understand: we are not trying to make people love us when we go to court; we are trying to keep them from killing us."

Among the numerous incidents involving racial violence with which NAACP attorneys concerned themselves in 1960 (aside from those involving sit-ins) were the defense of six Negro students who were teargassed and arrested in Tallahassee, Florida; the police beating of a 12-year-old girl in Batesville, Mississippi, whose father's life was threatened; the stoning of Negro bathers on the beach at Biloxi, and the defense of Dr. Gilbert Mason and others who took part in the wade-in demonstrations there; the appeal to United States Attorney General Rogers to release the FBI report on the Mack Parker lynching in Mississippi after a federal grand jury failed to return a true bill; and a demand that the Department of Justice conduct a thorough investigation of the attempted assassination of Z. Alexander Looby in Nashville.

Charges of barratry against lawyers handling NAACP cases and attempts at their disbarment have not been uncommon. Samuel W. Tucker of Emporia, Virginia, a member of the legal staff of the NAACP's State Conference, faced disbarment proceedings in 1960 in retaliation for defending civil-rights cases. "The NAACP Board," stated the *Annual Report,* "aware of the seriousness of this case, pledged its full resources in Mr. Tucker's defense. The case came up for hearing in November, after a series of legal maneuvers which apparently weakened the state's case so severely that the Commonwealth's attorney decided to drop the proceedings. . . . But for the effort, time and talent spent in seeking to develop a constitutional theory to support Mr. Tucker's right to use his legal services in the support of a cause of social justice, it is unlikely that Mr. Tucker would have been permitted to practice law in Virginia."

The general counsel of the NAACP and a top-ranking member of its executive staff is Robert Lee Carter. Born in Florida, Carter was graduated from Lincoln University in Pennsylvania, and took his law degrees at Howard and Columbia. He came to the Association from the Army, where he served as lieutenant during World War II. Carter was chief counsel in the Lyman Johnson case which opened the University of Kentucky to Negro students, and also in the suit brought in 1949 to secure equal salaries for Negro teachers in Mississippi. That year he also participated in the United States Court of Appeals case against the Southern Bus Lines which resulted in outlawing segregated seating on interstate buses. He argued the McLaurin case in Oklahoma, and assisted in preparing the briefs in both it and the Heman Sweatt case in Texas. In those cases, the United States Supreme Court agreed with the NAACP that intangible factors, such as sitting in a classroom instead of just outside the door (McLaurin) and associating on campus with potential professional competitors (Sweatt) were essential to educational equality. These two cases were direct forebears of the school segregation cases decided in May, 1954. Carter was also a participant in one of them, *Brown v. Board of Education,* both in preparing the brief and in arguing the case.

Lloyd Garrison, a descendant of the great abolitionist, is chairman of the National Legal Committee, whose forty-odd members include Morris Ernst, Osmond K. Fraenkel, Harry Bragg, Earl B. Dickerson, Sidney A. Jones, Edward P. Lovett, Loren Miller, Robert Ming, James M. Nabrit, Louis L. Redding, Herman Zand, Jawn Sandifer, A. T. Walden, and Frank Reeves. From the time of its first president, Moorfield Storey, who was also president of the American Bar Association, the NAACP has had the assistance of many of America's outstanding lawyers. Besides Clarence Darrow, these have included Arthur Garfield Hays, William H. Hastie (now a federal judge), Charles Houston (formerly dean of the Howard Law School), Louis Marshall, Francis Biddle, Frank Murphy, Spottswood Robinson, Leon A. Ransom, George M. Johnson, Jack Greenberg, Constance B. Motley, George E. C. Hayes, and Edward R. Dudley, formerly United States Ambassador to Liberia and now Borough President of Manhattan. No wonder that, with such an array of legal talent, by 1952 the NAACP had won favorable decisions in 34 out of the 38 cases it argued before the Supreme Court. And there were more victories later.

That hundreds of thousands of Negroes recognize the value of these gains is shown by the financial and moral support the NAACP receives. This support continues to amaze bigoted white Southerners. But, as an editorial in *Ebony* stated:

> Confronting them is a Negro willing to go hungry if it means his children would attend decent schools, willing to lose his job rather than withdraw his membership from the NAACP, who would rather mortgage his farm than to deny himself the right to vote—a Negro who would even be willing to die, if it meant that other Negroes might live in a race-free America. . . . In the North there is rejoicing and a new kind of determination, one that emanates from the hip as well as the lip. All across the country, the Negro is backing up his Southern brother with dollars and dimes and food and clothing and shouts of unadulterated joy. A wealthy Detroit medical group raised $31,000 at one dinner. Employees of a Los Angeles factory collected $900 during their lunch hour. A Richmond spiritual advisor donated a bus. At a Harlem church, according to a New York newsman, a woman cupped her hands to sneeze and somebody dropped a $5 bill into them . . . . The white South is angry. Her Negroes have ceased to play the accustomed role of humble servitude. They no longer need to hide their emotions, still their tongues. On their side is the God they have never forgotten. The law, slow in its processes, has at last included them in the circle of its strong right arm.

Thanks largely to the NAACP and its lawyers, this statement concerning the law has in it a degree of truth.

Mr. Desegregation

Thurgood Marshall has been called "Mr. Civil Rights" by many, "Mr. Desegregation" by others, and just plain Thurgood by hundreds who know him as hail-fellow-well-met outside of court. Inside the halls of justice, Marshall is a Lincolnesque sort of persuader whose rough-hewn eloquence has moved many a judge to search his conscience and come up with decisions he probably did not know he had in him. Fame and greatness are not always synonymous, but Marshall assuredly has both. The rugged simplicity of his oral presentation in court masks a mind as sharp as a steel trap. And like Clarence Darrow he has a depth of compassion coupled with a clarity of argument that makes logic and emotion seem compatible bedfellows.

An old saying has it that genius is nine-tenths perspiration. To a great degree the successful outcome of most of Marshall's cases may be ascribed to the enormous amount of preparatory work done before they were presented in court. Months were spent on research, evaluation of precedents, consultation, writing and rewriting of trial briefs. Everything possible was done to make a Supreme Court argument foolproof. Obscure decisions were studied. The most scholarly assistants were employed for documentation. The most minute facts were checked and rechecked for accuracy. Only the most respected and authoritative sources of opinion were quoted. Then, it is reported, the case in question might be presented before a mock court of young law students who acted as judges, questioning, inquiring, looking for loopholes. The entire presentation and the accompanying briefs might subsequently be revised by Thurgood Marshall and his associates after this run-through. Then, on the eve of the trial, with whatever materials he might still wish to look at, Marshall sat down in a room somewhere, the door closed, to think through his case alone. These time-tested procedures continue to be standard practice for the NAACP legal staff.

Marshall grew up in Baltimore. He went to nearby Lincoln University, where he was the noisiest student in his class. During Cab Calloway's brief stay at Lincoln, Cab and Thurgood could be heard scatting jubilantly up and down the dormitory halls beating out rhythms on tin pans long after midnight. Rough and ready, loud and wrong, good-natured and uncouth—these are phrases some of his Lincoln classmates still use to describe the raucous undergraduate. Yet Marshall was smart, too. At Howard Law School under Charles Houston's tutelage, he buckled down and became one of the most brilliant men in his class, meticulous in research, with a prodigious memory. It was Houston who first recognized Marshall's great potential and put him in contact with the NAACP.

After three years of private practice in Baltimore, Marshall joined the Association's legal staff in New York. In 1938 he was appointed special counsel in charge of all cases. The salary was small, but the work was challenging, exciting, dramatic, and sometimes dangerous. Soon Marshall was appearing with local counsel in southern courts where a Negro lawyer had never pleaded a case before, where hostile whites packed the court and the Negroes in town were too frightened to give the NAACP attorneys food or lodging. In 1941, when Marshall was asked to defend a man in Hugo, Oklahoma, against what seemed to be a framed-up murder charge based on prejudice, the Negro residents provided him with a bodyguard. They offered him a different place to sleep in each night and advised him to keep out of sight as much as possible. But for a man six feet two inches tall, this is very hard to do in a small town; furthermore, Marshall himself thought such precautions absurd. So after the first week he walked about the town as if he were an old resident, winning grudging admiration from the whites for his bravery. His courtroom arguments were so brilliant that on the day of his summation to the jury the local high school dismissed its seniors so they might hear the "Nigra" lawyer talk. Marshall lost the case, but the town had a new respect for Negro intelligence.

As Thurgood Marshall's legal fame grew, opportunities to earn much more money outside the field of civil rights were certainly available to him, but he remained with the NAACP until late in 1961 when he accepted a federal judgeship on the Circuit Court of Appeals.

The High Cost of Justice

The financial costs of justice in America can be enormous. In 1925 in Detroit the first Sweet trial, which ended in a hung jury, cost the NAACP $21,897.67. The costs of the second trial the following year, which brought acquittal, totaled $37,849.00. Preparing and defending a similar case today would cost perhaps twice as much. Even the cost of preparing and typing briefs in appeal cases amounts to a pretty penny. On its four of the five school desegregation cases—which resulted in the momentous Supreme Court decisions of 1954 and 1955—the NAACP expended more than $100,000.

Obviously, to raise such huge sums from dues-paying NAACP members was impossible, to say nothing of obtaining funds for maintaining the host of other vital activities. Because the NAACP attempted to influence public opinion and to prevail upon Congress to make and change laws, and because it maintained a lobby in Washington, gifts to it were never tax-deductible. To quote its brochure, *Toward Equal Justice:* "The public had contributed toward the NAACP legal work when shocking events—lynchings, riots and unjust accusations of crime—had caused widespread indignation. But to carry forward the slow, systematic and unsensational fight for equal opportunity to education, the right to vote and other practical proofs of Constitutional guarantees demanded other means of financial support. Toward this end, it was decided to establish a separate fund apart from the Association's precarious treasury. The purpose of the new fund would be to obtain new sources of income which could be devoted exclusively to the legal program, hitherto one subsidiary portion of the Association activities. On October 11, 1939, the NAACP Legal Defense and Educational Fund, Inc., was formed as a membership corporation under the laws of the State of New York." Its purpose is to support "those portions of the National Association for the Advancement of Colored People program which have been judged by the U.S. Treasury to be clearly eligible for tax-deductible contributions." As always, however, the Association itself is free to "continue to influence legislation and carry on a program of direct action in every public forum."

The NAACP's legal cases are expensive to carry through, but until the goals are attained there will be more cases that require heavy financing. Not only lawyers and legal clerks but traveling expenses must be paid; and experts must often be drawn on as consultants or witnesses. "Many of America's leading social scientists, historians, educators and attorneys, the men and women whose studies of race-relations aspects of sociology, anthropology, psychology, and psychiatry are considered definitive, have testified in trial court hearings at the request of the NAACP Legal Defense and Educational Fund. Dozens have served the Fund on scholarly assignments. Scores of these experts are now advising the Fund how its work may now promote adjustment of communities expected to adapt their school systems to the Supreme Court's decision that racial segregation in public schools is unconstitutional." Among many authorities on the American social scene who have provided invaluable aid to the NAACP are Otto Klineberg, Dr. Charlotte Babcock, Professor Allison Davis, Dr. Horace Mann Bond, Dean Kenneth D. Johnson, Dr. Kenneth Clark, Dr. Mabel Smythe, Professor John Hope Franklin, Dr. Lillian Dabney, Dr. Robert C. Weaver, Professor Ira DeA. Reid, Dr. Mamie P. Clark, and Dr. Hugh Smythe.

To raise the funds for cases involving constitutional rights and the strengthening of American democracy, a volunteer group of citizens called the Committee of 100 has since 1943 sponsored monetary appeals for the Legal Defense Fund. Such distinguished people as Harry Emerson Fosdick, Archibald MacLeish, Karl Menninger, Ralph Ellison, John L. Saltonstall, Jr., Lillian Smith, Ralph Barton Perry, Channing Tobias, and Bruno Walter have served on this committee.

At the St. Louis convention in 1953, Dr. Tobias called for the creation of a Fighting Fund for Freedom. Amassing a million dollars a year for ten years would push the fight for freedom far enough along to justify the slogan "Free by '63" by the time the centennial of Emancipation rolled around. Although it took several years to reach a million-dollar total, the stimulus to NAACP fund raising has been unmistakable. Freedom Fund chairmen have included Jackie Robinson, Duke Ellington, Marguerite Belafonte, and Floyd Patterson. Top-ranking figures in the world of music and the theater have gladly lent their talents to the cause. Lena Horne, Sammy Davis, Jr., Marian Anderson, Harry Belafonte, Camilla Williams, Leontyne Price, Miles Davis, Nat King Cole, Ossie Davis, Ruby Dee, Count Basie, Mahalia Jackson, Max Roach, Abbey Lincoln, Julian Cannonball Adderley, Michael Olatunji, Cab Calloway, Thelma Carpenter, Brock Peters, Larry Steele, Sarah Vaughan, and Oscar Brown, Jr., are only a few of the personalities whose zeal for racial justice has brought them to support the NAACP's work directly.

Every branch, youth council, and college chapter of the Association is assigned a Freedom Fund quota each year. Raffles, dinners, tag days, fashion shows (which Mrs. Belafonte has built into a tremendous drawing card), theater benefits, and direct solicitations help to swell the contributions to the Freedom Fund.

Freedom Is Not Free

One of the most ardent individual fund raisers for the Association is the Boston industrialist Kivie Kaplan, a man of boundless energy and enthusiasm. The NAACP is seldom out of his mind. On a recent vacation trip abroad he sold seventeen life memberships. On the beach at Vineyard Haven where he sometimes goes for a swim, he enrolled six new members. A life membership costs $500 and of course includes a lifelong subscription to *The Crisis*. Memberships may be paid for by a partial payment plan. Fully paid members are called the Honor Guard and their names are emblazoned in bronze on the walls of the Association's national office. Roy Wilkins says, "Life Memberships form a kind of limited endowment for the NAACP . . . in the event a depressed economic cycle should come upon us. In this sense, Life Members are the bedrock of the Fight for Freedom."

The first fully paid life member was John B. Nail, the father-in-law of James Weldon Johnson; he enrolled in 1927. Dr. Ernest Alexander, noted Harlem dermatologist, was the second. But until 1952 when Kivie Kaplan came along, the Association had only 300 life members. Kivie Kaplan changed this. Believing that "the security of the future depends on the security of today," he became a voluntary traveling salesman of life memberships in the NAACP. He signed people up, at the point of a smile, for life. His genial personality and unabashed interest in civil rights made it hard for those he approached not to enlist in the Fight for Freedom. To aid him he corralled some able lieutenants. Jackie Robinson and Atlanta University President Benjamin Mays served as co-chairmen with him of the National Life Membership Committee. The membership of this committee is nation-wide, and includes such energetic workers as Dr. Walter Darden of New Jersey, Kelly M. Alexander of North Carolina, Judge Hubert T. Delany and Dr. George Cannon of New York, Earl Dickerson of Illinois, Dr. J. L. Leach of Michigan, Dr. James Levy of Ohio, Dr. Maurice Rabb of Kentucky, Ike Smalls of Iowa, George Beavers of California, Mrs. Pauline Weeden of Virginia, and Mrs. Katherine Watson Frederick of Massachusetts.

Within eight years the NAACP had 1500 fully paid life members and 5000 subscribing members. In 1958 Mrs. Nettie Scott King of Indianapolis became the 1000th life member. Alpha Kappa Alpha was the first sorority to take out a national membership, and Alpha Phi Alpha was the first fraternity; these were soon joined by others. The first union local to vote as a body to take out a membership was Local 858 of the International Longshoremen's Association. Churches, lodges, and social clubs joined as fully paid units, as did 68 local branches of the NAACP. Some even took out double memberships. The young Aga Khan joined while at Harvard. Prime Minister Nehru of India, Averell Harriman, and Sammy Davis, Jr., also became members. In 1960, Senator and Mrs. Herbert Lehman, Harry Golden, Harry Belafonte, and Floyd Patterson became members. As one of the three co-chairmen of the National Life Membership Committee, Jackie Robinson voluntarily made a cross-country tour for the committee and recruited 300 new life members. At the Annual Life Membership luncheon held in Philadelphia in July, 1961, Kivie Kaplan was able to report 2163 paid-up memberships; in addition, 7312 individuals and organizations were in the process of purchasing membership certificates. During 1960 life membership payments brought the Association the sum of $390,000; this includes the 40 percent retained by the branches as their share.

In 1958 the Kivie Kaplan Life Membership Awards were established to be rewarded each year to the top six branches in recruitment. In 1959 the small branch in Greensville County, Virginia, with only 95 members, reported eight new life memberships and five subscribing memberships; this put it at the top for a branch of its size. In 1961 the awards went to Detroit, Boston, Savannah, Sacramento, Alexandria, Virginia, and Sumter, South Carolina. Freedom Fund dinners have been of great value in the drive for life memberships. In 1956, a dinner in Detroit, with Dr. Alf Thomas as chairman, brought in 200 new members. A dinner in New York, at which Dr. George Cannon was dinner chairman and Franklin H. Williams coordinator, signed up 600 life members. Besides giving numerous recruiting speeches in the Boston-Cambridge area where he lives, Kivie Kaplan during 1960 flew to St. Louis, St. Paul, Philadelphia, New York, and other cities on behalf of his pet project.

The roster of life members now includes Marian Anderson, Governor Nelson A. Rockefeller, Congressman Adam Clayton Powell, Eleanor Roosevelt, the Reverend Howard Thurman, Alan Paton, Poppy Cannon White, Nat King Cole, Chester Bowles, Count Basie, G. Mennen Williams, poet Ivor Winters, Irving Thalberg, Jr., and blues singer Joe Williams. But Senator Eastland, Gerald L. K. Smith, and William Faulkner are not yet enrolled—perhaps because Kivie Kaplan has not met them; if he had, he probably would have signed them up. Once members are enrolled, Kaplan is a great one for getting them to recruit additional life members. An appeal he asked Professor Ralph Harlow of Smith College to write goes in part like this: "Freedom is not easily or casually won. Blood, sweat and tears are demanded. It is more than your sympathy or a passing contribution to ease your conscience that we plead for. . . . You can support our lawyers, our Freedom Riders, our students willing to go behind prison bars in this cause. Will you?" With hundreds of sit-in and freedom riders cases to be defended in court, it is difficult for NAACP income to match outlay. As Dr. DeWitt Burton of the Detroit branch expressed it quite simply, "Freedom is not free."

Massive Desegregation

When the NAACP decided to get at the roots of segregation by court action that sought to destroy a whole tree—rather than whittling away at this or that evil branch eternally—discrimination in the public-school system was the specific tree chosen. The Association had been whittling legally at discrimination in education in one way or another for a long time. This, its executives realized, could go on forever, with one isolated case after another coming up. The day had come, they felt, to attack the entire system; to attempt to clarify the law in at least one area *all* the way down the line; to start with the smallest child, with the kindergarten and the grammar school, with the basic ABC's themselves—and the *C* could stand for Constitution.

Southerners did not like the NAACP's basic new approach. Following the Supreme Court's famous decision on school desegregation, there arrived in the mail one day at the national office of the NAACP a box that was too light to contain a bomb. Postmarked Perry, Florida, it had been sent anonymously and was wrapped like a gift. When Roy Wilkins opened the package he found a lynch rope with the slipnoose tied. Inside the box was a note:

THEY TELL ME IF YOU GIVE A NIGGER ENOUGH ROPE, HE WILL HANG HIMSELF. SO HERE IT IS.

There was no signature. But there was a P.S. that read: PLEASE USE AND PASS ON. Even though Wilkins did not hang himself, the senders in Florida must have been gratified to learn from the press that he received their gift safely, for many papers carried a photograph of the skeptical Mr. Wilkins holding his own lynch noose aloft.

Thurgood Marshall refuses to take the credit for initially masterminding the idea of a massive legal attack on school segregation. According to him, it resulted from the collaboration of many minds and many related factors. Charles Houston was very influential in plotting the strategy that successfully led to the Supreme Court's ruminations on the possible fate of children forcibly separated from one another by outmoded laws. The Nine Old Men who heard *Plessy v. Ferguson* in 1896 had gone to their glory. That decision set up the "separate but equal" rigmarole that affirmed Jim Crow but never worked out. It cost the white South more than it could afford to pay, and the Negroes more heartache than they could take. Perhaps Charles Houston realized before his death that it was about time for a change in high court thinking—as indeed it was.

Beginning as part-time attorney for the NAACP in 1930, and a few years later devoting all his time to it, Charles Houston "set the pattern for fundamental attacks on barriers to equal justice, in place of the former practice of meeting emergencies and opportunities as they arose. While emergencies would still arise, Houston preferred to plan affirmative actions systematically. One of his primary objectives was to widen educational opportunities. The first major victory was won in Baltimore City Court in 1935 when a young Amherst graduate of color was refused admission to the University of Maryland Law School. The applicant was Donald Murray." The case, argued by Thurgood Marshall, was won in the Maryland Court of Appeals. Murray received his diploma, practiced in Baltimore, and volunteered his services to the NAACP throughout his career.

Following in his old teacher's footsteps, Marshall "continued Houston's systematic pursuit after equal opportunity in education. One of the most glaring inequities was the wide gap between white and colored teachers' salaries. The first teachers' pay case was filed against the Board of Education in Montgomery County, Maryland, on behalf of William Gibbs, who was an acting principal in county schools at a salary of $612 per year. Had he been white, his annual pay would have been $1475 at that time. The court ordered salaries equalized throughout the county. This decision set a precedent for other counties where the NAACP and teachers groups could afford to undertake legal action toward the same goal." In nine counties in Maryland the added pay won for Negro teachers in 1938 amounted to over $100,000. After winning fifty such cases in various southern and border states, the NAACP's efforts added more than $3,000,000 annually to the payrolls of Negro teachers within a fifteen-year period. Incidentally, white women teachers in Kentucky were also aided, for their pay, which was less than that for men teachers, was equalized as a result of these suits.

Wider vistas opened when the case of *Lloyd Gaines v. University of Missouri* was brought before the United States Supreme Court by the NAACP. Gaines, a qualified Negro student, had been refused admission by the University of Missouri graduate law school. The registrar urged Gaines to attend a law school outside the state, which was willing to pay his tuition. On December 12, 1938, Chief Justice Charles Evans Hughes handed down the court's majority ruling that this procedure involving travel would not be equal treatment under the Constitution.

But breaking down educational barriers has been a slow process, as is evident from the following:

> Courts draw their decisions as narrowly as possible. They order changes in existing practices reluctantly. . . . The Supreme Court decision in 1938 requiring Missouri to offer Lloyd Gaines a legal education within his state was an important step. It did not rule out, however, many other means of confining Negro students to educational facilities far inferior to those furnished white students. . . . Ada Lois Sipuel sued the University of Oklahoma in April, 1946, for refusing her admittance to its law school. . . . The NAACP carried Ada Sipuel's case up to the U.S. Supreme Court. . . . The Court unanimously ruled that Oklahoma had to provide a legal education for her "as soon as it does for applicants of any other group." . . .

The next step was to attack the false theory that separate graduate schools for Negroes offered anything like an equal opportunity for professional training. Heman Sweatt applied for admission to the University of Texas law school in May, 1946. He was refused, and sued. . . . June 6, 1950, the U.S. Supreme Court unanimously ordered the University to admit Heman Sweatt to its hitherto all-white law school, holding that the Negro school could not possibly provide him with an equal education. This decision established the precedent for opening all State-operated graduate professional schools to Negroes.

G. W. McLaurin had been admitted to the University of Oklahoma graduate school of education to study for his doctorate of philosophy degree. Once there, to isolate him from white students he was forced to sit in an anteroom outside the classroom, to use a separate table in the library and to eat in the cafeteria at separate hours. Being branded an inferior humiliated him and brought mental strain which interfered with his ability to study. On the same day as the Sweatt decision, the Supreme Court decided by a second 9–0 ruling that such segregated practices denied McLaurin the equal protection of the laws guaranteed by the 14th Amendment to the Constitution. It ordered the University to abolish these regulations. Another long stride thus brought the power of the Constitution behind the proposition that Negro graduate students must be subject only to the same rules which apply to all other students.

"Victories at the highest levels of education caused jubilation, of course," wrote Walter White, "but all who were engaged in the fight knew that these victories would be of little value to Negroes generally or to democracy itself unless the cleansing process was extended downward to the lowest elementary schools. The gross disparities in both quantity and quality of training afforded Negroes in grammar schools and high schools as well as at the college level fitted only a small percentage of Negroes to qualify for more advanced courses."

Said Mordecai Johnson in 1952, "An examination of the whole structure of American education a few years ago showed that in New York State the average primary and secondary schools had a support of $4000 a year for a classroom of twenty-three, while the average Negro school all over the former slave states received $400 for the same classroom of twenty-three students. . . . If a Negro with one son started walking from Mississippi . . . by the time he got to New York he would have multiplied his child's educational advantages by ten."

In the summer of 1950 a national conference in New York of lawyers associated with the NAACP decided to attempt a bold, all-out frontal attack upon educational segregation. It was unreasonable and unjust, they maintained, to expect Negro children to wait for twenty, thirty or forty years for the Jim Crow school to wither away. For it was not just the physical inadequacies and curriculum deficiencies of most Negro schools in the South that were in question. Marshall argued that the very fact of segregation itself caused undeniable personality damage and serious injury to the human personality subjected to such inequalities.

Sponsored by the NAACP and convened by Marshall, a long series of meetings and conferences, some lasting for days, began to lay the groundwork for the Supreme Court appeals that eventually ended in historic victory. In meeting after meeting, the nation's leading sociologists, psychologists, and educators, white and Negro, prepared the social and psychological arguments that might be put before the court. To these preparations and to material later incorporated in briefs, Dr. Kenneth Clark made an invaluable contribution based on his studies of the deleterious effects of segregation upon the psyche of the Negro child.

In June, 1953, the Supreme Court ordered that five school desegregation cases be reargued before it. It issued five groups of questions on whether the Fourteenth Amendment had contemplated the abolition of segregation in public schools, whether the overthrow of segregated schooling was within the court's power, and how it could act if it decided to do so. Reargument was heard in December, 1953. In his capacity as counsel for South Carolina, John W. Davis, a former United States ambassador to Great Britain and presidential candidate, the attorney who had pleaded more Supreme Court cases than any man living or dead, led a battery of attorneys which included the legal officers of the southern states. The NAACP lawyers opposing them were Thurgood Marshall, Robert L. Carter, Jack Greenberg, Louis T. Redding, James Nabrit, George E. C. Hayes, and Spottswood W. Robinson, III. Their brief had been exhaustively prepared with the assistance of many of the nation's leading experts in constitutional history and the social sciences. Their main thesis was that racial segregation imposed by law is a violation of the United States Constitution.

Thurgood Marshall stated to the court: "Now is the time, we submit, that this Court should make it clear that that is *not* what our Constitution stands for." On May 17, 1954, by a 9–0 decision delivered by Chief Justice Earl Warren, the United States Supreme Court declared: "Liberty under law extends to the full conduct which an individual is free to pursue, and it cannot be restricted except for a proper governmental objective. Segregation in public education is not reasonably related to any proper government objective." The old *Plessy v. Ferguson* philosophy was laid to rest with the words: " . . . In the field of public education the doctrine of 'separate but equal' has no place. Separate educational facilities are inherently unequal."

Thus, after a generation of struggle in the courts, in relation to one area of Negro freedom the NAACP had at last pinned the law down. And it did so, not as a victor with his foot on the neck of the vanquished, but as a redeemer of the nation's best promise. In a message to NAACP leaders who were assembled in Atlanta a few days after the decision to discuss desegregation plans, Board Chairman Tobias said: "It is important that calm reasonableness prevail, that the difficulties of adjustment be realized, and that without any sacrifice of basic principles, the spirit of give and take characterize the discussions. Let it not be said of us that we took advantage of a sweeping victory to drive hard bargains or impose unnecessary hardships upon those responsible for working out the details of adjustment."

5

Victory Poses Problems

Nine O'Clock Bell

HIGH COURT BANS SCHOOL SEGREGATION
"Separate But Equal" Doctrine
Held Out of Place in Education

So read the banner headline across the front page of the *New York Times* on May 18, 1954. Another front-page headline proclaimed: "'VOICE' SPEAKS IN 34 LANGUAGES TO FLASH COURT RULING TO WORLD." James Reston's column was headed: "A SOCIOLOGICAL DECISION—Court Founded Its Desegregation on Hearts and Minds Rather Than Laws." The *Times* that day published an unprecedented eight pages of news and comments concerning the pronouncement, including the complete text of the Supreme Court decision. Beneath a charming photograph of Negro children in school was a running caption: "EQUAL OPPORTUNITIES—'We come then,' said the decision, 'to the question presented: Does segregation of children in public schools solely on the basis of race, even though physical facilities and other tangible factors may be equal, deprive the children of the minority group of equal education opportunities? We believe it does!'"

But a page of condensed opinions from all over the country quoted Alabama's *Birmingham News* as stating editorially, "The *News* believes that the considerations of public interest and states' rights which underlay the superseded decision of 1896 still apply and would better serve progress in racial relations and education." And Senator James O. Eastland of Mississippi was reported as saying flatly that the South "will not abide by nor obey this legislative decision by a political court."

Just before the school bells began to ring in September, the *New York Times* carried a report from Georgia's Governor Herman Talmadge which stated: "No force whatever could compel" admission of Negroes and whites to the same schools. Earlier he had called the Supreme Court decision a "step toward national suicide." Louisiana, the first state officially to defy the Supreme Court's edict, passed bills during the summer to preserve segregated schools by police power. On October 2 the *Times* ran a front-page headline: "FLORIDA OPPOSES FAST INTEGRATION IN HIGH COURT BID. Warns of Uncurbed Violence if Segregation in Schools Is Ended Immediately." On an inside page: "BALTIMORE CROWD ATTACKS 4 PUPILS. Negro Boy Punched in Fight Over Integration." Another article stated that the Milford, Delaware, Board of Education suspended 11 Negro high-school pupils, leaving them with no school to go to, after rioting by whites against integration. These suspensions were hailed by Bryant Bowles, president of the National Association for the Advancement of White People, as "a great victory." The National Association for the Advancement of Colored People, however, called them "a surrender to the illegal actions of a lawless mob."

The Negro high school nearest Milford was twenty miles away. At a pro-segregationist rally Bowles declared, "My 3-year-old daughter will never attend a school with Negroes as long as there is breath in my body and gunpowder will burn." Sheriff Wills McCall flew from Florida to Delaware to address the anti-integrationists. Three years before, McCall had wounded a Negro prisoner, Walter Lee Irvin, by gunfire and killed Samuel Shepherd, another Negro prisoner, as they sat handcuffed to each other in his police car. In his speech McCall praised the white racists of Milford for protecting the Delaware school system from Negroes, and boasted of "victories" in Florida and of how the home of NAACP organizer Harry Moore had been dynamited on Christmas night in 1951. McCall told how flaming crosses were burned in Negro neighborhoods. During the demonstration, motorcades drove through the streets shouting racial insults, mobs surrounded the school, and the state troopers had to be called out.

At White Sulphur Springs, West Virginia, 700 white parents voted "to remove bodily any Negro who tried to attend classes." In Mississippi, a state legislator said, "The white people in certain counties are organizing to protect themselves. Practically every county in the state has organized or is organizing. If we fail, the temper of the public may produce something like the Klan." In Baltimore 600 extra police had to be called out on October 4, 1954, to cope with jeering adults in front of schools, and some 2000 teenagers carrying placards reading WE DON'T WANT NE-GROES and KICK 'EM OUT attempted to march on the mayor's office. The same day in Washington, almost within the shadow of the Supreme Court, 4000 white students cut classes to demonstrate. Some carried

Confederate flags and signs that read: WE WHITES DEMAND OUR RIGHTS. White students who did not boycott classes were jeered at and taunted: "Don't be a Communist!" Meanwhile, Vice-President Nixon said, "My own youngsters will continue to go to Washington public schools . . . and grow up in an atmosphere where they realize we have attempted to provide equal opportunities for all."

This is how it was in some places in the autumn of 1954, a few months after the Supreme Court's desegregation ruling. Public and press reaction outside the South was overwhelmingly favorable, both because people felt that it was the right thing and because of its immediate harvest of international good will. Even in the South there were some signs that desegregation was seen as inevitable, however repugnant. It is possible that, given immediate enforcement, the ruling would have been grudgingly obeyed in all but the hardest-core areas. But the court did not put its ruling into effect; instead, it ordered new briefs and arguments on the most suitable ways of implementing the decision.

Meantime, however, there was considerable desegregation. Topeka, Kansas, and Washington, D.C., which had been directly involved in the litigation, proceeded immediately to desegregate, as did numerous schools and school districts in Delaware, West Virginia, Oklahoma, Arkansas, Missouri, Kentucky, Maryland, Texas, and Tennessee. There was some disorder, as has been noted, but for the most part it was short-lived. The rioting whites in White Sulphur Springs, West Virginia, for example, were put on their good behavior by a judge who threatened to fill the jail with them "until their feet stuck out the window."

In the spring of 1955 the *New York Times* carried a headline: "U.S. URGES DELAY IN DESEGREGATION. Solicitor General Tells High Court It Lacks Material for School Judgment Now." This front-page article reported that the southern states "warned the Supreme Court that an abrupt end to segregation might mean trouble." The attorney general of Texas argued before the court that it would be "rash, imprudent and unrealistic," and the assistant attorney general of North Carolina asserted that it might provoke "racial tension and animosities unparalleled since those terrible days that gave rise to the original Ku Klux Klan." Nevertheless, following Thurgood Marshall's request that the Supreme Court end school separation "not later than September, 1956," the court on May 31, 1955, ordered that educational integration be achieved "with all deliberate speed" compatible with "practical flexibility."

All Deliberate Speed

Three months after the Supreme Court's implementation order, another *New York Times* headline read: "SCHOOLS IN THE SOUTH STAY SEGRE-GATED." According to a United Press summary of school openings in the fall of 1955:

> At Beckley, West Virginia, more than forty Negro children were turned away when they attempted to enroll. . . . At Farmville, Virginia, white chil-dren went to one high school and the Negroes to another. . . . At Guil-ford College, North Carolina, site of a Quaker college, about fifty resent-ful white residents assembled at the town's public school determined to prevent registration of any Negro pupils. No Negro applicants appeared. Sheriff's deputies dispersed the crowd, which had surrounded a car be-longing to a couple who were among thirty-four signers of a petition urg-ing integration as "just and wise." . . . Federal Judge Hobart . . . granted the University of Alabama a four-month delay in the admission of Negro students. . . . Texas finance laws have provided that state aid funds be paid on a separate white-Negro school basis.

Headlines on March 12, 1956, proclaimed, "96 IN CONGRESS OPEN DRIVE TO UPSET INTEGRATION RULING." Nineteen southern Senators and 77 Representatives issued a "Declaration of Constitutional Princi-ples" (known also as "The Southern Manifesto"), which stated: "The unwarranted decision of the Supreme Court in the public school cases is now bearing the fruit always produced when men substitute naked power for established law. . . . The Supreme Court of the United States, with no legal basis for such action, undertook to exercise their naked judicial power and substitute their personal, political and social ideas for the established law of the land." The 96 Congressmen contended that the decision had "planted hatred and suspicion where there has been heretofore friendship and understanding," that is, between the two races in the South. But seemingly these lawmakers had forgotten that exactly a month before this statement, a Negro girl who sought to enter the University of Alabama had been greeted by a howling stone-throwing mob. Thereupon the university, Thurgood Marshall stated before a fed-eral court in Birmingham, had "punished" the student, Miss Autherine Lucy—who was acting within the law—by suspending her, but had done nothing about those who had broken the law by rioting and had cost the city and state thousands of dollars. Miss Lucy never got to study at the University of Alabama.

The day after the Congressmen's attack on the Supreme Court, the *New York Times* reported, "A cross was burned in front of the University of Florida law school tonight. It was ignited just before midnight and burned about ten minutes." New Orleans marked the second anniversary of the Supreme Court's decision, the *New York Post* observed, " . . . in the most vivid fashion of all. Somebody burned a cross on the lawn of Archbishop Joseph Francis Rummell, a Catholic prelate who has fought segregation both in Louisiana's parochial and public schools." In 1960, when four little Negro girls entered the first grade in two formerly all-white schools in New Orleans, howling white mothers screamed curses at the 6-year-old youngsters, and mobs blocked traffic in front of the schools. In Atlanta that fall, the Ku Klux Klan bombed a Negro school after a hooded demonstration in the downtown area.

Nor had feelings in Milford, Delaware, changed either by 1961—except that Bryant Bowles was no longer there to add fuel to the flames. He is serving a 99-year prison sentence in Texas for the murder of his brother-in-law. The town of Milford is still hate-ridden. The *New York Times* of August 12, 1961, reported a leading citizen as saying that "Negro parents are afraid to enroll their children in white schools. They are put under strong pressure—economic and social—not to do so." The Reverend David DeBerry, a Negro minister, says, "This is a closed town. You have an authoritarian situation. The white people are dominant, they are ruling." And City Manager J. Robert Green, speaking of Negro children, says, "I don't think we would give them police protection. I think we'd leave that up to the state police."

In Warren County, Virginia, where the *Northern Virginia Daily* constantly calls for "total war on the NAACP," Local 371 of the AFL-CIO Textile Workers Union helped subsidize private schools for white pupils until pressure from union headquarters forced them to cease. The public schools of Prince Edward County, Virginia, closed in 1959 rather than desegregate, and are still closed as of this writing. South Carolina, Alabama, and Mississippi have admitted no Negro children to their white public schools, nor have most of the rural areas in the rest of the South. In 1960 only about 6 percent of the Negro pupils below the Mason-Dixon line were in non-segregated classes. According to an NAACP pamphlet (here condensed):

It is more than six years since the Supreme Court declared racial segregation in public education to be unconstitutional. Commendable progress in implementing the decision has been made in most of the border states affected. Unfortunately, in many other states the Negro children have encountered not occasional denial of their rights by individual schools, but a massive rebuff by those very governments, state and local, whose constitutional duty it is to protect them. In these circumstances it is not the rights of individuals alone that are impaired or denied; the very processes of orderly government are challenged and flouted. . . .

Negro children denied their rights are indeed injured parties, but to require them to bear the whole burden of seeking redress of their injury through costly and prolonged litigation, to compete against the massive weight of official state opposition, is to deny justice. In five states not a single Negro child is as yet receiving the kind of education to which the Constitution entitles him; in five others the total numbers but a handful. After six years, even under the most liberal interpretation, this can hardly be deemed to meet the test of "deliberate speed."

Official Harassment

Not only have the southern states been busy since 1954 trying to devise "legal" means of barring Negroes from educational institutions, they have been busy seeking "legal" ways of putting the NAACP completely out of business. To segregationists, the initials NAACP are synonymous with the devil. As far back as 1946, the late Senator Bilbo of Mississippi wrote in his book, *Take Your Choice: Separation or Mongrelization:* "Unless you believe in and are willing to encourage or tolerate your sons and daughters, relatives, neighbors and friends associating with and marrying into the Negro race, then you must turn thumbs down on the NAACP and all its activities, branding it as Public Enemy No. 1 of the white race in America."

The several so-called legal ways by which the South attempts to cripple or kill the NAACP include legislative investigations, the enforced registration and submission of records, the publication of membership lists, the barring of teachers and municipal and state employees from membership, special taxes levied against it but not against other organizations or the unduly harsh application of existing tax laws, intimidation of lawyers and indiscriminate use of contempt of court proceedings, the passage of special emergency power statutes aimed directly at the NAACP (although it may not be named), and the use of existing laws, even those already pronounced unconstitutional by the Supreme Court, to hinder and harass the NAACP and cause it to spend thousands of dollars defending itself in court. The southern states would like nothing better than to break the NAACP by forcing it to deplete its funds in numerous and costly court cases. For example, as an aftermath of Little Rock, the Association was involved in 75 separate pieces of litigation in Arkansas through 1961.

Since the Negro vote is weak or almost nonexistent in many parts of the South, Negroes have no control over state legislative committees. Such committees seek to "investigate" any organization out of existence by subpoenaing their officers to attend highly publicized hearings, seizing their books and records, and then releasing the names of their members to the White Citizens Councils or the Klan, thus exposing the members to loss of jobs as well as physical danger. States that have conducted such vicious and one-sided investigations against the NAACP include Mississippi, Arkansas, Louisiana, Florida, and Virginia.

Just fighting to stay alive in the South is a problem. In 1956 the State of Texas accused the NAACP of failure to pay taxes as a profit-making organization, and of lobbying and barratry; by means of a "temporary" injunction it banned the Association from operating in the state. Louisiana issued an injunction for refusal to disclose membership lists. So also the State of Alabama issued an injunction and then found the NAACP in contempt and fined it $100,000 for refusing to disclose its membership lists. The $100,000 fine was fought all the way to the United States Supreme Court which in 1959 reversed the lower court and voided the fine. The court made it clear that the names of NAACP members cannot be divulged by state fiat. This ruling, obtained by Robert L. Carter, was of historic significance as a landmark in the judicial protection of the basic right to organize and associate for redress of grievances without molestation. The Alabama courts willfully delayed processing the ruling and did not proceed to hold a hearing in the "temporary" injunction against the NAACP until forced to do so by the Supreme Court. This injunction was made permanent in December, 1961, after a farcical hearing, but the way is now cleared for appeals which are expected to reach the top federal court again. This vicious circle of legal moves was of course designed with malice aforethought to kill the NAACP in Alabama, and to prevent any of its legal staff from defending its members or arguing anti-segregation cases in the Alabama courts. In Texas and Louisiana, however, the NAACP was successful in removing the legal barriers to its operation.

Since lawyers are a necessity in lawsuits and in defense against court action, the southern states of course seek every possible means of charging NAACP lawyers personally with irregularities or illegalities. Charges that attorneys incite clients to start cases for the attorney's own gain—

in other words, barratry—are common against Negro lawyers. Efforts to disbar militant Negro and white civil-rights lawyers are also common. South Carolina and Virginia passed laws which in effect prohibit lawyers from accepting fees from any person or organization fostering anti-segregation suits; and Mississippi has a law designed to keep out-of-state attorneys from practicing in the state. If new and hastily passed laws fail, there is always intimidation. Demagogues love to incite to violence, and bigots are eager to carry out their wishes. Thurgood Marshall reports being threatened in Mississippi by a tough-looking white with a gun on his hip who told him he had better be out of town before sunset. Since the legal business that had brought him there was completed, Marshall says that he wrapped his constitutional rights in cellophane, put them in his pocket, and caught the next train north.

But for Negroes who live in the South, there is no such thing as catching the next train, unless they want to leave their family, home, and friends behind. To cut off all help for them is, of course, the reason for the South's "legal" fight against the NAACP. Twenty-four Negro teachers in Elloree, South Carolina, were fired when they refused to sign a statement that they were not members of the NAACP and that they did not believe in integration of the public schools. When the NAACP lawyers representing the teachers argued in a federal court hearing that the state law violated the constitutional guarantees of freedom of speech, association, and petition, the attorney general of South Carolina stated: "The NAACP has reached a point of no return as far as South Carolina is concerned. They are disturbing the domestic tranquillity and causing enmity and bad feelings between people who have always lived together. We do not wish to have its members teaching in our schools." Nevertheless, the state repealed the law, anticipating an adverse decision. The attorney general of Georgia declared that the NAACP is an "organization subversive to the Constitution and the laws of the state of Georgia." And the Georgia Board of Education passed a resolution decreeing, "Any teacher in Georgia . . . who is a member of the NAACP, any allied or any subversive organization shall have his or her license revoked and forfeited for life."

The NAACP and Communism

Attempts to label the NAACP subversive, Communist-influenced, or out-and-out Communist have continued for a long time. The late Negro professional witness, ex-Communist Manning Johnson, since discredited, testified before two southern legislative committees to the effect that the NAACP was "a vehicle of the Communist Party designed to overthrow the government of the United States." Upton Blevis, president of White Men, Inc., described the NAACP as "the most subversive and successful of all Communist-front organizations ever set up in this country." Utterly disregarding the truth, these malicious and irresponsible accusations ignore evidence, so clearly on the record, that the NAACP is not and was not Communist and has never even remotely been under Communist influence. Since its earliest years, its top officials from Joel Spingarn and James Weldon Johnson to Walter White and Roy Wilkins have attacked communism in no uncertain terms in both speaking and writing, and in turn have been subjected to leftist attacks, sometimes being denounced as "Uncle Toms." Until recently, the official Communist program for Negroes called for the establishment of a separate Negro nation, an idea that was directly opposite to the NAACP's philosophy of integration.

The 41st Annual Convention of the NAACP in Boston in 1950 passed a long anti-communism resolution. It condemned attacks on the NAACP by Communists and fellow-travelers, denounced any left-wing infiltration uncovered in any branches, and called for the formation of a committee to "investigate and study the ideological composition and trends of the membership and leadership of local units . . . and if necessary to suspend and reorganize, or lift the charter and expel any unit, which, in the judgment of the Board of Directors, upon a basis of the findings of the aforementioned investigation and study of local units comes under Communist or other political control and domination."

This resolution was given wide publicity. Nevertheless, after the Supreme Court decisions of 1954, Circuit Court Judge Tom P. Brady of Mississippi stated that behind the NAACP and its "questionable" activities there were "87 Communist-front organizations." Meanwhile the attorney general of Georgia dug into the files of the House Committee on Un-American Activities to support a claim that some NAACP officials had once been associated with organizations listed as radical. He concluded that since the Communist party stood for "full racial equality," the NAACP had allowed itself to become "part and parcel of the Communist conspiracy to overthrow the democratic governments of this nation and its sovereign states." He overlooked, among other things, that the NAACP, its policy and program, were established long before the Communist party came into existence.

That J. Edgar Hoover does not agree with the Communist smear of the NAACP is shown by the fact that he devotes the major part of a chapter in his book, *Masters of Deceit,* published in 1958, to an account of the NAACP's success in shutting the Communists out. The Communists have smeared and vilified the Association as much as the most rabid anti-Negro newspaper in the South.

A more subtle form of attack on the Association that appeared recently was described in the keynote address delivered by Bishop Stephen Gill Spottswood, chairman of the NAACP Board of Directors, at the 52nd Annual Convention in Philadelphia.

> In a way, the newly revealed John Birch Society is more of a threat than iron-pipe mobsters in Alabama, for the Birch Society wears the robe of respectability and does not conduct its campaigns in gutters and alleys. But do not be deceived. Its number-one objective is the impeachment of Chief Justice Earl Warren of the United States Supreme Court for handing down the school segregation ruling. The Birch Society is also against federal civil-rights action and for leaving such matters to the states. Finally, the Birch Society believes in restricting voting rights to those who, in its judgment, are "qualified." Most of us do not need a crystal ball to tell how many Negro Americans the Birch Society would find to be "qualified." As far as Negro voting rights are concerned, the John Birch Society is much more than a kissing cousin of the State of Mississippi, where only 3.89 percent of the Negro citizens of voting age are permitted to register.

Little Rock Rocks

On the platform in Philadelphia as Bishop Spottswood spoke sat Mrs. Daisy Bates of Little Rock, Arkansas. This very pretty Negro housewife, co-editor of the *Arkansas State Press,* made headlines around the world with Orval Faubus, the governor of her state, on the same day—and together—because one stood for protection of children from a mob and the other stood for their vilification and degradation; one stood for education for all youngsters, the other for humiliation and ignorance for Negro children; one stood for constitutional and human rights, the other for states' rights and willful bigotry; one stood for democracy, the other for white autocracy. One stood for life, the other for death. Like John Shillady in 1919, Alex Wilson, the *Chicago Defender*'s Negro reporter on the scene of the Little Rock riots, never quite recovered from the shock of the kicking and beating he received at the hands of mobsters. He died a few years later.

Because state officials refused to provide protection for the Negro children but instead used the militia to bar them from school, President Eisenhower finally ordered federal troops—the 101st Airborne Division—to be sent in to insure enforcement of federal court orders. Alex Wilson was not the only newsman to suffer violence. White reporters were attacked as well. Three members of the *Life* staff were arrested. An Arkansas newsman, mistaken for a "damn Yankee," was slugged and knocked down twice before he could make his identity known. The managing editor of Harlem's *New York Amsterdam News* was chased down the street past several policemen who did nothing to protect him.

"It's that goddamn NAACP that's causing all the trouble," the mobsters yelled. "Them and these goddamn Yankee newspaper reporters. We ought to take all of them and scrounge up the ground with them." The whole world was astounded at the incredible behavior that white segregationists were permitted in Little Rock, and at the bravery of Daisy Bates, president of the Arkansas Conference of NAACP branches, who saw to it that nine Negro teen-agers passed through jeering stone-throwing mobs shouting unprintable obscenities and reached the gates of Central High School.

Television films of these events had to be very carefully edited to keep the dirty words off the nation's screens. Such conditions lasted three years—1957–1958–1959—while Governor Faubus spouted imprecations, President Eisenhower hemmed and hawed, troops went back and forth to and from Little Rock, 44 of the city's school teachers were discharged, the high school opened and closed and finally opened again under government order, and—whenever classes were held—the nine Negro teen-agers went to school through the mobs, after having first been barred by the Arkansas National Guard. White students inside the school shouted:

Two—four—six—eight,
We don't want to integrate!

In an interview for *Look* magazine, Minnijean Brown described life at Central High for the Negro pupils. In French class a white student put his feet across the aisle and said, "Nigger, if you want to go by me, you'll have to kill me, or walk around the room." At the lockers in the hall, "Don't touch my locker, nigger, or I'll kick the —— out of you." Whenever a bowl of hot soup or chili was deliberately spilled on a Negro student in the lunchroom, the white students would give fifteen "rah's" for the youngster who did it. White teen-agers made a practice of stepping on the heels of Negro girls and boys, or spitting on them as they changed classes, and daring them to do anything about it. "The Bill of Rights seemed to be a joke in Little Rock," said Minnijean, "like it was planned for white people, and they didn't expect us to get in on it."

When asked why the white students who molested the Negro students were not expelled, Superintendent of Schools Virgil Blossom replied, "Our job is to educate, not eliminate." Meanwhile, two Negro boys, Terrence Roberts and Jefferson Thomas, were slugged; one was knocked unconscious inside the school. Carloads of white youths waited outside after classes to throw rock-centered snowballs at the Negro kids. When the mid-winter term began, a stick of dynamite was found in a locker near the lunchroom. The few white youngsters who wanted to be friendly with the Negro students were jeered by the rest of the whites if heard saying even "Hello" to a Negro classmate. Several white students who occasionally sat with Negro students in the cafeteria were forbidden to do so by the vice-principal.

When Central's star football player, Bruce Fullerton, suggested that the school hold a panel discussion on integration to help dispel some of the false ideas commonly held about Negroes, the authorities prohibited it. One white girl was finally expelled for inciting student segregationists to continue their misdeeds; she was reinstated. A Negro girl was expelled for resisting taunts and physical abuse; she was not reinstated. Ernest Green was pushed down a flight of stairs, and twice whipped with hot wet towels in the shower room. No one was punished for this, but Ernest was barred from taking any active part in pre-graduation activities in the spring. His parents were deluged with threatening phone calls as June approached: "You don't think we'll let Ernest graduate, do you?" But he did graduate, the first of his race to receive a diploma from an integrated public school in Arkansas.

The picture window in Daisy Bates' home was smashed by stones from passing cars. Crosses were burned on the Bates' lawn and guards had to be hired for protection. Because of her work in connection with NAACP branches in Arkansas, Daisy Bates was subjected to violent radio and newspaper attacks. Abusive, obscene, and threatening phone calls to both her and her husband were frequent, and the mail brought threats and denunciations each day. One such communication said:

MRS. L. C. BATES IF YOU HAVE ANY BUSYNESS TO TEND TO YOU BETTER GET DONE FOR YOUR DAYES IS SHORT

Just before midnight on the September day in 1957 that the nine Negro children registered at Central, a caravan of segregationist cars headed for the Bates home. On searching the cars, the police found enough dynamite to blow up the whole neighborhood. During the following years there were three bomb attacks on their house. In August, 1959, according to a wire service, "A car filled with white men roared down the street toward the home of Mrs. Daisy Bates, Negro leader, spraying bullets. . . . Three bullets entered the living room of a house across the corner occupied by a white family. Three small children were in the room watching television. . . . One bullet missed one of the children by a foot."

That year bombs shook the mayor's office and the school board offices, and exploded in front of the fire chief's home. Barricades had to be placed around Central High School. After Washington took some action in the situation and the local police finally decided to give the harassed Negroes of Little Rock some small measure of protection, the city officers were called "puppets of the illegal forces of the Federal government" by Governor Faubus. "We are a nation that is being taken over by parlor pinks who have no moral scruples and no love for this country," he moaned.

Born in a sawmill town in Arkansas and educated at Philander Smith and Shorter Colleges in Little Rock, Daisy Lee Getson Bates was the first and only woman pilot in the Arkansas Civil Air Patrol during World War II. She had written publicity for a unit of the Air Patrol based at a Negro college, and decided to enroll herself. In 1941 she and her husband embarked on publishing a weekly newspaper, the *Arkansas State Press*. A crusading journal that fought segregation and second-class citizenship, it became the state's most influential Negro paper, and during its eighteen years of life was a strong supporter of the NAACP. School desegregation killed it. The year after the nine Negro children entered Central High, the paper lost $10,000 worth of advertising. White-owned firms, both local and national, canceled their contracts for fear of the boycotts threatened by the White Citizens Councils if they advertised in the *State Press*. Even Negro businessmen in Arkansas were so intimidated by the whites that they withdrew their ads. City taxes were raised on the Bates' new home as a further harassment. Newsboys who sold the *State Press* in Little Rock were robbed of their papers and beaten, the paper's agents in the rural areas were threatened, and the white bank that owned the building in which the newspaper was located demanded that it vacate the premises. The *Arkansas*

State Press, the Bates' only means of livelihood, was forced to go out of business.

At the 49th Annual Convention of the NAACP in Cleveland in 1958, Daisy Bates and the Little Rock Nine—Minnijean Brown, Elizabeth Ann Eckford, Ernest Green, Thelma Mothershed, Melba Patillo, Gloria Ray, Terrence Roberts, Jefferson Thomas, and Carlotta Walls, all teen-agers— received the Spingarn Medal for "their pioneer role in upholding the basic ideals of American democracy in the face of continuing harassment and constant threats of bodily injury."

Strange Years

Like Little Rock, the mountain town of Clinton, Tennessee, also had its years of trials and tribulations. Its high school was wrecked by hate bombs. "The South Learns Its Hardest Lesson," an article that one of the teachers wrote from her heart and which appeared in the *New York Times Magazine,* tells this story. The same autumn that the nine Negro children faced the mobs in Little Rock, twelve Negro youngsters trod an equally thorny path to school in Clinton, faced equally hate-twisted faces, heard the same oaths. The oldest, a senior named Bobby Cain, protected the others as best he could and determined to stick it out himself until spring, and graduation. Each night, tremblingly he prayed to be able to get through the next day. He did. He was graduated—the first Negro to receive a high-school diploma from an integrated school in Tennessee. "If Bobby can do it, we can," said the other Negro teen-agers.

So many youngsters were pioneers of democracy in those strange years from 1954 to 1962. A tiny Negro child attended the Hattie Cotton School in Nashville for a single session. Integrated on one day, the $540,000 school was bombed the next day and almost totally destroyed. Just a few hours before the bombing, John Kasper, an itinerant northern-born racist agitator, harangued a crowd of 500 in a downtown square. In Jacksonville, Florida, a Negro grammar school was dynamited. A Jewish synagogue in Atlanta was bombed because its rabbi was thought to be sympathetic to desegregation. In October, 1958, Rabbi Emmet A. Frank, who had denounced segregation, was intimidated in Alexandria, Virginia, and there were threats to bomb a Unitarian church in Arlington at which he was scheduled to speak. A portion of his own congregation moved to censure him for his views, but in his Sabbath sermon he replied, "A Jew who remains silent in the face of prejudice leveled at another group of God's children is traitorous to the basic principle of Judaism. . . . I will not divorce justice from Judaism. I will not be intimidated. I will not betray my heritage."

That same week in Birmingham, Alabama, a Christian minister, the Reverend F. S. Shuttlesworth, and 13 other Negro leaders were held incommunicado in jail for several days on unstated charges, and denied legal advice and medical services. The minister had been beaten by mobsters the year before and his home had been bombed when he attempted to register his children in an all-white school. In Bessemer, Alabama, Asbury Howard, a middle-aged Baptist deacon and civic leader, was fined $150 and sentenced to 180 days in jail for reproducing a poster from the *Kansas City Call;* it showed a Negro man in chains and called the attention of Negroes to things they could not do in the South, including "You can't study here." After filing notice of appeal and posting bond, Mr. Howard, who was just outside the courtroom but still inside the City Hall itself, was set upon and beaten by a large number of white men. Police gave him no protection; instead, they arrested his son, a young Korean War veteran, when he came to his father's defense. His appeal denied, a few weeks later Asbury Howard began serving his six-month sentence on the prison road gang.

"RACE VIOLENCE IN SOUTH GROWING, SURVEY FINDS—530 Killings, Beatings, Bombings Since 1955 Are Laid to Tension." So read a front-page headline in the *New York Herald Tribune* on June 15, 1959. The Associated Press story, which was also carried in the *New York Times,* stated: "Law and order have deteriorated in the South since the United States Supreme Court's outlawing of school segregation, a report by three agencies said today. . . . The record pointed to a widespread erosion of individual liberties. . . . Resistance groups, typified by the White Citizens Council born in Mississippi in 1954, have spread across the South. . . . Gunpowder and dynamite, parades and cross burnings, anonymous telephone calls, beatings and threats have been the marks of their trade."

The fact that the police and the entire judicial machinery of the South were collaborating with the segregationists resulted in case after case which soon taxed the NAACP's legal resources to the full. Not to mention the distances covered by others of its lawyers, Thurgood Marshall traveled some 40,000 miles in a single year, advising, counseling, or defending civil-rights cases or people persecuted and prosecuted because of color. In North Carolina during this period there was an example of strange judicial behavior that grew out of white resentment but was perhaps not directly related to the school situation. A few months after a pregnant Negro woman had been kicked down the courthouse steps in Monroe by whites, two Negro boys, aged 8 and 9, were arrested, tried, and sentenced to reform school for allegedly kissing or allowing themselves to be kissed by a neighborhood playmate, a 7-year-old white girl! The NAACP spent months getting the two children released.

Stories of all these strangely uncivilized doings directed to children were headlined around the world. In Denmark the *Dagens Nyheder* said. "Every white man in the whole world is experiencing the mob against the colored people like another stain on the white man's already heavily-stained conscience." The *Giornale d'Italia* in Rome called Arkansas "as morally backward as the Middle Ages." After Little Rock, the *Indonesian Times* in far-off Jakarta editorialized: "Americans must ask themselves whether Governor Faubus should not be haled before the Un-American Activities Committee for alienating half the world from the United States." The Iron Curtain countries, of course, had a field day, as witness Hungarian Premier Kadar's statement, "Those who tolerate that a people should be persecuted because of the color of their skin have no right to preach human liberty and human rights to others."

In the United Nations, a brown-skinned delegate from Ceylon joined in censuring Russia about Hungary, whereupon a Bulgarian representative, looking at the Ceylonese diplomat, cried, "Something worse could happen to you today if you went to Little Rock." The editorial page of Harlem's *New York Amsterdam News* added its own "FOOTNOTE TO HISTORY: Let the historians' record show that in the week in which the Russians hurled the first living earthly thing into outer space, the Big Story in U.S. newspapers was how and when the people of Little Rock, Arkansas, U.S.A., were going to throw Mrs. Daisy Bates and other NAACP leaders into jail for upholding the right of nine Negro children to develop and cultivate their brains in a school which their parents helped to pay for through blood, sweat, and tears."

In a recent article in the *Harvard Educational Review,* John Morsell, assistant to the executive secretary of the NAACP, commented as follows concerning segregated education in the State of Georgia:

> The state provides four junior colleges for whites and none for Negroes, two area trade schools for whites and none for Negroes, a medical school and graduate university facilities for whites and none for Negroes. . . . In the city of Atlanta, despite repeated queries, there are no ROTC units in Negro high schools. Students in Negro schools have been known to at-

tend classes for weeks without being able to secure the textbooks required for their courses; meanwhile the practice continues of supplying Negro students with used or out-dated texts discarded by Atlanta's white students. Double sessions continue in about half the Negro public schools, and many Negro children travel ten miles a day to reach a school that will admit them. . . . It is still nearly impossible for Negro youth to secure first-class modern vocational training.

"The plain truth is that the Deep South states are still cheating 2,500,000 Negro children of the equal education they can receive only in integrated schools," states the NAACP. "The segregationists are harming the South as a region and damaging the United States as the leader of the free world nations. . . . Segregated schools based upon color are not democratic. . . . The United States needs . . . every trained man and woman of whatever color, race, or religion. She needs these to survive. It is as simple as that. In addition to committing a moral wrong against colored people, the segregationists are sabotaging the security of their country."

Justice and Jobs

Segregationists both inside and outside labor unions sabotage the Negro's right to work wherever they can, particularly when they find him protesting segregation. Sabotage increases in periods of recession or depression, for when white folks need what have traditionally been "Negro" jobs, they find some way of getting them. For example, in the South during the Great Depression, unverified charges of Negro bellhops flirting with white women guests provided a pretext for numerous hotels to give those jobs to whites. But after the depression the whites kept the jobs, and the displaced Negroes had to scuffle as best they could.

"The NAACP carries on a continuing campaign to enlarge employment opportunities for Negro workers," states an official release. "The Association constantly works for enactment of Fair Employment Practices laws at the local, state and national levels. In turn, the Association represents victims of job discrimination before such FEPC groups or appropriate boards. It cooperates with the organized labor movement in efforts to eliminate discrimination within trade unions and to open up new job opportunities for minority group workers."

The 50th Annual Convention of the NAACP in New York was attended by 118 union leaders, including A. Philip Randolph, Cleveland

Robinson, and Walter Reuther, president of the United Automobile Workers; all of them spoke at the labor session. Herbert Hill, the Association's dynamic young labor secretary, reported on, among other things, the semi-segregated situation of the 6000 Negro and Puerto Rican stevedores on the New York water front, and the systematic exclusion of Negro longshoremen at the Brooklyn Army Terminal resulting from the discriminatory practices of the hiring agency that handled government contracts there. *No Harvest for the Reaper,* Hill's beautifully illustrated booklet on the migratory agricultural workers in the United States which the NAACP brought out, is one of the best accounts of these wandering farm laborers yet published. It is used by government agencies investigating the plight of these men and women whom Senator Paul Douglas has called "the lowest group in the American social order . . . the lowest paid, the most insecure, the most poorly housed, the most socially declassed and the most ignored." About a third of these migrants are Negroes. From the lettuce fields of California and the bean fields of Florida to the truck farms of the North, the NAACP is working for their betterment.

Hill often goes out into the field to keep in touch with municipal and state FEPC units, government agencies, and management and labor executives. Under his direction surveys are made, data assembled, and pamphlets written to make concrete what Negroes in general already know—namely, that, in spite of FEPC's and the President's Committee on Equal Employment Opportunity, there is still nation-wide discrimination against Negro workers. The unions themselves often throw up the major barricades in the path of these workers, especially the old-line craft unions that control the most lucrative areas of employment.

According to an NAACP pamphlet, *Racism Within Organized Labor,* unions affiliated with the AFL-CIO are guilty of four categories of discriminatory racial practices: outright exclusion of Negroes, segregated locals, separate race-based seniority lines in collective bargaining agreements, and exclusion of Negroes from apprenticeship training programs controlled by labor unions. The Ku Klux Klan and White Citizens Council forces, especially in Alabama, have penetrated many local unions and made them, in effect, virtual extensions of segregationist organizations. As a result, Negro workers throughout the South are experiencing an acute sense of alienation from and rejection by organized labor.

Today in virtually every large urban center, Negro workers are barred from or restricted in employment in the building trades. Local 26 of the International Brotherhood of Electrical Workers in Washington, D.C., provides a typical example of the use of union power to exclude Negro workers from obtaining employment on vast federal construction projects. This local controls all hiring for electrical installation work in Washington. For many years Negro workers have sought to be admitted to it, but as of December 31, 1961, there were still no Negro members, although one Negro had been given a temporary work card as a result of intensive pressure. The collective bargaining agreements negotiated by many major unions base promotion on separate lines of seniority. The employment of Negroes is restricted to unskilled or menial classifications, thus denying these workers equal seniority and preventing them from developing skills which would permit their employment for work in better-paying and more desirable classifications.

The continued exclusion of Negroes from apprenticeship training is particularly disturbing because many traditional sources of employment for Negroes are rapidly drying up as a result of automation and other technological changes now taking place in the nation's economy. Thus this group is forced to remain as marginal employees. Both the railroad craft unions and the operating Brotherhoods bar apprenticeship opportunities to Negro youth. Almost equally exclusive are the printing trades unions, the Sheet Metal Workers Union, the Ornamental and Structural Iron Workers Union, the Glass Workers, the Tile Setters, the Machinists, and the Bricklayers Unions. Through NAACP efforts, however, the first Negro was admitted to the apprenticeship training program of the Sheet Metal Workers in St. Louis and of the Plumbers Union in the State of New York.

Call the Undertaker

Small wonder that tension—and blood pressure—run high in the South. For a week every autumn one young physician, born and trained in the North, donates his services to a small Negro college in the South; he examines the entering freshmen. The first time he appeared on the campus, the local doctor, a Negro, said to him, "Son, don't be alarmed if you find the blood pressure of the average young Negro down here a bit higher than you would find it in the North. Pressures are higher all over the South—the tensions we live under, I suppose." These tensions exist from birth to death.

There was only one hospital in a small town in Texas. Negro doctors had to send all their surgical patients to it, although these physicians could not operate or practice there, and there were no Negro nurses. No private rooms were available to Negroes, regardless of how much they could pay. Instead, they were assigned to a gray depressing ward in the basement, with flimsy curtains separating the men's side from the women's. When the wife of the town's leading Negro physician had to have an emergency appendectomy, her husband had to rush her to this Jim Crow hospital and turn her over to a white physician for the operation. Feverish and half-delirious after surgery, she wanted water and rang her bell. When there was no response, she rang a second time, whereupon a white nurse appeared, said, "Nigger, can't you wait until I get here?" and slapped her.

There was a terrible automobile accident on a Mississippi road, in which a woman's arm was almost torn off. A passing motorist drove her to the nearest hospital. "Why didn't you tell us she was colored before you brought her here? We don't take Negroes. Drive to Clarksdale or somewhere." The woman died on the way to Clarksdale. She was Bessie Smith, the great blues singer.

A similar thing occurred in Georgia, near Dalton—a car crash, a woman who was bleeding badly, and a hospital that said, "No Negroes." An ambulance had to be summoned from Chattanooga 66 miles away, to take her there. The woman died. She was Juliette Derricott, a national executive of the YWCA and former Dean of Women at Hampton and Fisk, widely known and beloved by students.

On a bitterly cold night some twenty years ago an ambulance pulled up to the doors of a hospital in New York City with an elderly woman who had had a cerebral hemorrhage. Before she was brought inside, the admitting desk phoned her physician, Dr. Farrow Allen. "Doctor, you did not tell us that the patient was colored."

"Color has nothing whatsoever to do with it. I gave the diagnosis and symptoms over the telephone and that is all that was necessary."

"We do not accept colored patients in our private wards, and since you did not tell me that she was colored, you misrepresented the case." The woman remained in the ambulance for nearly an hour before the hospital finally admitted her. She died a short time later. She was the wife of W. C. Handy, the great composer of *The St. Louis Blues*.

In another accident case, the victim was 70 years old; his skin was white, his eyes blue-gray. He did not see the car speeding toward him, trying to beat the light on Piedmont Avenue in Atlanta one rainy day. The motorist struck him, stopped, picked him up unconscious, and rushed him to the new Grady Municipal Hospital. Physicians there worked to save his life; meanwhile his relatives were notified. A son-in-law was the first to arrive at the hospital. When the doctors saw the son-in-law, who was a Negro, they cried, "What! Have we put a nigger in the white ward?" Still unconscious, the patient was wheeled across the street through the rain to the Negro wards in the old building, where he died. He was the father of Walter White, executive secretary of the NAACP.

The NAACP has long been concerned with the problem of segregation relative to hospitals, patients, nurses, and doctors. With very few exceptions, white hospitals in the South that may allot *some* space to Negro patients do not allow Negro doctors to practice there. At such hospitals a Negro surgeon must assign his patient to a white surgeon to be operated upon. Negro interns and nurses are barred from hundreds of hospitals in the United States. Negro patients are barred from many hospitals; in some their number is limited to only a few beds. If these beds are occupied, a patient is not admitted, regardless of how critical his condition is.

Shortly after World War I, the NAACP concerned itself with an extreme example of southern high-handedness in connection with an Alabama hospital. The Veterans Administration announced that it intended to build a large segregated hospital in Tuskegee. Although the Board of Directors of the NAACP opposed the erection of such facilities for Negro veterans in the hate-ridden South, Tuskegee Institute approved the plans, and, upon being assured that there would be Negroes on the hospital staff, gave the government 300 acres of land for the site. When the buildings were completed, however, the president of Tuskegee, Dr. Robert R. Moton, was ignored and earlier promises were forgotten. An Alabama segregationist, a Colonel Stanley, was placed in charge, and the plant was staffed from top to bottom with southern white doctors and nurses, except for some Negroes who acted as combination nurses and maids and did the dirty work. When Negroes protested at an all-white staff in a Negro hospital, the Ku Klux Klan marched through the grounds of Tuskegee Institute in full regalia in a vain effort to intimidate its president, the faculty, and its students. Thereupon the NAACP sent Walter White to Washington to confer with the Veterans Administration. Tension between Negroes and whites continued to mount in Tuskegee, and the War Department finally decided to make a change. The most rabid Southerners were removed, and Negroes were put on the hospital staff.

A similar situation had arisen in New York City not long before that. Harlem Hospital, one of the city's largest hospitals, in the very heart of the growing Negro community, had no Negro doctors or nurses on its staff. At that time—the early 1920's—Negro physicians did not practice in tax-supported municipal hospitals in New York City. Negro patients in Harlem Hospital often complained of prejudiced and unfriendly treatment. "Before you enter Harlem Hospital, call the undertaker," was a common saying. As a preliminary to attempting to remedy conditions at this hospital, funds were raised by the North Harlem Medical Association, under the leadership of Dr. Louis T. Wright and the NAACP, so that attorney William N. Colson could be employed to gather the facts concerning discrimination there. A dossier was presented to Mayor Hylan, who ordered an investigation. As a result, qualified Negroes now serve on the staffs of all municipal and of many private hospitals in New York City.

Dr. Wright eventually became head of the surgical department at Harlem Hospital, as well as chairman of the Board of Directors of the NAACP. When awarded the Spingarn Medal in 1940, he was cited "for his courageous, uncompromising position held often in the face of bitter attack that Negro men of medicine should measure up to the most absolute standards of technical excellence and as a corollary, that having done so, Negro medical men and nurses should be accorded every opportunity to serve without discrimination on account of race or color."

"The Negro medical man has had to work out his problems in a nationally dispersed professional 'ghetto.' The two Negro schools, Howard University Medical School in Washington, D.C., and Meharry Medical College in Nashville, Tennessee, graduate and from their inception have trained the large majority of Negro physicians." So states an NAACP booklet, *Medical Care and the Plight of the Negro,* by Dr. W. Montague Cobb, distinguished anatomist at Howard University. At the end of World War II, including the two Negro institutions, there were 77 medical schools in the United States which, Dr. Cobb contended, should have "a priority of competence, not race. Fifty years ago, Howard and Meharry might have been the only solution to a difficult problem, but this is no longer the case. The present indication is for Howard and Meharry to open their doors to more white students and for the other 75 medical schools to admit such qualified Negro applicants as might appear. It is only through a program of intelligent integration that the health needs of the Negro, which are inseparable from those of the general population, can be met."

The battle for medical integration still goes on. In 1960 the Greensboro, North Carolina, chapter of the NAACP revealed that there was discrimination against both Negro physicians and patients in the hospitals of that city. The Association filed there, on behalf of Dr. Reginald Hawkins, the first lawsuit to be brought in the South against professional organizations which bar Negroes from membership. The suit charged the North Carolina Dental Society and the Second District Dental Society with depriving Negro dentists of their right to practice in local, state, and federal clinics and hospitals. An injunction was sought to restrain the two societies from excluding qualified Negroes from membership. To become a member of the national society, one had first to belong to the local society. This meant that North Carolina Negroes could never attain national membership, since they were barred on the local level.

Two hospitals in Greensboro receive federal funds under the Hill-Burton Act, but bar Negro doctors and dentists from their staffs. One hospital accepts only a limited number of Negro patients; the other, which is allotted $1.5 million of government money, accepts none. In submitting a summary of facts concerning the Greensboro situation to the Secretary of Health in Washington, Dr. George Simpkins, president of the local NAACP branch, stated, "We believe that it is morally wrong and legally indefensible that federal funds may be constitutionally granted to these two hospitals in such a way as to deny to one-fourth of Greensboro's population, *just because of race,* access to the healing arts and to the privileges and opportunities which these federal funds make possible." Subsequently the NAACP Legal Defense Fund filed a federal suit to end this discrimination.

Speaking on the general welfare of the sick in our country in September, 1961, Secretary Ribicoff of the Department of Health, Education, and Welfare, said, "Many are uncared for because the scattered and uncoordinated services in their cities and towns are not geared to the many different chronic illnesses they suffer. If a man does not happen to have the 'right' disease (favored on television, perhaps, by the most popular movie star, or sponsored by his town's most important citizen) he may be out of luck when it comes to care or treatment." Secretary Ribicoff might well have added, "In any case, he may be out of luck if he is colored."

The National Health Committee of the NAACP is headed by Dr. W. Montague Cobb and consists of distinguished physicians from all parts of the country. One of its recent statements says:

> Despite a spectacular rise in Negro health and a corresponding decline in the mortality rate, Negroes still are more commonly sick and die faster

than white people. The many economic and social factors contributing to this condition include low income, poor housing, inadequate education and Jim Crow practices. Health services available to Negroes are below par throughout the country. . . . Negroes have been condemned to die on the steps of hospitals which refused to admit them solely because of their race. Other hospitals admit Negro patients to Jim Crow wards or impose upon them the heavy financial obligation of single rooms. Constant work by the NAACP Washington Bureau has resulted in a breakdown of segregation in the hospitals the government maintains for veterans. Pressure by local branches has eliminated segregation in some publicly owned hospitals in the North. . . . Meanwhile, an educational program must be consistently pursued to demonstrate that no man's health is safe as long as anyone's is neglected. Germs and viruses scorn the color line.

The Watch on the Potomac

For nearly twenty years, through the administrations of four presidents and the sittings of ten Congresses, the NAACP has kept its eye at close range on the workings of the federal establishment in the nation's capital. At 100 Massachusetts Avenue, a stone's throw from the Capitol, The Washington Bureau has its office. Under Clarence Mitchell, its director, and J. Francis Pohlhaus, its counsel, the Bureau has earned well its reputation as a relentless watchdog over all matters in which the civil rights of Negro Americans are, or may be, affected through legislative and administrative action by government. No figure is more familiar on Capitol Hill, whether in the offices of Congressmen and Senators, or in the sprawling agencies that play so vast a role in the lives of our citizens, than Clarence Mitchell's.

The complaint of a colored service man needing a phone call to the Pentagon; the news of a violation of justice in a Mississippi town; a conference of fellow civil rights lobbyists from other organizations when a pertinent bill is pending; testimony before congressional committees; and the analysis of new proposals for congressional or executive action; these and a hundred other matters are the daily and monthly grist of the Bureau mill. Everybody in Washington who counts knows that the NAACP is there, in person, and on call.

6

Making Democracy Work

"Mr. Wilkins Whales!"

When Chet Huntley, the NBC-TV commentator, in 1959 reviewed the South's violent resistance to school desegregation, he suggested that the National Association for the Advancement of Colored People should withdraw from the struggle since "the NAACP may have outlived itself." Roy Wilkins asked for equal time to reply. It was granted. The speech Wilkins made when he appeared on TV deeply impressed hundreds of thousands of listeners throughout the nation. "Roy Wilkins on that screen was the best advertisement the NAACP has had for a long time," one viewer said. One of the hundreds of letters Wilkins received the week after the show came from a Negro who wrote: "You put a spring in people's feet when they walk down the street." And a man who was watching TV in a bar on Harlem's Lenox Avenue and heard his moving reply to Chet Huntley's implication that an NAACP was no longer needed in America yelled proudly, "Mr. Wilkins whales!"

In jazz parlance the word *whale* means to get down with it, to swing out strong, to be on a righteous kick, to really go to town, to play with soul. Unlike James Weldon Johnson, Dr. Du Bois, and Walter White, Roy Wilkins does not write his own publicity. That is, he is not the author of self-revealing books, magazine articles, and pamphlets, nor has he yet written his autobiography. James Weldon Johnson wrote one, Walter White wrote two, and the second Mrs. White wrote a biography of her husband; all are interesting reading. Arthur Spingarn once said that if Walter White had not been executive secretary of the NAACP, he could have become one of the greatest public relations men in the world. Not unlike Adam Clayton Powell, White had a flair for getting into the news and remaining there. Certainly, he was unsurpassed as a press agent for himself and for the Association.

But Roy Wilkins is content to leave his own publicity to the public relations department of the NAACP which is headed by Henry Lee Moon. Its releases are devoted almost exclusively to the work and problems of the NAACP; Mr. Wilkins' part therein—which is considerable—is of course not neglected. Stressing himself as a personality, however, does not seem to concern him at all. He is a modest man, his modesty matched only by his ability. When asked recently if he considered himself the leader of the Negro people in America he replied, "In 1937 James Weldon Johnson said the idea of one Negro leader is out. There are too many Negroes in this country with too many talents on too many levels, with too many objectives that are not necessarily your objectives or my objectives, for any one man to say, 'I am the Negro leader.'"

Roy Wilkins—he has no middle name—was born in St. Louis in 1901. His father was a Methodist minister whose irrepressible resentment at the treatment of Negroes had made it advisable for him to leave his home in Mississippi. On his mother's death when Roy was four years old, the boy was sent to an uncle and aunt in St. Paul, Minnesota, who brought him up. Unlike the earlier NAACP secretaries James Weldon Johnson and Walter White, Wilkins was not reared in the South. As a young man in Minnesota he faced a much milder form of the Negro problem than even New England–born Du Bois did; the latter had spent many years in Nashville and Atlanta before coming to the Association. Wilkins early showed signs of leadership quality by becoming manager of his elementary-school baseball team in St. Paul and editor of his high-school magazine. He received his college diploma across the river at the University of Minnesota, where he majored in sociology. There he won an oratorical prize for a speech on the Duluth lynching in 1920, and was appointed night editor of his college paper, the *Minnesota Daily.* After graduation he became a reporter on the *Kansas City Call,* the militant midwestern newspaper, and rose to be its managing editor.

In Missouri he met and married a beautiful girl named Aminda Badeau, whom everybody calls Minnie. Wilkins today is a sports car enthusiast, but for years Minnie would not allow him to own one; she felt he lived at a fast enough pace as it was.

In St. Paul Wilkins had lived in an integrated neighborhood and gone to unsegregated schools and college. But in Missouri he came face to face with the harsh realities of segregation for the first time—segregated schools, segregated theaters, Jim Crow restaurants from which all Negroes were barred, and state colleges that admitted no Negro students. One of the events in Kansas City which he covered as a newspaper man was William L. Dawson's graduation from Horner Institute of Fine Arts. Although this already well-known young Negro composer had played in the Chicago Civic Orchestra and was graduating with honors—one of his compositions was played on the program—because he was a Negro he was not allowed to sit on the platform during the ceremonies. Wilkins, watching Jim Crow in action, sat beside him in the audience as Dawson watched his white classmates on the platform.

As editor of the *Call,* Wilkins received a steady stream of news regarding race violence, lynchings, riots, and other horrors. He became active in the local NAACP. He headed the Association's successful campaign against the reelection of Kansas Senator Henry Allen, who had voted in 1930 to confirm John J. Parker for the United States Supreme Court. Wilkins' zeal in fighting the Negro cause in the Midwest soon brought him to the attention of Joel Spingarn, then president of the NAACP, and its national office. In 1931 he became assistant secretary, working with Walter White. Wilkins and his wife moved to New York and have remained there ever since. In 1934 he was appointed editor of *The Crisis.* On the death of Walter White in 1955, the Board of Directors named Wilkins executive secretary after twenty-four years of service. Said President Arthur Spingarn at the time, "There was never any question about Roy succeeding Walter. We only pondered over how soon the appointment should be made."

The way Wilkins analyzes his present job is, "You can't help but have a gang of irons in the fire. You have to be a combination diplomat, trouble-shooter, administrator, budget-maker, speech-maker, and smoother-overer, testify before Senate committees, appear at city council meetings, lecture at women's clubs, talk at churches, and travel around the country conferring with branches. We have a thousand chapters, and just about all their work is done by volunteers who are doing a great job. Besides these duties, you have to keep up with all the race literature being published to know what others are thinking and saying and doing." Wilkins puts in about a twelve-hour day, has given up cigars, and never drinks. At home he relaxes after dinner by reading sports car magazines and whodunits. He is usually in bed before midnight, even on Saturdays.

"What the Negro in America wants," Roy Wilkins declares, "is to establish his status as a citizen. The NAACP has insisted since it was founded that segregation must go. It has maintained this position during years of violent attack which branded it as radical and irresponsible. With the proper harnessing of all our forces and skills—new and old— success is inevitable. We don't hate the Southern white people. There's no malice. But the Negro has taken all he can. Now he wants what's due him."

Dynamic Branches

"NAACP branches and youth groups in 45 states have kept up a constant battle for freedom on every front, year in, year out," wrote Roy Wilkins in his Foreword to the *NAACP Report for 1960*. "It is a record of persistent, continuing attack and of partial and complete victories in a vast variety of fields. Being human (and volunteers) they may have missed an opportunity here or there, or have been dilatory, or have made errors. But their glories (often unsung in headlines) far outweigh their shortcomings. In dogged struggles too numerous to mention, they have won changes in the rules that make maneuver now possible and triumph a certainty. The civil rights victory is just around the corner." This tribute to the courage and tenacity of the branches of the NAACP is by no means undeserved. From Alaska to Florida scores of local branches, as Wilkins says, have gone through "struggles too numerous to mention."

Witness Brownsville, Tennessee, as reported in the press on May 7, 1961:

> A young woman who fled this southern town with her parents twenty-two years ago returned here today to continue the work they started. Mildred Bond, national Life Membership Secretary, presented the charter to the newly reorganized NAACP branch here following a welcome-home parade down Jefferson and Jackson Streets to the First Baptist Church. Brownsville, county seat of Haywood County, continues as one of the nation's major civil rights storm centers, following Negro voter registration activity. But the present Haywood-Fayette County story goes back to Sunday evening, June 23, 1940, and even before when the body of Elbert Williams, NAACP leader, was fished from the river. Williams had aroused the ire of Haywood County whites by encouraging Negroes to vote. Miss Bond's father, Ollie S. Bond, founded the Association's first unit here in 1938. But when Negro leaders expressed an interest in voting (61 percent of the county is Negro) they ran into untold hardship. The Bond family was forced to flee for their lives on Christmas Eve, 1939. Their escape was unknown to elements of the white community that burned the Bond home to the ground that same evening. Mr. Bond, in his New York home early last June, read of Negroes successfully registering to vote recently in his native Brownsville. "I never thought I'd live to see Negroes vote in Brownsville," said the pioneer NAACP leader.

Witness New Orleans in 1961, where not only Negroes but whites are intimidated:

Mrs. Mary E. Sand, leader of Save Our Schools, Inc., told the NAACP that many white parents would return their children to desegregated schools if allowed to. Local white parents fear economic pressures and physical violence from extremist segregationist groups, if they choose to obey the law. At present the average attendance at William Franz elementary school is eleven—one Negro and ten white. The McDonough 19 School continues to be completely boycotted by whites, making the three Negro tots there the only students. These two public schools were ordered open to all students by a Federal district court, after arguments by NAACP attorneys.

Witness Savannah. There follows the partial text of a wire sent President Kennedy on September 16, 1961, and signed by Bishop Spottswood, chairman of the Board of Directors.

THE BOARD OF DIRECTORS OF THE NATIONAL ASSOCIATION FOR THE ADVANCEMENT OF COLORED PEOPLE VOICES VIGOROUS AND EMPHATIC PROTEST AGAINST THE DISMISSAL ON TRUMPED-UP CHARGES OF WESTLEY W. LAW FROM HIS POST AS LETTER CARRIER IN THE SAVANNAH, GEORGIA, POST OFFICE. MISTER LAW IS A MEMBER OF OUR BOARD OF DIRECTORS AND IS ALSO PRESIDENT OF THE GEORGIA STATE ORGANIZATION OF THE NAACP AND OF ITS SAVANNAH UNIT. HE HAS DIRECTED FOR FIFTEEN MONTHS A CAMPAIGN TO WITHHOLD PATRONAGE FROM LOCAL MERCHANTS BECAUSE OF THE SHABBY TREATMENT ACCORDED NEGRO CUSTOMERS AND THE REFUSAL TO LIFT BARRIERS AT LUNCH COUNTERS AND TO EMPLOY NEGRO CITIZENS IN ANY EXCEPT THE MOST MENIAL CATEGORIES. THE SAVANNAH MERCHANTS CHANGED THEIR POLICIES AND THE WITHHOLDING CAMPAIGN RELAXED. BUT HARDLY HAD THE REPORTS OF A SETTLEMENT BEEN PUBLISHED BEFORE THE OFFICIALS IN THE SAVANNAH POST OFFICE BEGAN A CAMPAIGN TO DISMISS LAW. THIS SHAMEFUL EFFORT, PLEDGED IN ADVANCE TO A WHITE CITIZENS COUNCIL AUDIENCE BY A CAMPAIGNING GEORGIA CONGRESSMAN, RECEIVED THE SUPPORT OF PERSONS IN THE POSTMASTER GENERAL'S OFFICE IN WASHINGTON. IF THE GOVERNMENT IS TO BECOME A PARTNER IN ECONOMIC REPRISAL AGAINST A GOVERNMENT EMPLOYEE WHO EXERCISES HIS RIGHT AS A CITIZEN TO SEEK THE REDRESS OF NOTORIOUS GRIEVANCES SUFFERED BY HIS RACIAL GROUP, THEN WE HAVE COME, AS A NATION, TO A LOW ESTATE INDEED. OUR BOARD OF DIRECTORS RESPECTFULLY BUT MOST FIRMLY URGES IMMEDIATE ACTION ON THE ADMINISTRATIVE LEVEL TO RESCIND THE DISMISSAL AND TO ORDER A COMPLETE AND DETAILED INQUIRY WITH A VIEW TO DETERMINING THE STEPS TO BE TAKEN AGAINST THOSE RESPONSIBLE FOR THIS INJUSTICE.

The vigorous NAACP representations achieved their aim. A department review board voted 2 to 1 to reinstate Law, and he is back at work. Only the stern pressure and vigilance of the Association was responsible for nipping in the bud this ignominious persecution of a Negro letter carrier.

But Law and the members of the Savannah NAACP made other history. Before the settlement was reached, a news release from Savannah stated, "The economy in this city of 186,000 has been undergoing ordeal by boycott. For more than a year Negroes, who make up 35 to 40 percent of the population, have been boycotting white stores. No one knows exactly how many Negroes are refusing to shop at white stores or what their absence is costing white merchants." The Committee for Withholding Retail Patronage, as supervised by Curtis V. Cooper, made Lenten posters which read: WE'LL WEAR OLD CLOTHES THIS EASTER WITH NEW DIGNITY. The no-buying drive began in the spring of 1960 following the arrest of several Negro students for staking sit-ins at segregated lunch counters. There were beatings and riots. By the summer of 1961, however, the counters were integrated, city park facilities were open on a non-segregated basis, two Negro bus drivers had been hired, Jim Crow signs were removed from the buses, and NAACP members rode on front seats without incident, thereby encouraging other Negroes to follow suit. As a result of NAACP activity, the 228-year-old seaport city now has a new look.

Such movements aroused the concern of manufacturers and wholesale dealers in the North. New York's *Women's Wear Daily* carried a front-page story on "the boycott campaign spurred by the National Association for the Advancement of Colored People." It reported that in Charleston, South Carolina,

> The manager of a large chain store, which figures that normally about 30 percent of its customers are Negroes, said the figure has now dropped to about half that. . . . In Jacksonville, Florida, major retailers' sales are off several points, at least in part due to selective buying campaigns. At one major variety store, Negro business was off 50 percent. . . . In Greenville, S.C., a survey of retailers brought the response that a few "agitators" were not buying. . . . In Louisville, retailers dealing heavily in credit and lowend business were reportedly off as much as 50 percent in the face of a united Negro effort. . . . In New York, millinery syndicates which operate leased departments in the South, estimated that where boycotts were in effect department stores were losing 10 to 30 percent of volume. They claimed that the worst-hit cities were Louisville, Jacksonville, Jackson, Memphis and New Orleans.

"Selective buying" was not the only technique employed in many cities; sit-ins and picket lines were also used to good effect. TV screens

flashed daily the faces of marching pickets; papers carried more pictures of Negroes than they normally would had they been engaged in
less controversial activities, and the names of participants were widely
publicized—all this in order to render them liable to job loss or other
forms of intimidation. Nevertheless, some objectives were achieved in
various cities, among them the following: In Durham, where 18-year-old
John Edwards of the NAACP Youth Council is chairman of the drive
for jobs, 23 stores integrated their sales staffs; in Miami, local swimming pools were opened to Negroes after the successful conclusion of
an NAACP suit instituted by Attorney G. E. Graves; and in Nashville,
almost the entire downtown area ceased discriminatory practices. But in
Palm Beach, which the local branch points out is "the winter home of the
President," desegregation of public facilities has not yet been achieved.
And in Columbia, South Carolina, 192 college students and a number of
adults were arrested during a peaceful demonstration. A white freshman
from the University of South Carolina, seen shaking hands with a Negro
student, was asked by the police if he were a member of the NAACP.
When the youth replied that he had just joined, he was promptly arrested. Also jailed was the Association's field secretary, the Reverend
I. D. Newman. Lenny Glover, a student leader, was stabbed and seriously wounded by an unknown white assailant.

Of the less embattled branches, that at Las Vegas, Nevada, was responsible for a substantial step forward in its community recently. Formerly
Negroes were not welcome in the plush hotels and gambling casinos
of that desert playground. Even top Negro performers, except in rare
instances, could not stay in the hotels to which they brought overflow
crowds and record business. But that situation has been changed for
the better by the Las Vegas NAACP under the leadership of Dr. James
McMillan. Now Negro visitors, if they wish, may occupy $50-a-day
suites, see the floor shows, and bet as much money as they choose at
the gambling tables.

Detroit ranks as the top fund-raising branch of the NAACP. Cleveland
is also a very substantial contributor, as is Philadelphia with a dues-paying
membership of over 17,000. The fastest-growing small branch in the
nation has been that in Orlando, Orange County, Florida, which within
a year increased its membership from 173 to over 1000. The branch in
Atlanta, Georgia, has been tops in its voter registration campaign and
intensely active in its fight against segregated buses. The branches in
San Francisco and in Camden, New Jersey, and Jamaica, Long Island,
are foremost in publishing and distributing pamphlets and leaflets of

their own relative to improving race relations. Outstanding as a state conference unit is that of Virginia "for successful desegregation of public schools in six cities and five counties in addition to outstanding voter registration activity." For sheer courage in both a physical and a moral sense, laurels go to the Florida State Conference for refusing, in spite of arrests and fines, to release its membership lists when demanded by the legislature, and to the Mississippi Conference for its intensive voter registration campaigns in the face of continued intimidation, and for its gallant support of the Freedom Riders. Thus the struggles of the Negro, "too numerous to chronicle," continue.

A Baltimore Lady

She was born in Baltimore, educated in Baltimore, taught school in Baltimore, and has lived most of her seventy-odd years in Baltimore. She lives, works, eats, and sleeps NAACP. It is her heart and soul. They call her "Ma" Jackson, but her real name is Lillie—Dr. Lillie M. Jackson, since she was the recipient of an honorary degree from Morgan State College in 1956. Thousands of Baltimoreans know her as "that NAACP lady." She is a Baltimore lady—descendant of the Carrolls—small in stature, but a dynamo.

When Lillie Carroll was born, and for many years thereafter, Baltimore was a big old sleepy southern city, more Jim Crow than most, although it was only a little below the Mason-Dixon line and but four hours by train from New York. In many of its downtown department stores Negro women could not even try on hats or dresses. Some did not permit them to shop except by telephone. All public places where people congregated were strictly segregated, as were the schools and colleges and churches.

Lillie Carroll was graduated from the Colored Training School and taught in the Negro school system until she married Keiffer Jackson. Her husband was a traveling exhibitor of educational and religious movies, so she traveled about the country with him after their marriage, lecturing and singing. Thus she became conditioned to audiences, large and small, from those in country churches to huge gatherings in college gyms and lodge auditoriums. She has long been fully at ease before the public. Three of her four children were born on the road. One daughter became a concert singer, another a lawyer and well-known civic worker. Theirs is a family accustomed to public life. Lillie Jackson now has nine grandchildren—all of them are being brought up well. Baltimoreans wonder how, in the midst of so much family life, she has been able to devote so much time to the NAACP for more than a quarter of a century. But this she has done, besides being active in church life and the first woman member of the Trustee Board of the Sharp Street Methodist Church, as well as belonging to the National Urban League, the Council of Churches, the Elks, the YWCA, the Order of the Eastern Star, and the National Council of Negro Women. Her daughter Juanita, who is also active in Association affairs, married Clarence Mitchell, director of the NAACP's Washington Bureau. It is an NAACP family.

Lillie Jackson has been unanimously reelected president of the Baltimore branch of the NAACP since 1935. She is a mistress of the gavel. Her work with the Association began when she headed the reorganization of the then weak Baltimore branch which had only five active members. She soon headed a membership drive which brought in 200 new members. Under her dynamic presidency, the branch reached its peak membership—17,600—in 1946 and thus became the largest local unit of the Association in the country at that time. As organizer and president of the Maryland State Conference of NAACP branches, she was elected to the National Board of Directors in 1948.

The Baltimore branch has initiated history-making legal cases that opened the classrooms of the University of Maryland and other institutions to Negro students; opened the Enoch Pratt Library Training courses to Negroes and secured the appointment of Negro librarians in the state; secured the building of rural high schools for Negroes in Baltimore County; and equalized the salaries of Negro teachers in the state, with an estimated increase of $1.5 million annually. Lillie Jackson remembers that when she began to teach, her salary was considerably lower than that of a white teacher at the same level. The NAACP under her presidency put Negro policemen in uniforms for the first time; hitherto they had been plainclothes men who wore their own clothing when on duty. To get more Negroes on the city force, the Baltimore branch organized a police school to prepare candidates for the Civil Service examinations. It broke down the barriers against Negroes in the Bricklayers Union; secured the first appointments of Negro social workers in municipal departments; spearheaded, in conjunction with the City-Wide Young People's Forum, a successful drive for the employment of Negro clerks and cashiers in A&P supermarkets and other chain stores in Negro sections; and with the financial assistance of the Monumental Golfers Association instituted suit against the Park Board which resulted in all municipal golf courses being opened to Negro players. Under her leadership, the Baltimore NAACP has also made voter registration gains considered impossible a few years ago. Truly a busy quarter of a century for a little Baltimore lady!

More than once Lillie Jackson's name has been in headlines in the *Afro-American, Baltimore Sun,* and other papers. Widely displayed in the press of the entire city were photographs of her carrying a picket sign in front of famous old Ford's Theatre which for eighty-one years had segregated Negroes. For six years the Baltimore NAACP kept a picket line in front of its doors. Whenever Negro shows—like *The Green Pastures*—played there, the picket line was augmented with large numbers of Negro intellectuals frustrated at not being able to see actors of their own race on the stage. When *The Barrier,* an opera by Langston Hughes and Jan Meyerowitz which starred Lawrence Tibbett and Muriel Rahn, was playing in Washington, Lillie Jackson went to the theater with a delegation from Baltimore. She requested that the management refuse to present it at Ford's Theatre, where it was booked the following week, unless the theater dropped its policy of segregation. But the management would not cancel the engagement. Lillie Jackson then appealed to the cast, and all of them agreed not to perform—until the management informed them that they would be liable to legal action if their contracts were not fulfilled. Thereupon there was a meeting of the cast addressed by Lillie Jackson; as a result, Lawrence Tibbett and Muriel Rahn, the stars, and all the other members of the cast and the author agreed to picket Ford's Theatre themselves before and after each performance and between the acts, if they were forced to perform in Baltimore. An irate management thereupon canceled the engagement. The cast lost a week's salary and the author and composer their royalties, but Lillie Jackson won her point. The following week Ford's Theatre was dark, and the following year it dropped its longtime Jim Crow policy. Another victory for Lillie Jackson and the Baltimore NAACP.

On the dais at the Women's Luncheon at the Association's Golden Anniversary Convention in New York, Marguerite Belafonte presented to a "courageous and tireless fighter for freedom," on behalf of the Board of Directors, a certificate of merit which read in part: "To Lillie M. Jackson . . . in recognition of her long years of dedication to the cause of human liberty, in admiration for her sacrificial devotion to the Christian principles of universal brotherhood, and in grateful acknowledgment of her priceless contributions to the work of the National Association for the Advancement of Colored People."

A Mississippi Man

In 1959 a sworn and notarized affidavit from the County of Coahoma, Mississippi, was filed with the Department of Justice and the Civil Rights Commission in Washington. It stated:

> On Saturday, November 19, my daughter, Lynda Faye Kuykendall, was beaten severely in the town of Batesville, Mississippi, by a Mr. Leo Daniels, manager of the Sterling Variety Store, and the town marshal, Mr. I. C. Seales. Mr. Daniels accused my daughter, Lynda Faye, of stealing some candy from his store. Lynda Faye denied stealing the candy and told me she bought the candy from the Golden Rule Store. I went to the Golden Rule Store and asked whether the candy in question had been purchased from the Golden Rule Store and was informed by the lady there that she had sold the candy in question to Lynda Faye. All of this abuse took place after Lynda Faye told them she was my daughter. My trouble began with the local officials after I tried to register to vote. I was not permitted to register and have been bothered by them ever since in one way or another. Mr. Daniels and Mr. Seales slapped and hit Lynda Faye. Mr. Seales hit her with a blackjack. Her head and face were so swollen that she was required to remain in the hospital three days. Lynda Faye is just 12 years old. . . . Since the incident I have been harassed to no end. Telephone threats against me and my family are commonplace. Threats to burn the house down on us are prevalent. On Sunday night, November 27, somebody burned a cross near my home, the remains of which are still available. My name is Willie Kuykendall, Negro male. Whatever advice or assistance you can give me will be appreciated. If I can get assistance I plan to remain here on my own home and land. I cannot, however, cope with the lawless element of the white group alone. I feel that no act is beneath their dignity even to murdering me. I will be here as long as I can.

"I will be here as long as I can" is what young Medgar Evers, field secretary of the Mississippi Conference of NAACP branches, says too. When asked by an *Ebony* correspondent why he continued to live in Mississippi, native-born Evers replied, "The state is beautiful. It is home. A man's state is like his house. If it has defects, he tries to remedy them. That's what my job is. I live here to better it for my wife and kids, and for all the wives and all the kids who expect and deserve something better than they are getting from life."

As top NAACP executive in the state, Evers is often called upon to investigate incidents such as happened to the Kuykendall child and her father. He himself was slugged in a bus just after it had pulled out of the station in Meridian, Mississippi. He was struck full in the face by a white taxi driver who pursued the bus in his cab and stopped the vehicle because he noticed Evers sitting in a front seat.

Medgar Evers, born in Decatur, Mississippi, never heard of the NAACP until he was grown. During World War II he was drafted into the Army before he finished high school and served with a port battalion in Belgium and France. After D-Day he came back home. As a veteran he figured he could vote, so he and his brother and four other young Negroes registered. Soon his father was warned to tell his two sons to take their names off the books, and not to show up at the polls on voting day. All the local Negroes were frightened off the streets on election day, but the two Evers boys and the other four young Negroes went to the polls anyway. They never got to cast their ballots, however, because at the courthouse they were surrounded by a band of armed whites who drove them out.

Determined to finish his schooling, Evers went to Alcorn College where he was a football and track star and editor of the campus paper. He married in his senior year, and after graduation he became an insurance agent who traveled throughout the delta. The plight of the cotton-growing Negroes in the rural areas affected him deeply. He set up a branch of the NAACP in Cleveland, Mississippi, in the heart of the plantation country, and reorganized the moribund unit in Mound Bayou. He took part in the voter registration movement that led to the shotgun death of the Reverend George W. Lee, the wounding of Gus Courts, and the terrorization of Dr. T. R. M. Howard and his own brother, James. Both Dr. Howard and James Evers were forced to leave the state. Medgar Evers remained, although he was warned that his name was on the death list of the White Citizens Council. Today he and his wife Myrlie live in a housing development in Jackson. When a parcel comes for them and neither of them is home, the neighbors are afraid to receive it lest it contain a bomb. As for himself, Evers says he doesn't have time to be afraid.

His work with the NAACP causes him to travel extensively around the state; he usually drives himself, and his car registers an average of 40,000 miles a year. Evers was at the funeral of the Reverend George Lee, in Belzoni, and he attended the trial that cleared the confessed lynchers of 14-year-old Emmett Till. He investigated the Mack Parker lynching in Bilbo's home town, and the slaying of Lamar Smith at Brookhaven. He is constantly on call. The NAACP has more than twenty chapters in Mississippi. Its state office in Jackson is a busy place; this was particularly true during the months when the Freedom Rides were going on.

For sheer savagery, Mississippi is considered the worst state in the country. It has had more mob murders in recent years than any other state. It has the lowest percentage of Negro voters in the entire South— less than 4 percent of its 45 percent Negro population. Not one Negro child attends an integrated school in the entire state. In Yazoo City the names of all 53 Negroes who signed a desegregation petition presented to the school board were published in an inflammatory advertisement in the *Yazoo City Herald* paid for by the White Citizens Council. All but two of these Negroes lost their jobs, and a Negro plumber was forced to leave town. In Jackson, the capital of the state, officers use police dogs to disperse assemblies that are peacefully protesting racial indignities.

Justice in the Mississippi courts is decidedly one-sided. A white lawyer in Pascagoula raped a 17-year-old Negro girl who was baby-sitting in his home; he was given a suspended sentence of five years—and went free. But Clyde Kennard, who was arrested for allegedly receiving a few sacks of stolen chicken feed, was given seven years in prison. Kennard's real crime was attempting to enroll at the University of Mississippi. When Medgar Evers called Kennard's trial "a mockery of justice," he was arrested for contempt of court and fined $100. (Some Negro Mississippians are still shaking their heads over the Mississippi supreme court's unbelievable action in voiding Evers' conviction.) Yet no charges were brought against the *Yazoo City Herald* when it referred to the United States Supreme Court justices as "nine ninnies." Of course, nothing was done when Senator James O. Eastland told a Senatobia audience, in speaking of the Supreme Court's school ruling, "You are not required to obey any court which passes out such a ruling. In fact, you are obligated to defy it."

Senator Eastland is well aware that Medgar Evers lives in Mississippi, too. They are quite different men, however—one old, one young; one white, one black; one trying to turn back the clock, the other knowing that although now it is only midnight, the dawn cannot be far away. "Mississippi is a part of the United States," Evers says. "I'll be damned if I am going to let the white man lick me!" Evers is a Mississippi man—in all that the word implies—A MAN.

Love, Labor, and Laughter

There are many other NAACP officers and just plain members throughout the country whose lives are drama-packed and whose courage is great. Their everyday roles in the struggle for civil rights would make thrilling stories. Some day some writer should put as many of them down on paper as possible. On the national staff of the Association, too, there are people whose tasks are often too dangerous for comfort, and whose jobs require the greatest tact, bravery, mental agility and ordinary common sense. Ruby Hurley, a handsome and dynamic woman, shows no fear when she gets off a plane at a southern airport to take a local bus to a remote hamlet New Yorkers never heard of, where mobs have just roamed the streets smashing the windshields and slashing the tires of all Negro-owned cars or stoning churches and homes. She is southeast regional secretary, and her territory includes a large part of the least courteous South. Frequently enough, Gloster Current, director of branches; Herbert Wright, youth secretary; and field secretaries like DeQuincey Newman, Robert Saunders, W. C. Patton, and L. C. Bates find themselves in territories not unlike the Algerian villages of that you-never-know-what land on the Mediterranean. The insurance premiums of these fighters must be high, their hearts stout, and their nerves like steel. Theirs is a labor of love.

Less often exposed to danger but no less hard-working is the large and efficient staff in the national office in New York, some of whom have been with the Association for years and all of whom are on call for frequent trips to all parts of the country, north and south alike. Roy Wilkins' right-hand man is brilliant John A. Morsell. Robert L. Carter is general counsel, and Henry Lee Moon is director of public relations. James W. Ivy is editor of *The Crisis*. Lucille Black is the long-time membership secretary. Bobbie Branch is the office manager. It is Miss Branch and Miss Black who take on many of the behind-the-scenes duties and responsibilities of running the huge annual conventions—from seeing to the placing of furniture and telephones and the mimeographing of resolutions to helping a bewildered delegate find her lost badge or a famous speaker get his plane reservation changed. At convention time, these two work around the clock, seldom hearing any of the programs or meeting the celebrities; they are among the first of the national staff to reach the convention city and the last to leave for New York after the sessions close. They are the trouble-shooters, the solvers of petty problems, the "I've-lost-my-ticket-home" advisers. But it's a labor of love—and sometimes laughter.

Integration jokes go the rounds between delegates relaxing in lobby corners and during convention sessions and powwowing over late-night snacks in their rooms. Venerable President Arthur Spingarn is himself a great teller of jokes. Most integration jokes seem to have originated several years ago just after the Supreme Court decided to integrate the schools, so almost everyone has heard them in one form or another, but everybody laughs when one is told. One anecdote that is certain to get a laugh concerns the liberal young white Congressman from the North who became enamored of a very pretty Negro girl who was secretary in one of the legislative offices in Washington; when reproached for his interest by a politician from the Deep South, he countered, "I don't want to go to school with the girl—I just want to marry her."

Popular with Negro ministers at NAACP conclaves is the joke about the Negro in Virginia who in his quest for the higher things made up his mind to join a white church. At the door the frock-coated ushers officiating at the Sunday service suggested that the Negro return to the church office on a weekday and see the pastor. This the Negro did. The pastor, somewhat taken aback by a Negro Christian who wanted to worship in a white church, advised him to go home and pray.

"Tell God all about it first," the minister counseled, "and see what He says. Then come back and tell me."

The Negro went home, fell on his knees, and told God the whole story. The next day he came to the pastor's study again.

"What did God say?" asked the white minister.

"God said," the Negro replied, "that if He was to come to earth Himself, He couldn't join your church—so He told me, 'Don't worry about it.'"

Another joke concerns the nice old Negro lady who heard there were no longer any color bars in the Washington, D.C., restaurants, so she decided to test one of them. Putting on her best clothes, the old lady entered the dining room of a very plush establishment. She was treated with every courtesy, and both a waiter and the head waiter hovered over her to take her order. She asked for pig tails and black-eyed peas.

"I am most sorry, madam," the head waiter murmured politely, "that is not on our bill of fare."

"Then, son," said the old lady, "I'll take chitterlings, rutabagas, and corn bread."

Both men shook their heads. "So sorry, those dishes we do not have."

"Then I know you got ham hocks and collard greens," said the old lady.

"Regrettably, no," the waiters replied. "They are not on our menu."

The old lady rose. "Honey," she said, smiling, "I knowed you-all wasn't ready for integration."

The Sit-In Kids

The 52nd Annual Convention in Philadelphia in 1961 was attended by some 716 representatives of NAACP youth councils and college chapters from coast to coast. As in the Association's earliest years when white participants almost equaled Negroes, so today its youth groups include a large number of white students. The spirit of the old abolitionists seems to have come alive again, particularly as evidenced by white participation in the sit-ins and the Freedom Rides. The student sit-in movement was initiated by the NAACP's Wichita, Kansas, and Oklahoma City Youth Councils in 1958. The Councils were successful in more than fifty cases, and were honored at the 50th Anniversary Convention in New York in 1959. Of the sit-in demonstrators Roy Wilkins has written eloquently, "We owe them and their white student cooperators a debt for re-arming our spirits and renewing our strength as a nation at a time when we and free men everywhere sorely need this clear insight and this fresh courage, so quietly and so humbly offered. It is no extravagance to venture that they, in a sense, constitute another beacon in an Old North Church, another hoofbeat under a Paul Revere."

Today on many predominantly white campuses across the country—from Barnard College and the University of Rochester in New York to various branches of the University of California—there are energetic NAACP chapters. Both the Antioch College and the Indiana University chapters succeeded in eliminating discrimination in local barber shops against native and foreign students with dark skins. The NAACP sit-ins in Washington University in St. Louis in 1959 opened up service in nearby restaurants which formerly did not serve Negro, African, and Asian students. The University of Kansas chapter had been successful in this area some years before, after a popular young woman student from India had been served a hamburger in a paper bag in one local café, and Wilt Chamberlain, the basketball star, had been denied food in another. During 1960 the Oberlin College chapter, with almost no local segregation problem itself, raised $2790 to aid the indicted sit-in students of Fisk and of Tennessee A & I State College in Nashville. Other embattled southern students received various sums from many integrated campuses in the North.

Sit-ins as a mass movement were the big news of 1960. Begun on February 1 in Greensboro, North Carolina, by four A. & T. College students all of whom were members of the NAACP youth council, the movement spread across the South like wildfire. Many of these unique and highly effective protests were organized and led by NAACP youth of high-school and college age. The majority of those arrested were defended by attorneys of local NAACP chapters, and the chapters provided their bail bonds. In the North, NAACP units formed interracial picket lines of both young and old—Arthur Spingarn and Roy Wilkins and the entire staff of the national office picketed in New York—in protest against the southern Jim Crow policies of national chain stores. Many picket lines in the South were interracial, as were the sit-ins themselves. College students of both races had found something vital in their own communities to become aroused over, and in so doing they sometimes changed social customs faster than any court decrees could. Their elders have been amazed at the way some of the hoary Jim Crow barriers in public accommodations have crumbled from North Carolina to Texas, from Maryland to Florida. Several thousand students were arrested, a large number served jail sentences, and more than 200 were expelled for their part in achieving these civil liberties. But by the end of their first year of activity, they had seen segregation crumble at lunch counters and in other areas of public service in such divergent localities as Louisville, Kentucky, Petersburg, Virginia, Durham, North Carolina, Jefferson City, Missouri, and Baltimore, Maryland. "Negro youth is finished with racial segregation, not only as a philosophy but as a practice," said Roy Wilkins about the students who, by simply sitting on a stool at a lunch counter and waiting for service, had "forced the nation to take a *new* look at the old race problem."

Within six months after the sit-in movement began, NAACP lawyers were called to defend over 1600 students in twelve southern states; only a handful of them were acquitted, the others being fined or jailed. According to Thurgood Marshall, "Fines up to $500 and prison sentences of as much as six months have resulted. We are appealing convictions violating the constitutional rights of these students to higher courts and will contest them up to the U.S. Supreme Court, if necessary, to clear these young people of undeserved criminal records. With expenses pared to a minimum, legal costs for this great volume of litigation have required, in six months, financial commitments in excess of our full year's budget." The first sit-in convictions, from Baton Rouge, were upset by the United States Supreme Court late in 1961. Student trials and appeals continue today. The cost of justice is still high. Freedom is not free. Somebody has to pay.

Property bonds for the first 83 sit-in students arrested in Atlanta—charged with conspiracy, trespassing, and unlawful assembly in seek-

ing to be served food at various government and interstate transportation facilities—totaled $36,800. In Tallahassee, Florida, 12 students
whose cash bonds were $500 each were sentenced to 60 days or fined
$300. In Montgomery 21 students—8 Negro and 13 white—were ar-
rested for lunching together at a Negro café and fined $50 to $100
each. Governor Patterson forced the expulsion of more than 100 students and the firing of 11 teachers at the Alabama State College for
Negroes in Montgomery after 45 students staged a sit-in at the lunch
counter in the city courthouse. On campus, more than 1500 students
stayed away from their classes in protest. Said Bernard Lee, one of
those expelled, "If it takes us from now until 1965 to bring about
what was decided in 1865, we will do it. Education without freedom
is useless."

At Southern University in Baton Rouge, Louisiana, 2000 students
quit school in a sympathy strike when 18 student demonstrators were
expelled. Almost the entire student body of Bishop and of Wiley Colleges—both in Marshall, Texas—gathered on the courthouse steps in
prayer when 250 students of the two colleges were detained by the
police. In Orangeburg, South Carolina, over 500 Claflin and State College student members of the NAACP were arrested—too many for the
city jail to accommodate. Dripping wet in the chilly weather after their
demonstration had been hosed down and tear-gassed by the city firemen,
they were placed in an outdoor stockade where they remained for hours.

On Lincoln's Birthday, 1960, the students of Friendship Junior College in nearby Rock Hill staged their first sit-in at the lunch counters in
the local branches of two national chain stores. They were greeted with
homemade ammonia bombs in the hands of thugs. A year later, however,
the student sit-ins were still continuing. High-school pupils carried on
similar activities during the summer. Several teen-agers were arrested, as
was their adviser, the Reverend C. A. Ivory, the NAACP branch president, who was confined to a wheel chair. Police Captain Honeysucker
pushed the crippled minister off to jail where he was fingerprinted and
locked in a cell.

Early in 1961 nine college students were arrested at a Rock Hill lunch
counter. They were brought to trial on February 1, exactly a year after
the south-wide sit-in movement began. By that time these students knew
that more than $100,000 in fines had been levied against other students
from the Carolinas to Louisiana. When the Rock Hill students were sentenced to 30 days at hard labor or to fines of $100, they decided not to

pay the fines, which would further enrich the Jim Crow system, although the money was available. The court sent them to the York County workhouse, where, in prison stripes, they served their full sentences at hard labor. "You're on the chain gang now," Captain Dagler told them, as he made one of the students shave off his be-bop beard. "Boy, cut that thing from under your chin!"

Twice all nine were confined in one pitch-black cell, with only bread and water—the first time for singing hymns at unauthorized religious services they had initiated, the second time for slowing down working on the city dump rather than speeding it up. This time they went on a hunger strike, leaving their slabs of cold corn bread untouched on the floor. They were soon released from the cell. The textbooks they had brought with them to study were taken away—"This is a prison, not a damned school." On Sundays they were allowed visitors, and on the very first Sunday more than 300 visitors came—fellow students, friends, and parents. One of the boys, Clarence Graham, had written his father and mother, "Try to understand that what I am doing is right. It isn't like going to jail for a crime like stealing or killing, but we are going for the betterment of all Negroes." Their parents brought them candy and homemade cake and chicken and bananas and sweet potatoes.

As in many communities where whites felt they might be encouraging their children to take part in the sit-in movement, some of the parents were penalized by losing their jobs. A photograph released by United Press International showed sanitation workers in Montgomery removing from walls in the city a sign reading: HAVE YOU FIRED YOUR NIGGER YET? In Houston, Texas, the same press service made available to the papers a horrifying picture of a bruised and battered Negro, Felton Turner, with the initials K.K.K. slashed across his chest by a knife. Although he was hardly old enough to have teen-age children and had had nothing to do with any integration movement, he was attacked on the street at night by bigots, whipped with tire chains, slugged unconscious, and left tied to a tree. His masked attackers told him they were getting even for what Texas State University Negroes were doing in downtown Houston by sitting on white stools at white counters in white stores. Freedom is no respecter of persons. The attacked and the attacker pay, each in his way. Negroes may lose their jobs, their safety, or their lives; the whites lose their self-respect and the respect of millions around the world.

Picket Lines

Sit-in techniques were extended to include not only jail-ins but swim-ins, wade-ins, picnic-ins, read-ins, stand-ins, and pray-ins. An old cliché says that "the churches are the most segregated institutions in America." Thousands of miles of Atlantic and Gulf Coast beach fronts are denied to Negro bathers, as are tax-supported swimming pools. Hundreds of public parks in the South are not open to Negro taxpayers for picnicking, golfing, rowing, or looking at the animals in the zoos. And in many cities art museums and public libraries are closed to Negroes. In Jackson, Mississippi, college students who were members of the NAACP were arrested for reading books in the library. A library in Virginia closed rather than admit Negro readers. Numbers of Negro students in Memphis—almost half the population is Negro—were fined $50 each for seeking knowledge at the Cossitt Public Library. In Louisville the paddy wagons were kept busy carting Negro boys and girls off to jail because they stood in line at Jim Crow motion-picture theaters unable to buy tickets. As some stood in line, others picketed.

The following is a marching song by John Murray:

> Ol' Black Joe had his head bent low,
> And white folks said "That's fine."
> But if Ol' Black Joe were alive today
> He'd be on the picket line.

Almost all the sit-in, stand-in, swim-in activities were supported by picket lines. The pickets carry many signs that vary in accordance with local ingenuity. WEAR OLD CLOTHES WITH DIGNITY RATHER THAN NEW CLOTHES IN SHAME is common where selective buying is the object of the tactic. Others are: ONWARD TO JUSTICE; LET'S CRACK THE COLOR LINE; HIGH HOPES FOR HOT DOGS; I FOUGHT IN KOREA—WHY CAN'T I EAT HERE? WHAT DOES DEMOCRACY MEAN? or simply: JIM CROW MUST GO! In Memphis a young father pushed a baby carriage in which was his seven-month-old daughter down Main Street in a Freedom March. On her carriage was a sign: DADDY, I WANT TO BE FREE, TOO. One sign used in picketing chain stores in the North that have southern branches reads: WE WALK HERE SO THEY MAY SIT THERE. The NAACP prepared the following for the marchers on picket lines in some 300 northern cities to hand out to the uninformed:

Why We Picket

- In the stores in the South which belong to this chain corporation, Negro customers may buy any article, but they may not sit down and eat at the lunch counter.

- Hundreds of Negro college students who sat down to be served in Southern variety stores have been arrested, jailed and fined. Bail has been set as high as $1500 for each student. Fire hoses, tear gas and police dogs have been used.

- We picket this store because the profits made by it and by others outside the South help to maintain the insulting system against Negro customers in the Southern stores.

- Every dime withheld from this store is a blow against Jim Crow in the South.

- We picket to try to get these chain stores to treat all customers alike. If a Negro dollar is good at the Notions Counter it should be good at the Lunch Counter.

- We ask you to withhold trade from this chain of stores and thus support the Southern Negro students who seek fair play and dignity.

- This withholding campaign is in operation against the Woolworth, Kress, Kresge and W. T. Grant stores. They all have Jim Crow lunch counters in their Southern stores.

NATIONAL ASSOCIATION FOR THE
ADVANCEMENT OF COLORED PEOPLE

In New Haven more than 30 Yale medical students joined chain-store picket lines. In Saratoga Springs 200 Skidmore College girls and some 20 faculty members carried picket signs. In the Cambridge-Boston area there was a huge mass meeting of students in support of southern sit-ins. The National Student Christian Federation and the United States National Student Association supported the movement. Labor unions and other organizations participated in NAACP and Congress of Racial Equality (CORE) picket lines. As a result of southern sit-ins and northern picketing, one large chain of stores reported a drop of 18 percent in sales during a three-month period. Stockholders of all the major chains began to be concerned, and some urged that lunch counter segregation be stopped. The newspapers soon ran such statements as: "Four of America's leading variety chain store organizations including the F. W. Woolworth Company have announced after a series of conferences with government, state and local authorities and other interested groups that their luncheon facilities in 112 cities in the South have been integrated."

This must have been very gratifying to a young Negro Air Force veteran in North Carolina who was one of the first sit-ins. He had served in the Far East in an integrated flying unit and had trained, studied, eaten, and slept with his white fellow airmen. But when he returned to college in his native state—after listening to United States emissaries preaching democracy all over Indonesia and in Viet Nam—he could not get a sandwich in a Woolworth store. "It doesn't make sense!" he argued. Now he can get that sandwich. When 14-year-old Barbara Ann Posey started the sit-in demonstration in Oklahoma City in 1958, neither she nor any of the other 37,000 Negro citizens could eat in Woolworth's. Now 61 eating establishments in her home town are open to Negroes, and Barbara Ann feels better.

A campaign in Memphis led jointly by the adult group of the NAACP and its youth council resulted in the integration of the restaurants in both the Trailways and Greyhound bus terminals. In Atlanta 13 downtown restaurants and lunch counters have put an end to segregation, including Rich's department store which was a favorite with Negroes but whose Magnolia Room would not serve them. Several Texas cities have changed their policies in regard to segregation. In Dallas 36 eating places dropped their color bars. New lunchroom policies are in effect in the stores most frequented by Negroes in Nashville, Charlotte, Greensboro, Richmond, Norfolk, and some other cities, including Miami Beach where Negroes formerly found it difficult to buy even a glass of Florida orange juice. Racial progress is also being made in other areas than serving food.

The thirteen major downtown theaters in Kansas City now accommodate Negro patrons. After an intensive "Don't Buy Where You Can't Work" campaign by the NAACP youth council there, a number of places that formerly did not employ Negroes changed their hiring policy. The Kansas City Transit Authority hired 14 Negro bus drivers. In Jacksonville, Florida, 10 Negro drivers were employed. In Houston, Texas, a "Withholding of Patronage" boycott against supermarkets resulted in the employment of Negro men and women as clerks, cashiers, and supervisors. In Jefferson City, Missouri, two dairies that employed Negroes only as janitors changed their policies completely and employed Negro workers for all their departments after a "Selective Buying" drive initiated by Lincoln University students kept milk and butter from these dairies out of most Negro homes.

Students like those at Lincoln University, and other young people not in schools or colleges, have certainly given desegregation a *big* push in recent years. In recognition of this fact, when the NAACP voted to enlarge its Board of Directors at its 52nd Annual Convention, it also voted to raise from one to three the members "nominated by the youth section of the annual convention and elected by chartered youth councils and college chapters." Proudly President Arthur Spingarn told the young people: "I know that in your hands our Association is safe. In my 50 years with the NAACP, nothing has moved my heart more than the intelligence, the courage and the resolution you have shown. Don't stop. Don't delay. The time for advance is always *now!*"

Riding for Freedom

"The sit-in leader talks about being more Christian than the white is. He also thinks of himself as more American and more in accord with the highest principles of traditional American democracy than the white hecklers on the sidelines," said Dr. Jacob Fishman and Dr. Frederick Solomon at the Third World Congress of Psychiatry in Montreal. These two distinguished psychiatrists concluded that, with their non-violent approach, young Negro sit-ins had accomplished a remarkable psychological transfer, in that they provoked white extremists to "act out for them the very anger and resentment they themselves have felt."

The rampaging mobs that greeted the young CORE Freedom Riders in Alabama and Mississippi were certainly expressing hostility—even to the extent of setting fire to a bus filled with Negroes and whites, beating teen-age girls, slugging ministers of the church, and defying federal authority. Jim Peck, a white Freedom Rider, was beaten at the bus station in Birmingham on Mother's Day, 1961; more than 50 stitches were needed to close his wounds. Then, when he and other Freedom Riders were attempting to leave the city, they were surrounded by mobs at the Birmingham airport after their first plane canceled its flight and another was emptied by a bomb scare before take-off. In Jackson, Mississippi, policemen promptly hauled the first Riders off to court on a charge of disturbing the peace. Within a month after the Freedom Rides began, some 200 had been fined or jailed in Jackson. Many, including CORE director James Farmer, preferred to serve their sentences in jail rather than pay unjust fines. They were placed in the maximum security section of the Mississippi State Prison at Parchman in contradiction to

Mississippi's own laws, since they were convicted of misdemeanors, not of major crimes that called for imprisonment in the penitentiary. "Not only is Mississippi willing to ignore the United States Constitution, but it is also willing to ignore its own laws," said James Farmer.

It took two battalions of the National Guard, 22 cars full of highway patrolmen, three army reconnaissance planes, and a helicopter to escort one busload of 12 Freedom Riders and 17 reporters from Montgomery, Alabama, to the Mississippi state line. United States marshals had to use tear gas on a mob attacking the Negro First Baptist Church in Montgomery, where the congregation was being addressed by Martin Luther King; all were kept inside the church all night for their own safety. The city was placed under martial law.

In the ensuing months, Negroes and whites who were testing waiting-room, eating, and rest-room facilities at bus stations, air terminals, and railroad stations over most of the South were arrested. Several went on hunger strikes in prison, including a party of Jewish rabbis and Negro ministers who were arrested after they were refused service at the Tallahassee airport. All of this happened because states in the Deep South continued to ignore the 1955 Interstate Commerce Commission ruling and several Supreme Court holdings that segregation in interstate travel is unconstitutional. Governor Patterson of Alabama even went so far as to inform the Alabama State Highway Patrol that any state trooper who cooperated with the FBI in investigating violations of interstate travel would be fired.

For half a century southern carriers and terminals had ignored national regulations so far as they concerned Negro travelers. In some places in the South it was impossible for Negroes to buy sleeping-car tickets for overnight journeys or to eat in diners or to get service at Jim Crow ticket windows until all the whites at the opposite windows were taken care of; in some cases, as during World War II, they could not even get on a train when the one Negro coach was so crowded that one more passenger could not find space. At airports Negro passengers usually could get nothing to eat. Ralph Bunche of the United Nations once spent hours in the Atlanta airport without a meal. Dark-skinned Latin American and West Indian diplomats experienced the same difficulties.

The NAACP for years concerned itself with these travel problems. One by one the barriers have come down. Dining cars and Pullman accommodations became available without restriction and Jim Crow coaches went by the board. As a result of the NAACP's activities, segregated waiting rooms in railroad stations were outlawed for interstate passengers and segregated seating was banned even in intrastate travel. Finally, a Supreme Court decision forbade discrimination in any and all facilities (rest rooms, drinking fountains, lunch counters, etc.) that are maintained routinely for the use of interstate passengers.

But observance of these rulings was spotty, and they were often honored more in the breach than in the observance. NAACP branches in the South were instructed to test for compliance, and students in southern colleges were urged to avail themselves of their travel rights en route between college and home. When the Freedom Rides began in May, 1961, the NAACP gave the movement its full support. Many of the Riders were Association members. Almost until the departure of the first Freedom Riders, CORE director James Farmer was program director of the NAACP. Both national and local units gave the Freedom Riders legal aid, money for fines and bonds, and moral support, although the rides themselves were not sponsored by the Association. Late in 1961, CORE announced that the NAACP's Legal Defense Fund had assumed legal and financial responsibility for the 300-odd Freedom Riders who had been arrested in Jackson, Mississippi.

One immediate effect of the Freedom Rides was that two weeks after the Greyhound bus was burned outside Anniston, Attorney General Robert F. Kennedy requested the Interstate Commerce Commission to issue "as expeditiously as practical" nation-wide regulations banning segregation in interstate bus transportation and terminals, including waiting rooms, rest rooms, and restaurants. In September, 1961, the Commission ruled that all buses in interstate travel must display the sign: SEATING ABOARD THIS VEHICLE IS WITHOUT REGARD TO RACE, COLOR, CREED OR NATIONAL ORIGIN BY ORDER OF THE INTERSTATE COMMERCE COMMISSION, that the same statement must be printed on interstate bus tickets, and that drivers must report any interference with these regulations. Terminal facilities must also be open to all without discrimination. Roy Wilkins called this order "a gratifying amplification of the ICC ruling handed down in 1955 in response to a petition by the NAACP." To James Farmer it was "the Freedom Riders' vindication."

John Adams, one of the Founding Fathers of the United States, more than 175 years ago wrote a paragraph concerning the Boston Tea Party, when members of the young Revolution threw a whole cargo of British goods into the sea. Concerning this dramatic action against tyranny, Adams said: "There is a Dignity, a Majesty, a Sublimity in this last effort of the Patriots that I greatly admire. The People should never rise without doing something to be remembered—something noble and striking." This is exactly what the Freedom Riders did in so dramatically exposing the stupidity and inhumanity of the whole Jim Crow travel system in the South.

Tomorrow: We March

In 1910, when the NAACP was one year old, it had a national office, plus one branch in Chicago. When the NAACP was ten years old, it had 310 branches. When it was fifty years old, it had 1285 branches. In 1961 it had 1494 units all over America, including Hawaii and Alaska.

When the NAACP was one year old, it had 329 members. When it was twenty years old, it had 88,227 members. In 1961 it had 388,334 members, more than half of them in the South.

When the NAACP was one year old, it spent $6459.84. When it was ten years old, this had reached $30,348.33. When it was thirty years old, it was $60,220.46. In 1961 it reached $1,188,630.76.

During the Association's first year of activity, there were 90 lynchings. In 1920 there were 65. In 1930, 25. In 1940, only 5; and in 1950, none. One of the NAACP's major campaigns for almost four decades has been waged against lynching.

On a less spectacular but no less significant level, the NAACP's role as the prime source of help for the mistreated Negro, of information about his struggles and his progress, and of advice and counsel to others who are trying to help is underlined by the enormous volume of letters, wires, and other communications that pour into its national office alone. In 1961, there were 45,360 letters and telegrams (an average of 170 each working day). This was an increase of 3500 over 1960, and 20,000 more than in 1954, the earliest year for which these records are available in the national office. Letters have been delivered to 20 West 40th Street with only the address, "Colored Peoples Headquarters, New York City."

In 1910 Mary White Ovington and W. E. B. Du Bois had scarcely begun their public speaking, writing, and intensive propagandizing for the advancement of civil rights for the Negro. But by 1920 these two were in full swing, as was also James Weldon Johnson. In 1930 Walter White began adding fuel to the powerful propaganda fires that were to rouse America out of its lethargy regarding the mistreatment of the Negro people. Today Roy Wilkins' voice via radio and television reaches the farthest corners of the nation on behalf of racial justice. For more than fifty years *The Crisis* has gone into hundreds of thousands of homes.

When the NAACP first began its educational and legal crusade against discrimination, North and South, Negroes found it difficult to find food or lodging in most public places. Today Negro travelers may motor across the country from coast to coast and, except in the South, secure hotel or motel accommodations without great difficulty. Some of the barriers have begun to fall in the South, too, within the last two years. In 1910 school segregation was compulsory in many northern and western areas. Today de facto school segregation in the North is largely the result of residential segregation, and in the South—except for three hard-core states—there is at least token integration. In the field of employment, laws in a number of states now protect, albeit imperfectly, the Negro's right to work. In numerous areas real gains have been made. The Negro vote has greatly increased in the North, and slow but sure gains are being made in the South. The right to vote is still, however, a major fight below the Mason-Dixon line.

The legality of the restrictive covenant in housing can no longer be enforced by the courts, and anti-Negro residence laws in any form have been banned. However, barriers in private housing still remain. The great Negro ghettoes are still with us, but the barriers to escape are not as high as before the Association began its fight. Time after time the NAACP has gone to court—from the municipal to the county and state courts and to the Supreme Court—in seeking to buttress its objectives legally. The victories have been more numerous *by far* than the defeats. After half a century of NAACP activity in the field of civil rights, no one can deny that the moral climate of America today is immeasurably better. It can never again be what it was in 1910.

The centennial of the promulgation of the Emancipation Proclamation is 1963. The document to which Abraham Lincoln put his hand and seal—the seal of the government of the United States—declared that "all persons held as slaves within any State, or designated part of a State, the people Whereof shall then be in rebellion against the United States, shall be then, thenceforward, and forever free." That some portions of this country are still in rebellion against the laws of the United States as they affect the Negro is one of the problems with which the NAACP continues to wrestle. The Association faces this struggle with valor. A hundred years since freedom! It is time *now* that freedom be achieved. To that end, the NAACP has proclaimed its targets for 1963 as follows:

Employment: Equality of job opportunity remains the No. 1 problem confronting Negro Americans. The NAACP proposes to step up its drive to enlarge employment opportunities for Negro workers, and to push for additional enactment of FEPC laws. Our staff will continue working with trade unions to secure non-discrimination clauses in their contracts, to help implement these clauses, and to get them to insist upon enforcement of seniority provisions, irrespective of race, color, religion or national origin.

Housing: The NAACP will continue and intensify its efforts to have public assistance (including the federal backing of loans) withdrawn from any housing which restricts occupancy upon a basis of race, color, religion or national origin. When necessary and appropriate, the NAACP will institute legal action to ban discrimination in housing.

Voting: Lawyers will be available to challenge any denial of the right to register and vote. The continuing costly campaign to expand Negro voting will be intensified. Efforts will be continued to abolish the poll tax, both by Congressional action and by action at the state level.

Education: The NAACP's consistent and uncompromising legal, legislative, and educational attack will be stepped up in order to wipe out the last vestige of segregated education by the time of the 100th anniversary of the Emancipation Proclamation.

Transportation: The resources of the Association—legal, legislative, and community—will be mobilized to integrate all travel, intrastate as well as interstate.

Public Accommodations: Our branches and state conferences will continue to push for stronger civil-rights statutes and better enforcement of existing laws. They will encourage Negroes to seek to use public accommodations on the same conditions as other citizens. The local NAACP units will provide legal assistance whenever such services or accommodations are denied because of race.

Health: The Association supports the concept of a national health service for all the people, and will continue to fight racial discrimination in all health programs and facilities.

Church: The churches cannot be called to account in the courts for their rejection of the Christian doctrine of universal brotherhood, nor can legislation be imposed upon them. Education and an appeal to conscience must be strongly used. The NAACP, through its Church Division and its branches, will continue to urge the *practice* as well as the preaching of Christianity.

Filibuster: Senate Rule 22 is the biggest single stumbling block in the way of Negro progress. This rule permits anti-Negro Senators to talk to death any civil-rights measure before that body. Revision of this anti-democratic rule is a *must* in the NAACP program. Our branches everywhere have the responsibility to urge their Senators to vote for a change of Rule 22 in order to curb filibusters.

In brief, the National Association for the Advancement of Colored People has set as its target the complete elimination of second-class citizenship. This Fight for Freedom is not the Negro's task alone; it is the responsibility of every American. The NAACP invites all liberty-loving Americans to join in it.

Author's Postscript
Personal

I grew up with the NAACP, now in the second half-century of its existence as I am in mine. I learned to read with *The Crisis* on my grandmother's lap. The first movingly beautiful words I remember are those of the Bible and the editorials by Dr. Du Bois in *The Crisis*. My earliest memory of any book at all, except a school book, is *The Souls of Black Folk* by Du Bois. My mother, who worked for a time on Nick Child's *Topeka Plaindealer*, the Kansas Negro weekly, was an early member of the National Association for the Advancement of Colored People. I do not remember when my folks did not receive *The Crisis*. In Lawrence and Topeka and Kansas City I often heard them talking about the NAACP.

When I was in high school in Cleveland during World War I, I attended the 10th Anniversary Convention of the NAACP there, listened to its thrilling speakers, and met Pearl Mitchell who was a ringleader in its local work. I read *The Crisis*. In high school I had begun to write and to publish verse in the school magazine. But the height of my ambition was to have something published in *The Crisis*. From Mexico where I had gone to live with my father the summer after graduation, I sent some of my earliest poems to it. "The Negro Speaks of Rivers," written when I was 18, was the first of my poems to be published in a national magazine. From that time on, over a period of forty years, my poetry and prose appeared in *The Crisis*. That magazine, the official organ of the NAACP, gave me my start in the literary world. In 1925 I was awarded an Amy Spingarn Prize for creative writing, and in 1960 I received the Spingarn Medal.

During my time, the NAACP has won some great legal cases for civil rights. This is why the Sit-In Kids sit-in today, and why the Freedom Riders ride. They have read about these legal victories on paper—but if they live in Waycross, Georgia, for example, or Tupelo, Mississippi, they find these victories do not apply to them in their home towns. Not in real life. These noble promulgations are to them like the Fourth of July speeches I used to hear as a child in Kansas—"liberty and justice, freedom and democracy." I knew they did not apply to me because I could not even buy an ice cream soda at the corner drug store where my mother bought the family soap. I could not go to the movies in Lawrence, Kansas, because there was a sign up: COLORED NOT ADMITTED. And I could not take part in grammar-school track meets or swimming contests because the YMCA near our school, which the white students used for showers and swimming, would not admit Negro kids—the Young Men's *Christian* Association! So all those Fourth of July speeches I heard in my childhood went in one ear and out the other. I didn't believe a word of them.

The Sit-In Kids and the Freedom Riders now have, of course, a bit more to go on than I had. They have read or heard, or maybe even seen, that some of the court decrees and promulgations have begun to work a little in some ways in some places, and they know that some Washington officials have spoken out pretty clearly in support of civil rights, although counseling Negroes to wait a while. *What while,* of course, is what the youngsters want to know. *What while?*

Their daddies waited a while, their grand-daddies waited a long, *long* while. To the great-grand-daddies of these young Negroes today the white world owes *beaucoup* back money—lots and lots—for working and waiting *a while*—back pay for free labor, slave labor, hopeless expectations—payments long overdue—since 1619. Where is that money? Where is that freedom? And where is *this* freedom today? Those who are young want it now, before they get as old as those who will probably never have anything before they die. "All deliberate speed" is not *now.* If one cools off today he might be stone-cold dead tomorrow—and still no ballot, still no hospital to get well in or die in, still no hot dog at that bus station lunch counter.

Hot dog? Are you kidding? We want "what so proudly we hailed at the twilight's last gleaming." We want "my country 'tis of thee, sweet land of liberty." We want everything we ever heard about in all the Fourth of July speeches ever spoken. Don't say it—because you might be declared subversive—*but we want freedom.*

Bibliography

Aptheker, Herbert (ed.), *A Documentary History of the Negro People in the United States*, New York, Citadel, 1951.

Bardolph, Richard, *The Negro Vanguard*, New York, Rinehart, 1959.

Bontemps, Arna, *One Hundred Years of Negro Freedom*, New York, Dodd, Mead, 1961.

Bontemps, Arna, *Story of the Negro*, New York, Knopf, 1948.

Bontemps, Arna, and Conroy, Jack, *They Seek a City*, Garden City, Doubleday, 1945.

Botkin, B. A. (ed.), *Lay My Burden Down*, Chicago, Univ. of Chicago Press, 1945.

Broderick, Francis L., *W. E. B. Du Bois*, Stanford, Stanford Univ. Press, 1959.

Drake, St. Clair, and Cayton, Horace R., *Black Metropolis*, New York, Harcourt, 1945.

Du Bois, W. E. B., *The Amenia Conference: An Historic Negro Gathering*, New York, Troutbeck Press, 1935.

Du Bois, W. E. B., *The Souls of Black Folk*, New York, Blue Heron Press, 1953.

Embree, Edwin R., *Thirteen Against the Odds*, New York, Viking, 1944.

Franklin, John Hope, *From Slavery to Freedom*, New York, Knopf, 1947.

Hughes, Langston, and Meltzer, Milton, *A Pictorial History of the Negro in America*, New York, Crown, 1956.

Johnson, James Weldon, *Along This Way*, New York, Viking, 1933.

King, Martin Luther, *Stride Toward Freedom*, New York, Harper, 1958.

Moon, Henry Lee, *Balance of Power: The Negro Vote*, Garden City, Doubleday, 1948.

Muse, Benjamin, *Virginia's Massive Resistance*, Bloomington, Indiana Univ. Press, 1961.

Ottley, Roi, *The Lonely Warrior*, Chicago, Regnery, 1955.

Ottley, Roi, *New World A-Coming*, Boston, Houghton Mifflin, 1943.

Ovington, Mary White, *Portraits in Color*, New York, Viking, 1927.

Ovington, Mary White, *The Walls Came Tumbling Down*, New York, Harcourt, 1947.

Redding, J. Saunders, *The Lonesome Road*, Garden City, Doubleday, 1958.

Redding, J. Saunders, *They Came in Chains*, Philadelphia, Lippincott, 1950.

Simkins, Francis Butler, *The South Old and New*, New York, Knopf, 1947.

Wakefield, Dab, *Revolt in the South*, New York, Grove, 1960.

Weaver, Robert C., *Negro Labor: A National Problem*, New York, Harcourt, 1946.

White, Walter, *How Far the Promised Land?* New York, Viking, 1955.

White, Walter, *A Man Called White*, New York, Viking, 1948.

Reports

Annual Reports of the NAACP, 1911–

Civil Rights in the United States in 1950, New York, American Jewish Congress and National Association for the Advancement of Colored People, 1951.

Lynchings and What They Mean, Atlanta, Southern Commission on the Study of Lynchings, 1931.

Thirty Years of Lynching in the United States, New York, National Association for the Advancement of Colored People, 1919.

Magazines

Community
Crisis
Ebony
Jet
Life
Look
Nation
Phylon
Time

Appendix

National Officers, 1962

President

Arthur B. Spingarn

Chairman of the Board of Directors

Bishop Stephen Gill Spottswood

Treasurer

Alfred Baker Lewis

Assistant Treasurer

Dr. Harry J. Greene

Vice-Presidents

M. T. Blanton
Dr. Judah Cahn
Norman Cousins
Roscoe Dunjee
Grace Fenderson
Lewis S. Gannett
John Hammond
Dr. John Haynes Holmes
Dr. William Lloyd Imes
Dr. Allen F. Jackson

Dr. O. Clay Maxwell
Loren Miller
L. Pearl Mitchell
Hon. Wayne Morse
A. Philip Randolph
Ike Smalls
Joshua Thompson
A. T. Walden
Bishop W. J. Walls
Andrew D. Weinberger

Board of Directors

Kelly M. Alexander
Daisy Bates
Hon. Theodore M. Berry
Dr. Algernon D. Black

James Blake
Dr. Ralph Bunche
Betty Lou Burleigh
Dr. Nathan K. Christopher

Dr. W. Montague Cobb
Doretha Combre
C. R. Darden
Hon. Hubert T. Delany
Max Delson
Earl B. Dickerson
Dr. George D. Flemmings
Dr. Buell Gallagher
Dr. Harry J. Greene
Dr. S. Ralph Harlow
James Hinton
Dr. H. Claude Hudson
George K. Hunton
Dr. Lillie M. Jackson
Kivie Kaplan
Joseph P. Kennedy
Daisy E. Lampkin
Westley W. Law
Dr. J. Leonidas Leach
Hon. Herbert H. Lehman

Alfred Baker Lewis
Chester Lewis
Z. Alexander Looby
Dr. Benjamin E. Mays
Dr. James J. McClendon
William Robert Ming, Jr.
Carl Murphy
Dr. Eugene T. Reed
Walter Reuther
Jackie Robinson
Eleanor Roosevelt
Hon. Theodore Spaulding
Amy E. Spingarn
Arthur B. Spingarn
Bishop Stephen Gill Spottswood
James Stewart
Dr. J. M. Tinsley
Jessie M. Vann
Dr. Ulysses Wiggins
Samuel Williams

Executive Staff

Executive Secretary

Roy Wilkins

Assistant to the Executive Secretary

John A. Morsell

General Counsel

Robert L. Carter

Director of Washington Bureau

Clarence Mitchell

Director of Public Relations

Henry Lee Moon

Director of Branches

Gloster B. Current

Southeast Regional Secretary

Ruby Hurley

Southwest Regional Secretary

Clarence Laws

West Coast Regional Secretary

Tarea H. Pittman

Membership Secretary

Lucille Black

Life Membership Secretary

Mildred Bond

Youth Secretary

Herbert Wright

Labor Secretary

Herbert Hill

Church Secretary

Edward J. Odom

Director of Special Projects

Marguerite Belafonte

Director of Registration and Voting

John M. Brooks

Special Assistant for Housing

Jack E. Wood

Special Assistant for Education

June Shagaloff

Editor of *The Crisis*

James W. Ivy

Office Manager

Bobbie Branch

National Committee Chairmen, 1962

National Health Committee

Dr. W. Montague Cobb

National Legal Committee

Lloyd Garrison

National Life Membership Committee

Kivie Kaplan, Chairman
Dr. Benjamin E. Mays, Jackie Robinson, and
Dr. George Cannon, Vice-Chairmen

Recipients of the Spingarn Medal

1915   Ernest E. Just, for research in biology.

1916   Major Charles Young, for service to Liberia.

1917   Harry T. Burleigh, for creative music.

1918   William Stanley Braithwaite, for creative literature.

1919   Archibald H. Grimké, for service to his race and country.

1920   William E. Burghardt Du Bois, for founding the Pan-African Congress.

1921   Charles S. Gilpin, for excellence as an actor.

1922   Mary B. Talbert, for service to women of her race.

1923   George Washington Carver, for research in agricultural chemistry.

1924   Roland Hayes, for artistry in song.

1925   James Weldon Johnson, for achievements as author, diplomat, and public servant.

1926   Carter G. Woodson, for work as historian.

1927   Anthony Overton, for achievements in business.

1928   Charles W. Chesnutt, for creative literature.

1929   Mordecai Wyatt Johnson, for leadership as president of Howard University.

1930   Henry A. Hunt, for service to education.

1931   Richard B. Harrison, for excellence as an actor.

1932   Robert Russa Moton, for leadership and service to education.

1933   Max Yergan, for YMCA work in Africa.

1934   William Taylor Burwell Williams, for service to education.

1935   Mary McLeod Bethune, for leadership and service to education.

1936   John Hope, for leadership and service to education.

1937   Walter White, for anti-lynching work.

1938   No award.

1939   Marian Anderson, for artistry in song.

1940   Louis T. Wright, for contributions in the field of medicine.

1941   Richard Wright, for creative literature.

1942   A. Philip Randolph, for leadership in labor and national affairs.

1943   William H. Hastie, for career as jurist and champion of racial justice.

1944   Charles R. Drew, for outstanding work in blood plasma.

1945   Paul Robeson, for artistry in song and theater.

1946   Thurgood Marshall, for distinguished legal services.

1947   Percy L. Julian, for researches in chemistry.

1948   Channing H. Tobias, for leadership in defense of American liberties.

1949   Ralph J. Bunche, for scholarship and services to the United Nations.

1950   Charles Hamilton Houston, for legal leadership as champion of equal rights.

1951   Mabel Keaton Staupers, for leadership in nursing profession.

1952   Harry T. Moore, for martyrdom in cause of Negro rights.

1953   Paul R. Williams, for creative architecture.

1954   Theodore K. Lawless, for achievements in dermatology.

1955   Carl Murphy, for leadership and journalistic achievements.

1956   Jack Roosevelt Robinson, for his pioneer role in athletics.

1957   Martin Luther King, Jr., for outstanding leadership.

1958   Daisy Bates and the Little Rock Nine, for their pioneer role in upholding the basic ideals of American democracy in the face of continuing harassment and constant threats of bodily injury.

1959   Edward Kennedy (Duke) Ellington, for outstanding musical achievements.

1960   Langston Hughes, for creative literature.

1961   Kenneth B. Clark, for dedicated service and inspired research which contributed significantly to the historic Supreme Court decision of 1954 banning segregation in public education.

Other Writings
on Civil Rights

"Southern Gentlemen, White Prostitutes, Mill-Owners, and Negroes," *Contempo* (December 1, 1931): 1

If the 9 Scottsboro boys die, the South ought to be ashamed of itself—but the 12 million Negroes in America ought to be more ashamed than the South. Maybe it's against the law to print the transcripts of trials from a State court. I don't know. If not, every Negro paper in this country ought to immediately publish the official records of the Scottsboro cases so that both whites and blacks might see at a glance to what absurd farces an Alabama court can descend. (Or should I say an American court?) . . . The 9 boys in Kilby Prison are Americans. 12 million Negroes are Americans, too. (And many of them far too light in color to be called Negroes, except by liars.) The judge and the jury at Scottsboro, and the governor of Alabama, are Americans. Therefore, for the sake of American justice (if there is any), and for the honor of Southern gentlemen (if there ever were any), let the South rise up in press and pulpit, home and school, Senate Chambers and Rotary Clubs, and petition the freedom of the dumb young blacks—so indiscreet as to travel, unwittingly, on the same freight train with two white prostitutes . . . And, incidentally, let the mill-owners of Huntsville begin to pay their women decent wages so they won't need to be prostitutes. And let the sensible citizens of Alabama (if there are any) supply schools for the black populace of their state (and for the half-black, too—the mulatto children of the Southern gentlemen [I reckon they're gentlemen]), so the Negroes won't be so dumb again . . . But back to the dark millions—black and half-black, brown and yellow, with a gang of white fore-parents—like me. If these 12 million Negro Americans don't raise such a howl that the doors of Kilby Prison shake until the 9 youngsters come out (and I don't mean a polite howl, either), then let Dixie justice (blind and syphilitic as it may be) take its course, and let Alabama's Southern gentlemen amuse themselves burning 9 young black boys till they're dead in the State's electric chair. And let the mill-owners of Huntsville continue to pay women workers too little for them to afford the price of a train ticket to Chattanooga . . . Dear Lord, I never knew until now that white ladies (the same color as Southern gentlemen) travelled in freight trains . . . Did you, world? . . . And who ever heard of raping a prostitute?

"Brown America in Jail: Kilby,"
Opportunity 10.6 (June 1932): 174

The steel doors closed. Locked. Here, too, was Brown America. Like monkeys in tiered cages, hundreds of Negroes barred away from life. Animals of crime. Human zoo for the cast-offs of society. Hunger, ignorance, poverty: civilization's major defects woven into a noose for the unwary. Men in jail, months and months, years and years after the steel doors have closed. Vast monotony of guards and cages. The State Penitentiary at Kilby, Alabama, in the year of our Lord, 1932.

Our Lord . . . Pilate . . . and the thieves on the cross.

For a moment the fear came: even for me, a Sunday morning visitor, the doors might never open again. WHITE guards held the keys. (The judge's chair protected like Pilate's.) And I'm only a nigger. Nigger. Niggers. Hundreds of niggers in Kilby Prison. Black, brown, yellow, near-white niggers. The guards, WHITE. Me—a visiting nigger.

Sunday morning: In the Negro wing. Tier on tier of steel cells. Cell doors are open. Within the wing, men wander about in white trousers and shirts. Sunday clothes. Day of rest. Cards, checkers, dice, story telling from cell to cell. Chapel if they will. One day of rest, *in jail*. Within the great closed cell of the wing, visiting, laughing, talking, *on Sunday*.

But in the death house, cells are not open. You enter by a solid steel door through which you cannot see. White guard opens the door. White guard closes the door, shuts out the world, remains inside with you.

THE DEATH HOUSE. Dark faces peering from behind bars, like animals when the keeper comes. All Negro faces, men and young men in this death house at Kilby. Among them the eight Scottsboro boys. *Sh-s-s-s!* Scottsboro boys? SCOTTSBORO boys. SCOTTSBORO BOYS! (Keep silent, world. The State of Alabama washes its hands.) Eight brown boys condemned to death. No proven crime. Farce of a trial. Lies. Laughter. Mob. Music. Eight poor niggers make a country holiday. (Keep silent, Germany, Russia, France, young China, Gorki, Thomas Mann, Romain Rolland, Theodore Dreiser. Pilate washes his hands. Listen Communists, don't send any more cablegrams to the Governor of Alabama. Don't send any more telegrams to the Supreme Court. What's the matter? What's all this excitement about, over eight young niggers? Let the law wash its hands in peace.)

There are only two doors in the death house. One from the world, in. The other from the world, out—to the electric chair. To DEATH.

Against this door the guard leans. White guard, watching Brown America in the death house.

Silence. The dark world is silent. Speak! Dark world:

> *Listen, guard: Let the boys out.*
> *Guard with the keys, let 'em out.*
> *Guard with the law books, let them out.*
> *Guards in the Supreme Court! Guards in the White House!*
> *Guards of the money bags made from black hands sold in the*
> *   cotton fields, sold in mines, sold on Wall Street:*
> *Let them out!*

Daily, I watch the guards washing their hands.

The world remembers for a long time a certain washing of hands. The world remembers for a long time a certain humble One born in a manger—straw, manure, and the feet of animals—standing before Power washing its hands. No proven crime. Farce of a trial. Lies. Laughter. Mob. Hundreds of years later Brown America sang: *My Lord! What a morning when the stars began to fall!*

For eight brown boys in Alabama the stars have fallen. In the death house, I heard no song at all. Only a silence more ominous than song. All of Brown America locked up there. And no song.

Even as ye do unto the least of these, ye do it unto Me.

White guard.

The door that leads to DEATH.

Electric chair.

No song.

"One More Conference," LHP 821, Beinecke (1933)

Out of the First Amenia Conference [1916] seventeen years ago, held on the estate of Joel E. Spingarn at Amenia, New York, the National Association for the Advancement of Colored People was born. That noble old warrior for the rights of the race, the N.A.A.C.P., with its nation-wide branches, finds itself today with its head bloody and a bit bowed by the force of events since almost everybody's stock fell in 1929, including the N.A.A.C.P.'s in the eyes of the Negro peoples. Then came the Scottsboro Case. The N.A.A.C.P., instead of retiring gracefully when it lost in its desire to defend the boys, joined hands with Hamilton

Fish, Herbert Hoover, and the Governor of Alabama in denouncing the I.L.D., the Communist Party, and the other left organizations that had long been voicing demands for the betterment of the Negro with quite as much sincerity as the N.A.A.C.P. itself.

Strange then that the Second Amenia Conference, recently concluded, should release to the press this week its statement of findings containing paragraphs that might have been lifted whole and entire from Karl Marx. The thirty-one Negroes, largely young teachers, students, and writers, whose average age (in spite of the presence of Dr. Du Bois and James Weldon Johnson) was thirty-two, came to the conclusion that, "The primary problem is economic," thus setting, near the very beginning of their report, a Marxian note. They go on to say that "the whole system of private property and private profit is being called into question." They speak of the exploitation of Negro labor, the long hours and low wages. And they issue this warning to the white workers in America: "It is impossible to make any permanent improvement in the status and the security of white labor without making an identical improvement in the status and the security of Negro labor," which is really only a paraphrase of the famous line from Marx to the effect that "labor with a white skin can never emancipate itself as long as labor with a black skin is branded." And the young colored men and women at the Second Amenia Conference call for "immediate attention to the organizing of the great mass of workers both skilled and unskilled, white and black." They propose "such social legislation as old age pensions, unemployment insurance, the regulation of child and female labor, etc. These social reforms may go to the extent of change in the form of the government itself."

They give Karl Marx, however, no credit for having written all these things more than fifty years ago, nor the Communists for having upheld these principles in recent years in the face of the police clubs of the North and the lynch terror of the South. Indeed the Second Amenia Conference, towards the end of its report, dismisses Communism as "impossible without a fundamental transformation in the psychology and the attitude of white workers on the race question and a change in the Negro's conception of himself as a worker." It seems that they somewhat confuse psychology and economics, not realizing that a change in the ownership of the means of production would bring about a change in the national psychology of both white and black. Or perhaps this statement in regard to Communism, coming as it does after stealing much of the proletarian thunder in the body of the report, was inserted by the young people merely out of deference to Dr. Du Bois and the few conservative old die-hards present in their midst.

Or is there a more serious reason for their apparent conclusion in favor of what they call "Reformed Democracy," meaning evidently the NRA? Most of the young Negroes present at the Second Amenia Conference, radical as they may be, are nevertheless employed by such conservative organizations as the Y.W.C.A., the Urban League, the N.A.A.C.P., Fisk, Howard, and Hampton Institute. And one of them is a Society Editor for the *Pittsburgh Courier.* How could they, after advocating a program based to a large extent on Marx, actually come out and call it Communism? They would probably all lose their jobs. The young Negroes do not live on Mr. Spingarn's rich and beautiful estate at Amenia. After all, he who pays the piper calls the tune. The conference closed with no machinery devised for carrying its suggestions into action. And the thirty-one Negroes, whose average age (in spite of Dr. Du Bois) is thirty-two, left Amenia wagging a tail which is probably bigger than the dog. Anyway, we have had one more conference.

"Cowards from the Colleges,"
Crisis 41 (August 1934): 226–28

Let no one who reads this article write me a letter demanding, "But why didn't you bring out some of the good points?" For the express purpose and intention of this article is to bring out the bad points—some of the bad points—in many of our centers of Negro education today.

Two years ago, on a lecture tour, I visited more than fifty colored schools and colleges from Morgan College in Baltimore to Prairie View in Texas. Everywhere I was received with the greatest kindness and hospitality by both students and faculties. In many ways, my nine months on tour were among the pleasantest travel months I have ever known. I made many friends, and this article is in no way meant as a disparagement of the courtesies and hospitality of these genial people—who, nevertheless, uphold many of the existing evils which I am about to mention, and whose very geniality is often a disarming cloak for some of the most amazingly old-fashioned moral and pedagogical concepts surviving on this continent.

At every school I visited I would be shown about the grounds, and taken to view the new auditorium or the modern domestic science hall or the latest litter of pigs born. If I took this tour with the principal or some of the older teachers, I would often learn how well the school was getting on in spite of the depression, and how pleasant relationships were with the white Southerners in the community. But if I went walking with a younger teacher or with students, I would usually hear reports of the institution's life and ways that were far from happy.

For years those of us who have read the Negro papers or who have had friends teaching in our schools and colleges have been pretty well aware of the lack of personal freedom that exists on most Negro campuses. But the extent to which this lack of freedom can go never really came home to me until I saw and experienced myself some of the astounding restrictions existing at many colored educational institutions.

To set foot on dozens of Negro campuses is like going back to mid-Victorian England, or Massachusetts in the days of the witch-burning Puritans. To give examples, let us take the little things first. On some campuses grown-up college men and women are not allowed to smoke, thus you have the amusing spectacle of twenty-four-year-old men sneaking around to the back doors of dormitories like little boys to take a drag on a forbidden cigarette. At some schools, simple card playing is a wicked abomination leading to dismissal for a student—even though many students come from homes where whist and bridge are common amusements. At a number of schools, dancing on the campus for either faculty or students is absolutely forbidden. And going to dancing parties off campus is frequently frowned upon. At one school for young ladies in North Carolina, I came across an amusing rule which allowed the girls to dance with each other once or twice a week, but permitted no young men at their frolics. At some schools marching in couples is allowed instead of dancing. Why this absurd ban on ballroom dancing exists at colored schools, I could never find out—doubly absurd in this day and age when every public high school has its dances and "proms," and the very air is full of jazz, North and South, in inescapable radio waves.

One of the objects in not permitting dancing, I divined, seems to be to keep the sexes separated. And in our Negro schools the technique for achieving this—boys not walking with girls, young men not calling on young ladies, the two sexes sitting aisles apart in chapel if the institution is coeducational—in this technique Negro schools rival monasteries and nunneries in their strictness. They act as though it were unnatural for a boy and girl to ever want to walk or talk together. The high points of absurdity during my tour were campuses where young men and women meeting in broad daylight in the middle of the grounds might only speak to one another, not stand still to converse lest they break a rule; and a college in Mississippi, Alcorn, where to evening lectures grown-up students march like school kids in and out of the hall. When I had finished my lecture at Alcorn, the chairman tapped a bell and commanded, "Young ladies with escorts now pass." And those few girls fortunate enough to receive permission to come with a boy rose and made their exit. Again the bell tapped and the chairman said, "Unescorted young ladies now pass." And in their turn the female section rose and passed. Again the bell tapped. "Young men now pass." I waited to hear the bell again and the chairman saying, "Teachers may leave." But apparently most of the teachers had already left, chaperoning their grown-up charges back to the dormitories. Such regimentation as practiced in this college was long ago done away with, even in many grammar schools of the North.

Apparently the official taboo on male and female companionship extends even to married women teachers who attend summer seminars in the South, and over whom the faculty extends a prying but protective arm. The wife of a prominent educator in the South told me of being at Hampton for one of their summer sessions a few years ago. One night her husband called up long distance just to hear his wife's voice over the phone. Before she was permitted to go to the phone and talk to a MAN at night, however, she had to receive a special permit from, I believe, the dean of women, who had to be absolutely assured that it really was her husband calling. The long distance phone costs mounted steadily while the husband waited, but Hampton did its part in keeping the sexes from communicating. Such interference with nature is a major aim on many of our campuses.

Accompanying this mid-Victorian attitude in manners and morals, at many Southern schools there is a great deal of official emphasis placed on heavy religious exercises, usually compulsory, with required daily chapels, weekly prayer meetings, and Sunday services. Such a stream of dull and stupid sermons, uninspired prayers, and monotonous hymns— neither intellectually worthy of adult minds nor emotionally exciting in the manner of the old time shouts—pours into students' ears that it is a wonder any young people ever go to church again once they leave college. The placid cant and outworn phrases of many of the churchmen daring to address student groups today make me wonder why their audiences are not bored to death. I did observe many young people going to sleep.

But there are charges of a far more serious nature to bring against Negro schools than merely that of frowning on jazz in favor of hymns, or their horror of friendly communication between boys and girls on the campuses. To combine these charges very simply: Many of our institutions apparently are not trying to make men and women of their students at all—they are doing their best to produce spineless Uncle Toms, uninformed, and full of mental and moral evasions.

I was amazed to find at many Negro schools and colleges a year after the arrest and conviction of the Scottsboro boys, that a great many teachers and students knew nothing of it, or if they did the official attitude would be, "Why bring that up?" I asked at Tuskegee, only a few hours from Scottsboro, who from there had been to the trial. Not a soul had been so far as I could discover. And with demonstrations in every capital in the civilized world for the freedom of the Scottsboro boys, so far as I know not one Alabama Negro school until now has held even a protest meeting. (And in Alabama, we have the largest colored school in the world, Tuskegee, and one of our best colleges, Talladega.)

But speaking of protest meetings—this was my experience at Hampton. I lectured there the week-end that Juliette Derricotte was killed. She had been injured in an automobile wreck on her way home from Fisk University where she was dean of women, and the white Georgia hospitals would not take her in for treatment, so she died. That same week-end, a young Hampton graduate, the coach of Alabama's A.&M. Institute at Normal, was beaten to death by a mob in Birmingham on his way to see his own team play. Many of the Hampton students and teachers knew Juliette Derricotte, and almost all of them knew the young coach, their recent graduate. The two happenings sent a wave of sorrow and of anger over the campus where I was a visitor. Two double tragedies of color on one day—and most affecting to students and teachers because the victims were "of their own class," one a distinguished and widely-travelled young woman, the other a popular college graduate and athlete.

A note came to me from a group of Senior students asking would I meet with a student committee. When a young man came to take me to the meeting, he told me that it would concern Juliette Derricotte and their own dead alumnus. He said that the students wanted to plan a protest on the campus against the white brutality that had brought about their death.

I was deeply touched that they had called me in to help them, and we began to lay plans for the organization of a Sunday evening protest meeting, from which we would send wires to the press and formulate a memorial to these most recent victims of race hate. They asked me would I speak at this meeting and I agreed. Students were chosen to approach the faculty for permission to use the chapel. We were to consult again for final plans in the evening.

At the evening committee meeting the faculty had sent their representative, Major Brown, a Negro (who is, I believe, the dean of men), to confer with the students. Major Brown began by saying that perhaps the reports we had received of the manner of these two deaths had not been true. Had we verified those reports?

I suggested wiring or telephoning immediately to Fisk and to Birmingham for verification. The Major did not think that wise. He felt it was better to write. Furthermore, he went on, Hampton did not like the word "protest." That was not Hampton's way. He, and Hampton, believed in moving slowly and quietly, and with dignity.

On and on he talked. When he had finished, the students knew quite clearly that they could not go ahead with their protest meeting. (The faculty had put up its wall.) They knew they would face expulsion and loss of credits if they did so. The result was that the Hampton students held no meeting of protest over the mob-death of their own alumnus, nor the death on the road (in a Negro ambulance vainly trying to reach a black hospital) of one of the race's finest young women. The brave and manly spirit of that little group of Hampton students who wanted to organize the protest was crushed by the official voice of Hampton speaking through its Negro Major Brown.

More recently, I see in our papers where Fisk University, that great (?) center of Negro education and of Jubilee fame, has expelled Ishmael Flory, a graduate student from California on a special honor scholarship, because he dared organize a protest against the University singers appearing in a Nashville Jim-crow theatre where colored people must go up a back alley to sit in the gallery. Probably also the University resented his organizing, through the Denmark Vesey Forum, a silent protest parade denouncing the lynching of Cordie Cheek, who was abducted almost at the very gates of the University.

Another recent news item tells how President Gandy of Virginia State College for Negroes called out the cracker police of the town to keep his own students from voicing their protest as to campus conditions. Rather than listen to just grievances, a Negro president of a large college sends for prejudiced white policemen to break his students' heads, if necessary.

And last year, we had the amazing report from Tuskegee of the school hospital turning over to the police one of the wounded Negroes shot at Camp Hill by white lynchers because the share-croppers have the temerity to wish to form a union—and the whites wish no Negro unions in Alabama. Without protest, the greatest Negro school in the world gives up a poor black, bullet-riddled share-cropper to white officers. And awhile later Tuskegee's president, Dr. Moton, announces himself in favor of lower wages for Negroes under the N.R.A., and Claude Barnett, one of his trustees, voices his approval of the proposed code differentials on the basis of color.

But then, I remember that it is Tuskegee that maintains a guest house on its campus for *whites only!* It also maintains a library that censors all books on race problems and economics to see that no volumes "too radical" get to the students. And during my stay there several young teachers whispered to me that a local white trustee of the school receives his Negro visitors only on the porch, not in his house. It is thus that our wealthiest Negro school with its two thousand six hundred students expects to turn out men and women!

Where then would one educate "Uncle Toms"?

Freedom of expression for teachers in most Negro schools, even on such unimportant matters as to rouge or not to rouge, smoke or not smoke, is more or less unknown. Old and moss-backed presidents, orthodox ministers or missionary principals, control all too often what may or may not be taught in the classrooms or said in campus conversation. Varied examples of suppression at the campuses I visited are too numerous to mention in full in a short article, but they range all the way from an Alabama secondary school that permitted no Negro weeklies like the *Chicago Defender* or the *Pittsburgh Courier* in its library because they were "radical," to the great university of Fisk at Nashville where I asked a nationally known Negro professor and author of several books in his field what his attitude toward communism was, and received as an answer, "When I discuss communism on this campus, I will have a letter first from the president and the board of trustees."

There is at the Negro schools in the South, even the very well-endowed and famous ones that I have mentioned, an amazing acquiescence to the wishes of the local whites and to the traditions of the Southern color-line. When programs are given, many schools set aside whole sections in their own auditoriums for the exclusive use of whites. Often the best seats are given them, to the exclusion of Negro visitors. (But to insert into this article a good note, Mary McLeod Bethune, however, permits no such goings-on at Bethune-Cookman Institute in Daytona, one of the few campuses where I lectured that had not made "special provisions" for local white folks. A great many whites were in the audience but they sat among the Negroes.)

Even where there is no official campus segregation (such as Tuskegee's white guest house, or Hampton's hospital where local whites are given separate service), both teachers and students of Negro colleges accept so sweetly the customary Jim Crowing of the South that one feels sure the race's emancipation will never come through its intellectuals. In North Carolina, I was given a letter to the state superintendent of the Negro schools, a white man, Mr. N. C. Newbold. When I went to his office in Raleigh to present my letter, I encountered in his outer office a white woman secretary busy near the window quite a distance from the door. She gave me a casual glance and went on with what she was doing. Then some white people came into the office. Immediately she dropped her work near the window and came over to them, spoke to them most pleasantly, and ignored me entirely. The white people, after several minutes of how-are-you's and did-you-enjoy-yo'self-at-the-outing-last-week, said that they wished to see Mr. Newbold. Whereupon, having arrived first and having not yet been noticed by the secretary, I turned and walked out.

When I told some Negro teachers of the incident, they said, "But Mr. Newbold's not like that."

"Why, then," I asked, "does he have that kind of secretary?"

Nobody seemed to know. And why had none of the Negro teachers who call at his office ever done anything about such discourteous secretaries? No one knew that either.

But why (to come nearer home) did a large number of the students at my own Lincoln University, when I made a campus survey there in 1929, declare that they were opposed to having teachers of their own race on the faculty? And why did they then (and probably still do) allow themselves to be segregated in the little moving picture theatre in the nearby village of Oxford, when there is no Jim-Crow law in Pennsylvania—and they are some four hundred strong? And why did a whole Lincoln University basketball team and their coach walk docilely out of a cafe in Philadelphia that refused to serve them because of color? One of the players explained later, "The coach didn't want to make a fuss."

Yet Lincoln's motto is to turn out leaders! But can there be leaders who don't want to make a fuss?

And can it be that our Negro educational institutions are not really interested in turning out leaders at all? Can it be that they are far more interested in their endowments and their income and their salaries than in their students?

And can it be that these endowments, incomes, gifts—and therefore salaries—springing from missionary and philanthropic sources and from big Northern boards and foundations—have such strings tied to them that those accepting them can do little else (if they wish to live easy) but bow down to the white powers that control this philanthropy and continue, to the best of their ability, to turn out "Uncle Toms"?

A famous Lincoln alumnus, having read my undergraduate survey of certain deplorable conditions on our campus, said to me when I graduated there, "Your facts are fine! Fine! Fine! But listen, son, you mustn't say everything you think to white folks."

"But this is the truth," I said.

"I know, but suppose," continued the old grad patronizingly, in his best fatherly manner, "suppose I had always told the truth to white folks? Could I have built up that great center for the race that I now head in my city? Where would I have gotten the money for it, son?"

The great center of which he spoke is a Jim Crow center, but he was very proud of having built it.

To me it seems that the day must come when we will not be proud of our Jim Crow centers built on the money docile and lying beggars have kidded white people into contributing. The day must come when we will not say that a college is a great college because it has a few beautiful buildings, and a half dozen Ph.D.'s on a faculty that is afraid to open its mouth though a lynching occurs at the college gates, or the wages of Negro workers in the community go down to zero!

Frankly, I see no hope for a new spirit today in the majority of the Negro schools of the South unless the students themselves put it there. Although there exists on all campuses a distinct cleavage between the younger and older members of the faculties, almost everywhere the younger teachers, knowing well the existing evils, are as yet too afraid of their jobs to speak out, or to dare attempt to reform campus conditions. They content themselves by writing home to mama and by whispering to sympathetic visitors from a distance how they hate teaching under such conditions.

Meanwhile, more power to those brave and progressive students who strike against mid-Victorian morals and the suppression of free thought and action! More power to the Ishmael Florys, and the Denmark Vesey Forum, and the Howard undergraduates who picket the Senate's Jim Crow dining rooms—for unless we develop more and ever more such young men and women on our campuses as an antidote to the docile dignity of the meek professors and well-paid presidents who now run our institutions, American Negroes in the future had best look to the unlettered for their leaders, and expect only cowards from the colleges.

"Too Much of Race,"
Crisis 44.9 (September 1937): 272

Members of the Second International Writers Congress, comrades, and people of Paris: I come from a land whose democracy from the very beginning has been tainted with race prejudice born of slavery, and whose richness has been poured through the narrow channels of greed into the hands of the few. I come to the Second International Writers Congress representing my country, America, but most especially the Negro peoples of America, and the poor peoples of America—because I am both a Negro and poor. And that combination of color and of poverty gives me the right then to speak for the most oppressed group in America, that group that has known so little of American democracy, the fifteen million Negroes who dwell within our borders.

We are the people who have long known in actual practice the meaning of the word Fascism—for the American attitude towards us has always been one of economic and social discrimination: in many states of our country Negroes are not permitted to vote or to hold political office. In some sections freedom of movement is greatly hindered, especially if we happen to be sharecroppers on the cotton farms of the South. All over America we know what it is to be refused admittance to schools and colleges, to theatres and concert halls, to hotels and restaurants. We know jim-crow cars, race riots, lynchings, we know the sorrows of the nine Scottsboro boys, innocent young Negroes imprisoned some six years now for a crime that even the trial judge declared them not guilty of having committed, and for which some of them have not yet come to trial. Yes, we Negroes in America do not have to be told what Fascism is in action. We know. Its theories of Nordic supremacy and economic suppression have long been realities to us.

And now we view it on a world scale: Hitler in Germany with the abolition of labor unions, his tyranny over the Jews, and the sterilization of the Negro children of Cologne; Mussolini in Italy with his banning of Negroes on the theatrical stages, and his expedition of slaughter in Ethiopia; the Military Party in Japan with their little maps of how they'll conquer the whole world and their savage treatment of Koreans and Chinese; Batista and Vincent, the little American-made tyrants of Cuba and Haiti; and now Spain and Franco with his absurd cry of "Viva España" at the hands of Italians, Moors and Germans invited to help him achieve "Spanish Unity." Absurd, but true.

We Negroes of America are tired of a world divided superficially on the basis of blood and color, but in reality on the basis of poverty and power—the rich over the poor, no matter what their color. We Negroes of America are tired of a world in which it is possible for any group of people to say to another: "You have no right to happiness, or freedom, or the joy of life." We are tired of a world where forever we work for someone else and the profits are not ours. We are tired of a world where, when we raise our voices against oppression, we are immediately jailed, intimidated, beaten, sometimes lynched. Nicolás Guillén has been in prison in Cuba, Jacques Roumain in Haiti, Angelo Herndon in the United States. Today a letter comes from the great Indian writer, Raj Anand, saying that he cannot be with us here in Paris because the British police in England have taken his passport from him. I say, we darker peoples of the earth are tired of a world in which things like that can happen.

And we see in the tragedy of Spain how far the world oppressors will go to retain their power. To them now the murder of women and children is nothing. Those who have already practiced bombing the little villages of Ethiopia now bomb Guernica and Madrid. The same Fascists who forced Italian peasants to fight in Africa now force African Moors to fight in Europe. They do not care about color when they can use you for profits or for war. Japan attempts to force the Chinese of Manchuria to work and fight under Japanese supervision for the glory and wealth of the Tokio bourgeoisie—one colored people dominating another at the point of guns. Race means nothing when it can be turned to Fascist use. And yet race means everything when the Fascists of the world use it as a bugaboo and a terror to keep the working masses from getting together. Just as in America they tell the whites that Negroes are dangerous brutes and rapists, so in Germany they lie about the Jews, and in Italy they cast their verbal spit upon the Ethiopians. And the old myths of race are kept alive to hurt and impede the rising power of the working class. But in America, where race prejudice is so strong, already we have learned what the lies of race mean—continued oppression and poverty and fear—and now Negroes and white sharecroppers in the cotton fields of the South are beginning to get together; and Negro and white workers in the great industrial cities of the North under John L. Lewis and the C.I.O. have begun to create a great labor force that refuses to recognize the color line. Negro and white stevedores on the docks of the West coast of

America have formed one of the most powerful labor unions in America. Formerly the unorganized Negro dockworkers—unorganized because the white workers themselves with their backward ideology didn't permit Negroes in their unions—formerly these Negro workers could break a strike. And they did. But now both Negroes and whites are strong. We are learning.

Why is it that the British police seized Raj Anand's passport? Why is it that the State Department in Washington has not yet granted me permission to go to Spain as a representative of the Negro Press? Why is it that the young Negro leader, Angelo Herndon, was finding it most difficult to secure a passport when I last saw him recently in New York? Why? We know why!

It is because the reactionary and Fascist forces of the world know that writers like Anand and myself, leaders like Herndon, and poets like Guillén and Roumain represent the great longing that is in the hearts of the darker peoples of the world to reach out their hands in friendship and brotherhood to all the white races of the earth. The Fascists know that we long to be rid of hatred and terror and oppression, to be rid of conquering and of being conquered, to be rid of all the ugliness of poverty and imperialism that eat away the heart of life today. We represent the end of race. And the Fascists know that when there is no more race, there will be no more capitalism, and no more war, and no more money for the munition makers, because the workers of the world will have triumphed.

"The Need for Heroes,"
Crisis 48 (June 1941): 184–85, 206

The written word is the only record we will have of this our present, or our past, to leave behind for future generations. It would be a shame if that written word in its creative form were to consist largely of defeat and death. Suppose *Native Son*'s Bigger Thomas (excellently drawn as he is) was the sole survivor on the bookshelves of tomorrow? Or my own play, *Mulatto,* whose end consists of murder, madness, and suicide? If the best of our writers continue to pour their talent into the tragedies of frustration and weakness, tomorrow will probably say, on the basis of available literary evidence, "No wonder the Negroes never amounted to anything. There were no heroes among them. Defeat and panic, moaning, groaning, and weeping were their lot. Did nobody fight? Did nobody triumph? Here is that book about Bigger. The catalogue says it sold several hundred thousand copies. A Negro wrote it. No wonder Hitler wiped the Negroes off the face of Europe."

Another more thoughtful student of the year A.D. 2200, one engaged in research for a Ph.D. perhaps, might say, "But there is a book on the Nordic shelves by a writer named Vandercook that makes the blacks out as great fighters and heroes. It's called *Black Majesty* and concerns Toussaint L'Ouverture, Dessalines, and Christophe of Haiti."

"But he was a white man and probably inclined to romanticize," the first student will say. "Have you come across any good books the Negroes themselves wrote about their own heroes?"

"A few histories by Dr. Woodson," the second student would say. "But the facts are condensed and the color of the times is not there. Dr. Woodson was a Negro who did his best, with excellent scholarship but in a short space of time and with practically no funds, to put down the history of his people in America and to cover a very wide field— because practically nobody had done it before him. He had no time nor leisure nor funds to devote himself to a full exploration of the heroes of the race. Harriet Tubman, Sojourner Truth, Frederick Douglass, Nat Turner were worthy of an odyssey—a great creative series of biographies and novels—but I don't find them on the shelves of our library. What were the Negro writers doing in the Twentieth Century?"

"Perhaps Hitler burned their books," says the first student.

"He couldn't burn them if they didn't exist," says the second student. "Even now in literature the colored people have a need for heroes."

Heroes Ignored

And with that statement let us bring our conversation back through time to today. In our books and plays, our songs and radio programs, Negroes have a need for heroes, now, this moment, this year. The field of humor and fun has been widely explored, largely by white writers from Octavus Roy Cohen to whoever does the scripts for Rochester. The field of frustration and tragedy has been put on paper and on the stage by dozens of excellent writers, Negro and white, from Eugene O'Neill to Richard Wright, Gilmore Millen to Claude McKay, Walter White to Theodore Ward. The field of struggle is depicted by Du Bois, Johnson, and others of the sociologists and survey makers. The field of folk lore is covered and uncovered by A. C. L. Adams, Odum, Johnson, and Zora Neale

Hurston. Day to day achievement and the amazing practical progress of less than a century of freedom is recorded by Embree, Work, the late James Weldon Johnson—quiet, useful, factual records, invaluable to the scholar and historian. But where, in all these books, is that compelling flame of spirit and passion that makes a man say, "I, too, am a hero, because my race has produced heroes like that!"?

Where is the novel or biographical study of Frederick Douglass who defied death to escape from slavery, defied mob-wrath to resist Jim Crow, defied narrowness and convention to side with woman suffrage in a day when women were considered fit only for housewives, defied the racial chauvinism of both his own race and the whites in his second marriage? In other words, a MAN, strong and unafraid, who did not die a suicide, or a mob-victim, or a subject for execution, or a defeated humble beaten-down human being. Douglass lived greatly, triumphed over his times, and left a flaming pattern for the youth of all ages and all countries. But no Negro writes a novel about him. No, we write about caged animals who moan, who cry, who go mad, who are social problems, who have no guts.

We have a need for heroes. We have a need for books and plays that will encourage and inspire our youth, set for them examples and patterns of conduct, move and stir them to be forthright, strong, clear-thinking, and unafraid.

Abundant Hero Material

Do not say there are no living Negro heroes. Do not say there have never been any in the past. Those statements would be lies, enormously untrue. A few of our colored writers have tried to overcome such lies, misconceptions, or lack of knowledge: Arna Bontemps, Arthur Fauset, Carter Woodson, Elizabeth Ross Haynes, J. A. Rogers.

African history, slave history, reconstruction days are crowded with the figures of heroic men and women. Search out the old slave records and read them, the autobiographies in the Schomburg Collection or the Library of Congress with their yellowed pages, the stories told by slaves and ex-slaves themselves. Read the records of reconstruction, the memoirs of our Negro congressmen of that time, and the later books by Du Bois and others on the period. Then come up to today—but don't look for today in books because our few writers haven't gotten around to putting it down yet—but look in the back files of the Negro press:

The Chicago Defender in the riot days of 1919 in that tough and amazing city; or come on up to almost now and read about Sam Solomon and the first Negro voters in Miami in 1939; or come right up to today and look at the news story of the fourteen Negro boys of the United States navy who were not afraid to expose the chains of Jim Crow on the American battleships for which you and I pay taxes.

Present Day Figures

But why bother with the newspapers at all? Look around you for the living heroes who are your neighbors—but who may not look or talk like heroes when they are sitting quietly in a chair in front of you. Just to give you a clue (for you may search out your own heroes and heroines, since you have them in your own cities and towns) look into the stories behind the lives of persons like Hank Johnson, the union leader in Chicago; like Angelo Herndon, who stood trial for his life in Atlanta on a charge of sedition because he spoke against Jim Crow and hunger; like Mary McLeod Bethune, who built a school in the far South on whose campus no Jim Crow is permitted, not even when Roland Hayes sings there or Mrs. Roosevelt speaks and the white folks wish to come—for they may come *and sit side by side with all others*. (And if you think that is easy to achieve in the South and does not take bravery and gall and guts, try it yourself. Or else be humble like that college president reported recently in the *Courier*—of the male sex, too—who says he is sorry the white people of his community who wish to hear Mrs. Roosevelt speak on his campus cannot attend because the state law is against it! Thus meekly he accepts an obvious wrong and does nothing—not even verbally. Such men would accept Hitler without a struggle—but Mrs. Bethune wouldn't—not even in Florida.)

Another hero—if you still think there are no living ones: Roscoe Dunjee, who for twenty-six years has been the fighting editor of the *Black Dispatch* in Oklahoma City, a southern city, where the crackers and the Ku Klux have often dared a Negro to raise his voice—but Dunjee's voice is still raised against the wrongs of prejudice, Jim Crow, and oppression. But which of our novelists, black or white, have yet written a novel, a short story, or even a poem about a modern upstanding Negro editor who refuses in the face of threats to fold up shop and go down to defeat? The white writers can be excused. They have their own heroes to write about, their real heroes (and their built-up heroes) from George

Washington to Edison, Barbara Fritchie to Amelia Earhart, Robert E. Lee to General Pershing, Joe Hill to Harry Bridges, Buffalo Bill to Richard Halliburton.

Hollywood Caricatures

We have our heroes, too—but we keep so silent about them. Why? We glorify them so little, *never* on the screen in the miserable uninspired (seldom lacking a cabaret scene) movies that the "Negro" film companies turn out. We almost never honor the memories of our dead heroes with celebrations, songs, or programs: those who died in the slave struggle to make us free, those who died with John Brown, those who died in the Civil War, those who were beaten to death and murdered in reconstruction days trying to establish for us today the right to vote and live as Americans. And as to the living—if we don't happen to agree with their politics, or are piqued with them because they haven't time to socialize, or are jealous of them—myopia and the mole-hills often keep us from seeing the mountains of their statures—we keep silent about them.

It is the social duty of Negro writers to reveal to the people the deep reservoirs of heroism within the race. It is one of the duties of our literature to combat—by example, not by diatribe—the caricatures of Hollywood, the Lazy Bones of the popular songs, the endless defeats of play after play and novel after novel—for we are not endlessly funny, nor always lazy, nor forever quaint, nor eternally defeated. After all, there was Crispus Attucks. There was Denmark Vesey. There was Harriet Tubman. There was Frederick Douglass. There was Oliver Laws. There is James Peck. There are the Negro voters of Miami. There are the fourteen sailors of the U.S.S. *Philadelphia*. And there are you.

A Word to Youth

Listen, boys and girls at Tuskegee and Wiley, in the Dunbar and Booker T. high schools all across the South, in the kitchens and hotel pantries where you work to get the money to go back to school, in the CCC camps and the army camps where you've been drafted without Negro officers—listen, boys and girls, don't let anybody tell you your own race hasn't produced great men and women, that great men and women do not exist today, that you yourselves cannot be great, guiding and leading and inspiring our people. Don't let the motion pictures that show us always as humble servants, clowns, or silly fools kid you into believing that there never was a Nat Turner, or that the folks who marched to the polls to vote in Miami in spite of terror and sawed-off shotguns are not heroes. Don't let the radio sketches that give you only dialect comedians make you believe that lack of proper English is always attended by servility, grotesqueness, and stupidity. Remember that Sojourner Truth could neither read nor write and probably talked in dialect as well, but she was not servile or grotesque or always funny. More often her words were like a great flame to the human spirit in bondage.

And there are today in the South leaders of sharecroppers and tenant farmers whose English is by no means perfect, but who are helping to bring a new peace and a new unity to the plantations of the Southland. The radio never puts those Negroes into a sketch. But because of that lack, you yourselves must not forget that they are *here* with us today, living heroes, in danger of mob-law, arrest, and lynchings—still they are not cowards.

Ask for Books

Listen, young folks at Hampton and at Dillard, if the professors don't find for you books about the great black folks of the past, ask them where such books are. And if the Negro writers whose works are reviewed in the *New York Times* don't write the kind of books you need, then you must delve into history and write your own books yourselves, for we haven't many good Negro writers. And some of our best ones seem unaware of the heroism, past or present, of the Negro people. (I myself have not been sufficiently aware, so I accept here and now my own criticism.) I do not say that many of the tragic books and plays concerning our plight in America are not good plays or good books, having their place and their usefulness in arousing sympathy, interest, and discussion. But for ourselves who are colored and who know our plight too well, for ourselves there is a need, more than anything else, of great patterns to guide us, great lives to inspire us, strong men and women to lift us up and give us confidence in the powers we, too, possess. We ordinary people need in our books and plays and on our screens and over the air waves Negro heroes and Negro heroines—who may or may not always speak perfect English but who are courageous, straightforward, strong; whose gaiety is not of the "Yas, suh, boss" variety all the time; and whose words and thoughts gather up what is in our own hearts and say it clearly and plainly for all to hear.

Heroes Unafraid

We need in literature the kind of black men and women all of us know exist in life: who are not afraid to claim our rights as human beings and as Americans; who are not afraid of the mobsters, the crooked politicians, and the often ignorant, short-sighted, and dangerous white demagogues in places of power; who are not afraid of the sometimes venal black demagogues paid to fool and mislead their own people. We need in our books those who remember the past when one word of freedom was enough to bring the lash to our backs—*yet that word was spoken.* We need in our books those who have known the day-after-day heroism of work and struggle and the facing of drudgery and insult that some son or daughter might get through school and acquire the knowledge that leads to a better life where opportunities are brighter and work is less drab, less humiliating, and less hard—*yet for us that work was done.* We need in our books those who have lived through the days when even to move into a decent house outside the black slums in Detroit or Cleveland or Chicago was to bring out the mob, stones through the windows, bullets, and danger of death—*yet we moved into those houses.* We need in our books today the fourteen sailors *dishonorably* discharged from the United States Navy for trying to bring a little decency into the relations on shipboard between whites and Negroes—*yet those fourteen sailors spoke out unafraid.* Their example will not be forgotten a hundred years hence.

We know we are not weak, ignorant, frustrated, or cowed. We know the race has its heroes whether anybody puts them into books or not. We know we are heroes ourselves and can make a better world. Someday there will be many books and plays and songs that say that. Today there are strangely few. Negro literature has a need for heroes. Then it will come alive, speak, sing, and flame with meaning for the Negro people.

"What the Negro Wants,"
Common Ground 2 (autumn 1941): 52–54

Often in speaking with white friends about the so-called Negro problem, I am amazed at their lack of information concerning the failure of democracy in our regard. They in turn are often amazed to learn that the Negro is so badly and so generally ill-treated. Since, being a Negro, I do not rail and sweat and frown in anger, they seem vaguely to feel that things are not really very bad for us after all. And sometimes men of the best goodwill look at me and say, "Just what do you want?"

It would seem wise then to set down clearly and plainly what I and thirteen million other American Negroes desire. The things that I shall enumerate are basic and non-controversial; they are the things any self-respecting citizen of the United States desires for himself regardless of color.

First, we want a chance to earn a decent living. Even the most casual glance about you as you walk down the main street of any American city will show you that there are no Negroes employed as clerks in any of the shops you pass, none as tellers in any of the banks, none as motormen on the street cars or as drivers of buses. None as traffic cops. None in any of the working jobs that your eye can spot paying more than a minimum salary.

We are elevator boys, janitors, red caps, maids—a race in uniform, as far as your tour of the main street goes. In factories it is often the same story: a few Negro cleanup men who sweep out the trash under machines, or a scattering of Negroes among the unskilled laborers. Employers will often blame the unions which, it is true, frequently raise the color bar, refusing to accept Negroes either as skilled workers or as apprentices in the trades. But even where there is no union bar and many foreign-born workers are used, no Negro will be hired. And the employer, if pushed, will admit that he wishes to employ none, giving often, as a reason, that the white workers will not work with Negroes—a fact seldom true, especially in the case of the foreign-born who have not acquired the traditional American prejudice against color.

What we want then is, first, economic opportunity—the right to earn our money at any trade or profession open to other Americans. We want the chance to do, or learn to do, skilled labor in plants and factories alongside any workman of any other race, especially in the many plants now turning out billions of dollars' worth of defense orders with our Government money. We want no discrimination in Government employment or Civil Service after we have passed all the tests—except the test of being white. We want unionization not based on race, and we want laws making it illegal for labor unions to prevent any man from working or being unionized on account of race. Example in point, the Brotherhood of Locomotive Engineers, the Motion Picture Operators, the Stage Hands, and many others. We do not want a Jim Crow Army in which Negro units are officered largely by whites, or a United States Navy in which we may be only cooks and mess men.

Second, we want equal educational opportunities all over America. All schools supported by public funds should be open to Negro students whose parents, too, contribute to these public funds. In Mississippi twenty-five counties have no recognized high-school facilities for Negroes, and only one dollar is spent on Negro education to every $9.88 spent on white education—yet 51 per cent of the population of the State is Negro. We want equal pay for Negro teachers in the public schools. In certain states they are allotted only half the salaries paid to white teachers. We want all Christian schools open to us the same as to those of the white race, or else we want those schools to drop the word Christian from their catalogues. We want the right to study and teach anywhere that anybody else studies and teaches.

Third, we want decent housing. In the big cities we are very tired of living in the ancient abandoned sections deserted by the whites, for which we pay double rents. We are tired of residential segregation which prevents us from buying or renting where we choose, if we have the money to do so. We resent the ghetto system of the Black Belts and realtors' covenants which prohibit Negroes from purchasing lots at will. We resent being forced to live in slums and, because of color restrictions, being, therefore, at the mercy of landlords who can charge us what they choose since they know we cannot move. We resent not being able to get loans on our property, or loans for building or insurance after we build, simply because we are colored and live in colored neighborhoods. Street repairing, garbage removal, lighting, drainage, and other services in the Black Belts are the worst in the city, although we too pay taxes.

That is why, fourth, we want full participation in Government—municipal, state, and national. Only where we participate in Government have we any sure and effective way of remedying these unfortunate conditions. Therefore we protest gerrymandering and redistricting of neighborhoods to cut up and divide the Negro vote and thus prevent Negroes from electing their choice of representatives to city or state governing bodies. And in the South, we resent not being permitted to vote at all. For how can we fight bad housing, bad paving, bad sewage, and bad schools if we have no vote? And if, as in Texas, we cannot even belong to the Democratic party, the party that controls the State and all its citizens (of whom there are almost a million Negroes), how can we better our own conditions in a democratic way?

We want, fifth, a fair deal before the law. That means we desire Negroes on all jury panels, and that we be fairly called for jury service. We desire the right to elect judges (which means again that we must vote). We desire adequate legal representation. In some states, it is difficult, if not impossible, for a Negro to practice before the bar. We desire protection from police brutality, which is severe in Negro neighborhoods, and against which we often have no redress. We desire Negro policemen. In other words, we desire equality before the law, for otherwise the law imposes upon us—and seldom with majesty.

Sixth, we desire public courtesy, the same courtesy that is normally accorded other citizens. We desire polite service in the shops and at the gas stations and in restaurants and on the trains and buses. (Mexicans and other dark-skinned residents within our borders would appreciate this, too.) We wonder why, in the South, we are not accorded the courtesy of the customary "Mr.", "Mrs.", or "Miss" before our names. Why should shopkeepers feel free to call us merely "Mary" or "Jim" or "Hey, you"? We, too, are Americans, and we try to use good manners toward others.

And, finally, we want social equality in so far as public services go. White people have it. And certainly, in their case, there is no law forcing people to invite anyone else to dinner if they do not care for his company. Nor is there any law forcing people to marry who normally do not wish to do so. We Negroes do not wish to force ourselves into the private lives of other people. But we do want the right to use, and be protected in the use of, all the *public* conveniences that other Americans may use: the municipal parks, play grounds, auditoriums, hospitals, and schools. We want the right to ride without Jim Crow in any conveyance carrying the traveling public. We want the right when traveling to dine in any restaurant or seek lodgings in any hotel or auto camp open to the public which our purse affords. (Any Nazi may do so.)

We want nothing not compatible with democracy and the Constitution, nothing not compatible with Christianity, nothing not compatible with sensible, civilized living. We want simply economic opportunity, educational opportunity, decent housing, participation in Government, fairness at law, normal courtesy, and equality in public services.

There is nothing wrong in wanting these things, is there? If so, where-in lies the wrong?

There are thirteen million Negroes in America. We are men of good-will seeking goodwill from others.

"What to Do Now,"
Chicago Defender, September 4, 1943

People keep writing and asking me what to do NOW about the grievous racial situation in America. Unfortunately, I am no oracle. Neither am I George S. Schuyler, neither Dr. W. E. B. Du Bois. Those gentlemen have long been writing and speaking on the subject—while an oracle can look into the future and see what OUGHT to be done NOW in order to have what you want THEN.

Nevertheless, I make so bold as to put down here some of the things I humbly think colored people ought to do. (Others that I do not put down I will leave to your own initiative—which I reckon is as good as mine, if not better.)

I think every adult Negro able to work or fight, in uniform and out, ought to join the National Association for the Advancement of Colored People. It costs only one dollar a year. In case there is no branch in your town, the address of the national office is 69 Fifth Avenue, New York City, N.Y. They try mainly to break down discrimination through legal channels, by contesting unfair laws, by defending Negroes persecuted illegally, and by keeping their office in Washington busy putting pressure on the government.

I also think every Negro old enough to earn a dollar ought to join the National Urban League with branches in most large industrial centers. But if there is no branch in your town the address of their national office is 1133 Broadway, New York City. They have been, for a number of years now, working on the problems of discrimination in employment. They have opened up many new avenues of opportunity for colored people. They are a valuable and practical organization. With YOU as a member they can do even more than they have been doing.

March on Washington

People ask me what about the March on Washington movement. I am a member of it, too, but I have got two things against it. One is, they do not admit white people. And the other is that their leader, A. Philip Randolph, is always attacking Russia.

Now, Russia is the only predominantly white country in the WHOLE world that will not tolerate racial discrimination of any kind anywhere within its Soviet borders—not even when brought there by American tourists. It is also the only country of any color where the poor man has an equal break.

As to white people in America—there are so many of them here that I think we have to learn to work with them and they with us. Suppose John Brown, who laid down his life for freedom at Harpers Ferry, were alive today. Being white, he couldn't join the March on Washington movement—even if he wanted to lay down his life again. Anyhow, by being a member of it myself, I figure that maybe I can persuade the Movement to admit white folks and also to get Mr. Randolph to lay off our courageous ally, the Soviet Union. Therefore, I will pay my dime. If you are paying yours, see if you can get our organization to correct these rather out-moded defects.

After all, the world of tomorrow, if it is to be any good at all, has got to be a cooperative world with all races working together, not fighting and marching on each other like mad. It has also got to be a world in which the wealth of this earth—of which there is plenty to go around to all who work, farm, mine, or in other ways help create it—will be distributed so that you and me, poor as we be now, won't need to be so poor then. The Soviet Union has brilliantly pointed the way toward a more equal distribution of the benefits of this world. Let's not fight other races on a color basis. And let's not fight progressive social ideas.

Join Something

In your own neighborhoods, join the most progressive league, club, or church at hand. If they are all old fashioned and handkerchief-head, then create a club, a league or a church that believes in ending Jim Crow, that believes in working with the white people of good will in your town, that believes in international cooperation after the war, and friendship for Indians and Russians and Chinese and everybody else willing to act decent. See if you can't find a minister like Rev. Adam Powell of Abyssinia Baptist church around. If none, then develop one. Make your church a real center of PRACTICAL good as well as spiritual.

Sure, shout if you want to. And pray! But pray, not only for your OWN soul, but for the souls of the white folks. Also pray for the Allies to defeat Hitler, for the Klan-minded to get what's coming to them, for India to be free, for the NAACP to have six million members, and for the peace that passeth understanding to descend upon those of our congressmen who still uphold the poll-tax and oppose the right of Negroes to vote down home. When you stop praying, get up and help God to do something about conditions in this world.

"Walter White's First Twenty-Five,"
Chicago Defender, June 10, 1944

Last week at the Hotel Roosevelt in New York a dinner was given in honor of Walter White's first 25 years with the National Association for the Advancement of Colored People. In recognition of his distinguished services at the close of a quarter century of work, a distinguished crowd containing many of America's leading citizens filled the Grand Ballroom. Even the balcony was packed with tables.

The dinner began at seven and ended at midnight. It was a good dinner—for a public banquet. There was chicken. As usual at public dinners, there were too many speeches, but only a few of them were too long. Dr. William Allan Neilson was an able and amiable chairman, and by witty ribbing held most of the speakers to their allotted time. Almost everybody at the speakers' table was a platform celebrity in one way or another, so they made good use of their verbal time.

Mrs. Franklin D. Roosevelt brought greetings from her husband, and paid charming tribute to the work of Walter White and the NAACP. She sat at Mr. White's right. To the left of the toastmaster sat Mr. Wendell L. Willkie, who said he had a hard time competing with Walter's personal charm in Hollywood when they were there together. When he got serious, he said folks were tired of high proclamations and low performances. The applause of the audience said, "Amen!"

Praise for the Praiseworthy

The distinguished lawyer, Arthur Garfield Hays, told of how years ago when he and Walter White were in Detroit in connection with the famous Sweet case, the late great attorney, Clarence Darrow, mistook Walter White for a white man. And the present president of the Association's largest branch, the Detroit Branch, which sent a gift of Five Hundred Dollars, said that one of the fine things about Walter White was that the people knew he would never sell them out.

Miss Jean Muir spoke of the fine work Walter White did in Hollywood in educating the movie industry to abandon its old stereotypes of Negro caricature, but said that the furtherance of that work was really up to the moviegoers themselves. When you see a picture with decent Negro roles in it, Miss Muir said, write to the studio that produced the picture and commend them on it. When you see an abomination, to quote Miss Muir, like "Cabin in the Sky," write and tell the studios it stinks.

Mr. Arthur Spingarn, the President of the National Association for the Advancement of Colored People, told of how the late James Weldon Johnson, impressed with Mr. White's useful work and burning ardor in Atlanta years ago, had first recommended him to the National Office of the Association. Mr. Carl Van Vechten paid tribute to Walter White as a writer—and to his books *Flight, Fire in the Flint,* and *Rope and Faggot,* also his numerous pamphlets and magazine articles. He said that in Germany Hitler burns Walter White's books. Here in America those books burn people's souls.

An American Organization

Several speakers stressed the fact that the National Association for the Advancement of Colored People is much broader than its name implies in that it is an American organization composed of both Negroes and whites, and that its real work is sustaining the basic truths of American democracy by clearing away the prejudice and bigotry and antidemocratic debris at the base of the great pillars of our national faith. It was made plain that when democracy for any minority is in danger, then democracy for all is in danger.

The key speech of the evening was made by Dr. Mordecai Johnson, the President of Howard University, who reviewed the work of the NAACP and its many achievements. Mr. Johnson spoke like the venerable minister of the gospel that he is, with many a rolling period, that rolled on into a collection speech that caused the assembled gathering to come forth with Twenty Thousand Dollars—which is just about the largest collection I have ever seen taken up anywhere. The collection got off to a flying start with a check for Five Thousand Dollars. Various folks gave lesser checks, and that genial dean of Negro music, Mr. W. C. Handy, gave Five Hundred. And the Hundred Dollar checks and bills came in at a rapid rate.

For some strange reason, they stopped at a Hundred Dollars and never did get down any lower, which let me out, because everybody knows poor poets and writers are not in the upper income brackets. At my table three or four folks had their hands on five or ten dollar bills, but nary an usher asked for those.

One other thing that struck me as a bit strange these days and times about the dinner was that I did not see a single man or woman in military uniform at the Speakers' Table. Nor did I see a single representative of organized labor, neither AFL, the CIO, or the Pullman Porters. Among all those distinguished lawyers, judges, politicians, ladies, and race leaders, looks like to me there should have been some labor, too. Anyhow, it was a good dinner—I enjoyed myself.

"Simple and the NAACP,"
Chicago Defender, June 16, 1945

"You see this, don't you?" said my Simple Minded Friend, showing me his NAACP card. "I have just joined the National Organization for the Association of Colored Folks and, Jack, it is FINE."

"You mean the National Association for the Advancement of Colored People," I said.

"Um-hum!" said Simple, "but they tell me it has white peoples in it too."

"That's right, it does," I said.

"I did not see none at the meeting where me and Joyce went this evening," said Simple, "and there should have been some there because that FINE colored speaker was getting white folks told—except that there was no white folks there to be told."

"They just do not come to Negro neighborhoods to meetings," I said.

"Then we ought to hold some meetings downtown so they can learn what this Negro problem is all about," Simple said. "It does not make sense to always be talking to ourselves."

Shaking Cans

"Well, next time I go to a AACP meeting—"

"N-A-A-C-P meeting," I said.

"NAACP meeting, I am going to move that everybody get a can," said Simple, "and go from store to store and bar to bar and hash house to hash house and take up collection for the NAACP from all these white folks making money in colored neighborhoods. If they do not give, I will figure they do not care nothing about me. They are always taking up collections from *me* for the Red Cross or the Community Chest or something or other. They are always shaking their cans in my face. Why shouldn't I shake my can in their face?"

"It would be better," I said, "if you got them all to be members of the NAACP, not just to give a contribution."

"Every last Italian, Greek, Jew, also Irishman in Harlem, or the Southside, Chicago, or if it's Detroit from Paradise Valley to the West Side, ought to belong to the NAACP. But do you reckon they would come to meetings? They practically all live in the suburbans."

"They come to Harlem on business," I said, "so why shouldn't they come to meetings?"

"Because they go to the suburbans to get away from us Negroes they been selling groceries and victuals and beer to all day and half the night. They do not want to be bothered with me and my problems when they close up their shops."

"Do you blame them?" I said.

"I do," yelled Simple. "Long as the cash register is ringing they can be bothered with me, so why can't they come to NAACP meetings?"

"Have I ever heard of you going out to the Italian or Jewish neighborhoods to any of their meetings to help them with *their* problems?" I asked.

"I do not have any stores in the Italian or Jewish neighborhoods," said Simple. "Neither do I own nary pool hall in their neighborhood, nor nary Greek restaurant, nor nary white apartment house from which I get rent. I do not own no beerhalls where Jews and Italians come to spend their money. If I did, I would join the Jewish NAACP, and the Italian one, too! I would join the Greek NAACP, if I owned a hash house where nothing but Greeks spent money all day long."

Human Business

"You put it all on such a mercenary basis," I said.

"They would want me to have mercy on them if they was in my fix," said Simple.

"I did not say anything about mercy," I said. "I said *mercenary*—I mean a buying and selling basis."

"They could buy and sell me," said Simple.

"What I mean is, you should not have to have a business in a Jewish neighborhood to be interested in Jewish problems, or own a spaghetti counter to be interested in Italians. In a democracy, everybody's problems are related, and it's up to all of us to help solve them."

"If I did not have a business reason to be interested in their business," said Simple, "then what business would I have being interested in their business?"

"Just a human reason," I said. "It's all human business."

"Maybe that is why they don't join the NAACP," Simple said, "because they do not think a Negro is human."

"If I were you, I would not speak so drastic," I said, "unless I had some facts to go on. Have you asked any of the white businessmen where you trade to join the NAACP—the man who runs your laundry, or manages the movies where you go, or the Greek who owns the restaurant? Have you asked any of them to join?"

"No, I have not," said Simple. "Neither have I asked my landlord's landlord."

"Well, ask them and see what they say," I said.

"I sure will," said Simple, "then if they do not join the NAACP, I will know those white folks don't care nothing about me!"

"You make it simple," I said.

"The Accusers' Names Nobody Will Remember, but History Records Du Bois," *Chicago Defender,* October 6, 1951

[Active in the promotion of world peace and nuclear disarmament, Du Bois was chairman of the Peace Information Center, an organization that was declared subversive by the U.S. government at the height of the Cold War. Du Bois refused demands from the Department of Justice that he register as an agent of "foreign principle" and was indicted in 1951 under the Foreign Agents Registration Act of 1938. He was later acquitted because of insufficient evidence, but the Department of State refused to issue him a passport in 1952, preventing him from traveling abroad until 1958.]

If W. E. B. Du Bois goes to jail a wave of wonder will sweep around the world. Europe will wonder and Africa will wonder and Asia will wonder, and no judge or jury will be able to answer the questions behind their wonder. The banner of American democracy will be lowered another notch, particularly in the eyes of the darker peoples of the earth. The hearts of millions will be angered and perturbed, steeled and strengthened.

They will not believe that it is right, for Dr. Du Bois is more than a man. He is all that he has stood for for over eighty years of life. The things that he has stood for are what millions of people of good will the world around desire, too—a world of decency, of no nation over another nation, of no color line, no more colonies, no more poverty, of education for all, of freedom and love and friendship and peace among men. For as long as I can remember, Dr. Du Bois has been writing and speaking and working for these things. He began way before I was born to put reason above passion, tolerance above prejudice, well-being above poverty, wisdom above ignorance, cooperation above strife, equality above Jim Crow, and peace above the bomb.

Today the books of W. E. B. Du Bois are on the shelves of thousands of libraries around the world, translated into many languages, known and read by scholars everywhere. The work of his youth, his monumental *Study of the African Slave Trade,* is still the authoritative book on that nefarious traffic. His *The Souls of Black Folk, Dark Water,* and *The Quest of the Silver Fleece* are among the most beautiful and stirring of volumes about democracy's color problems ever written. Through those books in the first decades of this century the consciences of many young Americans were awakened.

As a co-founder of the National Association for the Advancement of Colored People, Dr. Du Bois gave America one of its greatest liberalizing organizations whose contributions to democracy through legal test cases and mass unity, history will list as invaluable. As the founder of the Pan-African Congress, he linked the hand of black America with Africa and Asia. As a teacher and lecturer in the colleges and forums of the nation, he has had an immeasurable influence for good upon young minds. As editor of *The Crisis* for many years, he developed the first distinguished, lasting journal of Negro opinion in the Western World. Dr. Du Bois is the dean of Negro scholars. But not only is he a great Negro, he is a great American, and one of the leading men of our century. At the age of eighty-three he is still a wellspring of knowledge, a fountain of courage, and a skyrocket for the great dreams of all mankind.

Somebody in Washington wants to put Dr. Du Bois in jail. Somebody in France wanted to put Voltaire in jail. Somebody in Franco's Spain sent Lorca, their greatest poet, to death before a firing squad. Somebody in Germany under Hitler burned the books, drove Thomas Mann into exile, and led their leading Jewish scholars to the gas chamber. Somebody in Greece long ago gave Socrates the hemlock to drink. Somebody at Golgotha erected a cross and somebody drove the nails into the hands of Christ. Somebody spat upon His garments. No one remembers their names.

"Be Your Own Santa Claus by Putting More Civil Rights in Your Stocking," *Chicago Defender,* December 8, 1951

An autumn visit to the South convinces me more than ever that the National Association for the Advancement of Colored People is just about the most important organization operating in America today in the field of democratic extensions. And what the NAACP is doing benefits not just colored people but the whole U.S.A. Certainly the NAACP is currently washing democracy's ears with legal wash cloths that are getting rid of some of the dirt that had been clogged there for a long, long time. It's also removing some of the scales from democracy's eyes.

For instance that old dining car curtain that the steward used to walk up and pull to shield from sight a Negro diner at the end table—it's gone! In the old days, if a hungry colored traveller was lucky enough to get into the diner at all, he would always be put at the end table. Then, with a rudeness that seemed to me uncivilized, they would pull a curtain in front of your face so white travellers would be spared the sight of a Negro eating under the same train roof with them. If the two end tables were full, Negroes simply had to wait. That is no longer true. A few days ago I had occasion to eat several meals on trains in Virginia, the Carolinas, and Georgia, and I was not always placed at the end table. No curtains were pulled. Whites ate at the same table with me. Once in Georgia I was seated in the very center of the car. There were other Negro passengers at other tables. There were Negroes being served refreshments in the club cars. As far as I could tell, from Washington to Savannah, the old Jim Crow in railroad service in relation to food and drink is gone. One more stupidity now a part of history, thanks to the NAACP and the individuals who fought their various cases right up to the United States Supreme Court.

As to education and the NAACP's various legal victories, local and federal, in that field, cities, counties, and states all up and down the Eastern seaboard are building schools like mad for colored students, trying quickly to "equalize" the classroom facilities for the races. This, of course, is a physical impossibility within foreseeable time and available tax budgets, so eventually our white folks in the South will have to let Negroes and whites study and teach together if they expect to keep up with the march of civilization. Meanwhile, new schools, even if Jim Crow, are better than the old overcrowded broken-down buildings so often allotted to Negroes. Thank the NAACP and the suits its lawyers have brought for this.

I visited some of these new school buildings, and some of them are very nice. What puzzles me, though, is why even new colored schools are so often placed in such remote places, and on such odd sites—often down in hollows instead of on the nearby hill where there is sunlight and air and the red clay couldn't run into the halls when it rains. And with all the vast lands in the South, why a colored school frequently has to sit right bang up on the highway, with busses and trucks roaring by to drown out the teacher's voice, is another thing that puzzles me. I asked some of the colored teachers about it and they said they guessed the white school boards just didn't give a damn. So I reckon it is now up to local NAACP chapters to get some Negro citizens on Southern school boards. As scared as Southern educators seem to be now of the NAACP I expect they'd let Negroes on the school boards just to keep them quiet, so why not try it and see?

There is a new sense of confidence among thinking Negroes in the South that something *concrete* can be done about things racial there, and a feeling that the Negro is beginning to have some influence on changing Southern mores for the better. A large part of this new optimism is due, I believe, to the courage and integrity of various local NAACP branches and their leaders, as well as to the legal victories won on the national front. Certainly civil rights in the South in some respects are definitely on the upgrade. And if you as a Negro want more civil rights in Dixie and throughout America, you could not do better this Christmas than by being your own Santa Claus—immediately join the NAACP, bring in more new members, make contributions, attend meetings, and thus stick some additional civil rights into your racial stocking.

"From Rampart Street to Harlem I Follow the Trail of the Blues," *Chicago Defender,* December 6, 1952

About a month ago I heard it on a juke box in New Orleans. The other day I found it in a shop in Harlem, and ever since it has been whirling around on my record player: Little Caesar singing "Goodbye, Baby" to music by Que Martyn on a Hollywood label, which bids fair to be classed among my favorite records. It is a little two-minute drama in blues with a cast of two, a guy and a doll. The guy catches his girlfriend waiting for another man. She thinks he is the other man when he knocks. Then the explaining begins while Little Caesar caterwauls his blues.

The explanations do not take. At the end he shoots her: BANG! BANG! Then moans, "I can't stay here by myself." And he is gone, too. BANG! Folks who liked Pearl Bailey and Jackie Mabley's recording of "Saturday Night Fish Fry" will like this one.

Years ago I spent the better part of a summer on Rampart Street, so I have a fondness in my heart for that long old roughneck thoroughfare and the songs it loves. I followed the Mississippi River down from Memphis, stopping in Vicksburg and Natchez and Baton Rouge that summer.

I arrived in New Orleans in a Jim Crow car and roomed with a lady on Rampart Street who ran Saturday night fish fries. I got a job on a banana boat and made a trip to Havana and other Cuban ports and back, where I lived in the French Quarter for a time, but soon gravitated back to Rampart where there are more colored people. Toward the end of the summer I left in a Jim Crow car for Mobile.

This time when I left New Orleans I departed in a private room on the deluxe Panama Limited. I was given the private room because I am colored. Formerly Negroes could not ride on this all-Pullman train at all, but the recent Supreme Court decisions have changed that for the better.

Now they will give a Negro passenger traveling between Southern stations on this train a roomette, drawing room, or bedroom without extra charge rather than seat him in the club or parlor cars when his ticket calls for a seat. There is sometimes some advantage in being colored—when the accommodations given are separate but better than whites receive for the same money.

In my experience, this only happens in Pullman travel, however. Before the recent Court rulings, it was the Southern railway custom to give a Negro "Lower 13," which meant a drawing room, rather than have him in the body of the Pullman car, providing the drawing room was not already sold.

This happened to me a few weeks ago traveling on the Gulf, Mobile and Ohio's fine little train, The Rebel, which runs between New Orleans and Jackson, Tennessee. I was going to speak at Lane College in Tennessee. My ticket called for a lower berth.

Although there were only two other persons, both white, in the Pullman car, the conductor gave me the bedroom, where I had complete privacy, even to my own washroom and toilet. This would have cost more than twice as much as my ticket, had I paid for it. But it was given to me free! Anything to keep Negroes segregated! Our white folks strike me as being real simple.

When the writer Melvin Tolson and I left the Literary Festival at Jackson College, Mississippi, the ticket seller took a very long time and held considerable consultation with others in the office before selling us seats on the Southbound Panama Limited.

Finally he gave us two seats in the Club Car, numbers 4 and 5. But when we went to board the train just as it was pulling out of the Jackson station, rather than seat us in the Club Car, the conductor held up the train for more than two minutes while he went from car to car until he found a coach that had an unsold drawing room in it where we would be separate from other passengers. In the rich privacy which our color gained us, we left Mississippi, vastly amused at the lengths to which Southerners go to preserve Jim Crow. A crack train held up that two Negroes might suffer segregation by being given its finest accommodations rather than permitted the democracy of the open coaches!

The many lawsuits brought by Negro travelers in recent years against Southern railroads, and the NAACP's legal battles, were demonstrated to me in an amusing fashion on my recent trip when I went alone into a diner in Mississippi to eat.

The former curtain screening the "Negro" table was gone. I was seated with great courtesy, but at an end table, nevertheless. I have always found dining car waiters all over the country most polite. This time, however, the white steward and the Negro waiters seemed to be giving me unusually attentive service.

The steward stopped twice at my table to ask me if everything was to my liking, and if I was enjoying my meal. Two waiters attended my every need. At the end of the meal, one of the waiters said to me, "We are delighted to have you on this train, Mr. Marshall."

"Mr. Marshall?" I asked. "Which Mr. Marshall?"

"Thurgood Marshall," said the waiter.

It turned out they thought I was the NAACP lawyer! I was sorry to have to say that I was not. Someday somebody is going to write a wonderful satirical Southern railroad blues about how it feels to be a Negro traveling in the South, even in these days of transition from the old Jim Crow to the new.

When you get off the Panama Limited in New Orleans and leave your fine free deluxe drawing room, being colored, you have to use the Jim Crow part of the Union Station—which is on Rampart Street, that old street of the blues. In the Jim Crow waiting room there is no news stand, no shoe shine stand, no clock, none of the refreshments to be found in the big main waiting room. No mirror or sink in the Men's Room, which is as dirty a toilet as I've ever seen. All of which is enough to give a colored traveler the blues.

"Langston Hughes Speaks,"
Crisis 60 (May 1953): 279–80

During a period in my life coinciding roughly with the beginning of the Scottsboro Case and the depression of the 1930's and running through to the Nazi-Soviet Pact, I wrote a number of poems which reflected my then deep sympathies with certain of the aims and objectives of the leftist philosophies and the interests of the Soviet Union in the problems of poverty, minorities, colonial peoples, and particularly of Negroes and jim crow. Most of these poems appeared only in booklet form and have long been out of print. I was amazed to learn that some of these outdated examples of my work are today being circulated in our State Department's overseas libraries. Written, some of them, partially in leftist terminology with the red flag as a symbol of freedom, they could hardly serve to present a contemporary picture of American ideals or of my personal ones.

I am not now and have never been a member of the Communist Party, and have so stated over the years in my speeches and writings. But there is in my family a long history of participation in social struggle—from my grandfather who went to prison for helping slaves to freedom and another relative who died with John Brown at Harpers Ferry to my great uncle, John M. Langston, only Negro representative in Congress from Virginia following the Reconstruction, and who had supported Abraham Lincoln in his recruiting Negro troops, and spoken for freedom on the same platform with Garrison and Phillips. In my own youth, faced with the problems of both poverty and color, and penniless at the beginning of the depression, I was strongly attracted by some of the promises of Communism, but always with the reservations, among others, of a creative writer wishing to preserve my own freedom of action and expression—and as an American Negro desiring full integration into our body politics. These two reservations, particularly (since I could never accept the totalitarian regimentation of the artist nor the communist theory of a Negro state for the Black Belt)—were among other reasons why I never contemplated joining the Communist Party, although various aspects of communist interests were for some years reflected in the emotional content of my writing. But I was shocked at the Nazi-Soviet Pact, just as I am shocked now by the reported persecution of the Jewish people. And I was disturbed by the complete lack of freedom of press and publication I observed in the USSR. In our own country I have been greatly heartened in recent years by the progress being made in race-relations, by the recent Supreme Court decisions relative to Negro education, restrictive covenants, the ballot, and travel. My work of the war years and my latest books have reflected this change of emphasis and development in my own thinking and orientation. This is, I think, clearly and simply shown in the last paragraph of my latest book:

> Our country has many problems still to solve, but America is young, big, strong, and beautiful. And we are trying very hard to be, as the flag says, 'one nation, indivisible, with liberty and justice for all.' Here people are free to vote and work out their problems. In some countries people are governed by rulers, and ordinary folks can't do a thing about it. But here all of us are a part of democracy. By taking an interest in our government, and by treating our neighbors as we would like to be treated, each one of us can help make our country the most wonderful country in the world.

"A Sentimental Journey to Cairo, Illinois,"
Chicago Defender, May 15, 1954

I have always been a blues fan.

Last year in its series of Americans, Audio Archives brought out a fascinating long-playing record of some of the compositions of W. C. Handy. With the "Father of the Blues" himself acting as narrator, playing both guitar and cornet, and singing parts of the songs, this record is a valuable addition to the history of American music, as well as being both informative and entertaining.

In telling how he became interested in Negro folk music, Mr. Handy says that when he was a little boy in a rock quarry in the Deep South, he used to hear the workmen singing a song that went something like this:

> Hey-ooo-oo-o! Heyooooo
> I wouldn't live in Cairo!

And this song made him wonder what was wrong with Cairo. Was it too far up North to be down South—or too far down South to be up North?

Years later when Handy wrote his greatest blues, he mentioned Cairo in that song. I first heard its name in "The St. Louis Blues" which the Negroes in Kansas City were singing when I was a little boy.

Cairo is a levee town three hundred and sixty miles south of Chicago, on the Mississippi, at the extreme southern tip of Illinois. Several months ago it was in the news a great deal when the legal battle to integrate the schools there was at its height. Then it was reported that mob violence was feared. When I told a friend of mine that I intended to visit Cairo, he told me a joke about a Negro who once got off a train in a strange Southern city. No sooner had the train departed than a group of white men walked up to him. One of them said, "Say Negro, don't you know we don't allow no colored folks to light here?"

The Negro replied, "No, sir, I didn't know."

"The last Negro that lit in this town, we hung him," the white man said. "But since you declare that you didn't know that we don't allow Negroes here, we will give you a chance—providing you catch the next train out of town."

The Negro said, "Since you'll give me a chance, boss, I won't wait for the next train. I'll catch the one that's just gone!"

Of course, nothing like that happened to me in Cairo. In fact, nothing untoward at all—until I was about to leave town. I had a very pleasant afternoon and evening there, and satisfied my curiosity about the place. Everyone I met kept asking me how come I had stopped over in Cairo. So I kept explaining that I was making a sentimental journey to a town I had always wanted to see ever since I first heard that line in "The St. Louis Blues" which goes, "If I get to Cairo, make St. Louis by myself."

On the train to Cairo was a Negro student from the university who introduced himself and, when we got to his home town, he took me to the high school to meet his former teachers and the principal.

I also met the principals and some of the teachers from the other colored schools—which are no longer segregated schools, since colored pupils may now, thanks to the NAACP, go to any school in the neighborhoods in which they live. Some of the teachers drove me about the city, another invited me to dinner with her family and saw that I got my train that night.

Just before catching the Panama Limited south, I was driven past the house of the white lawyer for the NAACP to see that now famous neon sign pictured in *Life* and *Jet* which his neighbor to the rear has put atop his garage, to flash off and on at night pointing to the home of the man who had the nerve to aid Negroes in breaking down the school barriers.

I had thought the sign was gone by the time of my visit. But, no, it was still there, pointing its red arrow of bigotry at this man's house. As we drove by, another car pulled up just behind us and slowed down. We continued to the corner where we turned to come back. The other car went by us picking up speed.

As we again passed the house, a white man ran out straight toward our car, in his shirt sleeves, one hand in his pocket and an angry look on his face. We stopped. Fortunately, he recognized the Negroes in the car as teachers whom he knew, and they recognized him as the lawyer who lived there. We were startled, naturally, at the wrath in his face, until he told us that someone had just thrown a rock through his front window—evidently an occupant of the car that had slowed down behind us.

This lawyer said that almost every week people drove by at night and threw rocks at his windows. But he said, "No one will drive me out of town!"

Meanwhile, as we talked, the beautiful red sign flashed off and on, off and on, atop his neighbor's garage, its arrow pointing to him. It was there in the dark street, a moment after a stone crashed through his window, that I met David Lansden, a courageous white man in Southern Illinois who believes in democracy, equality, and racial decency. It was my privilege to tell him how much I admire his courage and his integrity. Having seen Cairo, I can now never forget it—nor the stones that are still being thrown there at democracy.

"Emmett Till, Mississippi, and Congressional Investigations," LHP, Beinecke (September 16, 1955)

[Fourteen year old Emmett Till was abducted and killed in 1955 for allegedly whistling at a white woman in Mississippi. The NAACP immediately labeled the case a lynching, but despite organizing protests that became a rallying point for the Civil Rights Movement, an all-white jury acquitted the men responsible for the boy's death.]

OH, WHAT SORROW!
OH, WHAT PITY!
OH, WHAT PAIN
THAT TEARS AND BLOOD
SHOULD MIX LIKE RAIN
AND TERROR COME AGAIN
TO MISSISSIPPI.

Come again?
Where has terror been?
On vacation? Up North?
In some other section
Of the nation,
Lying low, unpublicized?
Masked—with only
Jaundiced eyes
Showing through the mask?

OH, WHAT SORROW,
PITY, PAIN,
THAT TEARS AND BLOOD
SHOULD MIX LIKE RAIN
IN MISSISSIPPI—
AND TERROR, FETID HOT
YET CLAMMY COLD,
REMAIN.

This is a poem written in memory of the dead boy, Emmett Till, whose body was found shot through the head, beaten and bruised, in the Tallahatchie River, 120 miles South of Memphis. Charlie Lang and Ernest Green were young Negro boys like Emmett Till, too, only fourteen years old when they were lynched in Mississippi on October 12, 1942. Their adolescent bodies were hanged together from the Shubuta Bridge over the Chicasawhay River. Mississippi leads all the states in the United States in lynchings. Since the year 1882 it has had 576 lynchings according to official count, and how many more there are that have never been recorded, nobody knows. Certainly, I think Mississippi must lead the world in the lynching of children.

I have never heard or read about any Congressional committee investigating lynching. But there have been almost five thousand recorded lynchings in the United States since Tuskegee Institute began keeping a list of lynchings and publishing them in the *Negro Yearbook*. Of course, Negroes who have been murdered, beaten to death by individual whites, or simply shot down by southern police are not included in Tuskegee's record. The lawless killing of black men and women is an old Southern custom going back to slavery days. In Ben Botkin's graphic book of slave memories published by the University of Chicago Press, "Lay My Burden Down," there is a quotation from a former slave who remembers, "My papa was strong. He never had a licking in his life. But one day the master says, 'Si, you got to have a whipping.' And my papa says, 'I never had a whopping and you can't whop me.' And the master says, 'But I can kill you.' And he shot my papa down. My mama took him in the cabin and put him on a pallet. He died."

Because nobody wants to die, thousands of Negroes stayed away from the polls at the last election in Mississippi—for fear of their lives if they tried to vote. If such intimidation of citizens of the United States—to the point where they are afraid to exercise the democratic right of the ballot—is not un-American, I don't know what is. Yet I have not as yet read or heard of the House Committee on Un-American Activities investigating such activities. Again, if the long-time lynch customs of the South are not un-American, I don't know what is. Yet I have never as yet heard or read of the Senate Permanent Committee on Investigations conducting any sort of probe into lynchings. In recent years Congressional committees have taken up a great deal of time, and used up a great deal of tax money, investigating the loyalty of various Negro citizens. Even such famous personages of color as Channing Tobias, Jackie Robinson, Josh White, and pretty Hazel Scott have gone to Washington to testify as to their loyalty and faith in democratic institutions.

It would seem to me sort of nice if the white politicians in Washington would now repay those distinguished colored Americans who have sworn and double sworn their allegiance to democratic ideals, by investigating JUST A FEW of the white folks who hang fourteen-year-old boys to bridges and throw them in rivers and who frighten and intimidate colored voters away from the polls—not to speak of those who continue to segregate the public schools, uphold Jim Crow on the railroads, and bar not only Negro citizens of the United States but East Indian diplomats from getting a decent meal in a public restaurant. Just one little small investigation of these things, using just a wee tinnychee bit of our mutual tax money, and showing just one lynched body on TV, or forcing just one Southern mobster to take refuge in the Fifth Amendment, seems to me long overdue. Senator Eastland from Mississippi might well consider calling such an investigation now while public interest is high. It ought to be even easier to catch lynchers than it is Communists, especially in Mississippi, where they are so bold about it, and where they have no respect for the legal age. Imagine lynching children! It makes me sick at the stomach. Have senators no stomachs?

"Du Bois: Greatness Has a Birthday,"
Chicago Defender, March 1, 1958

On Feb. 23 Dr. William Edward Burghardt Du Bois is ninety years old. This dean of Negro scholars was born at Great Barrington, Massachusetts, in 1868. He attended Fisk University, Harvard, and the University of Berlin.

In 1896 he published the first of his monumental studies, *The Suppression of the African Slave Trade,* as one of the volumes of the Harvard Historical Studies, and in 1899 he did a scholarly survey on *The Philadelphia Negro* consisting of over 2,000 pages of social and statistical information of great importance.

In 1903 his *The Souls of Black Folk* appeared to exercise its enormous influence on Negro intellectuals and writers for a half century thereafter.

Dr. Du Bois has been the greatest single influence on Negro thinking of our time, compared by Henry Steele Commager to Thomas Jefferson and Benjamin Franklin, and described by John Gunther as being "almost like Shaw or Einstein."

Du Bois was the author of the original call for "organized, determined, and aggressive action" on the problems of race that resulted in the famous Niagara Conference in 1905, and from it developed a movement that eventually led most of its leaders into the formation of the National Association for the Advancement of Colored People, destined to become one of America's most historic organizations.

Dr. Du Bois became the editor of its magazine, *The Crisis,* whose powerful editorials stirred the minds of thousands, excited the bigots to wrath, and were often quoted in papers throughout the world. The NAACP has stated officially that without Du Bois "the Association would never have been what it was and is."

Shortly after World War I Dr. Du Bois founded the Pan-African Congress. And no less a leader than the new Prime Minister of Ghana, Kwame Nkrumah, has declared that the Fifth Pan-African Congress "provided the outlet for African nationalism and brought about the awakening of African political consciousness."

In a recent article in *The Nation,* Truman Nelson declares that Ghana, Nigeria, French West Africa, and the Cameroons have all been "guided along the road of non-violent revolution by the founding stones of Du Bois."

Certainly William Edward Burghardt Du Bois has had an influence on the whole dark world from Alabama to Africa. Today at ninety, still vigorous of mind and body, greatness celebrates a birthday.

As the grand old man of American Negro life and letters approaches the century mark, we may well remember some of the things he said and wrote as far back as a half century ago. Here are quotations from the recently reissued *The Souls of Black Folk* that are as valid now as when they were freshly written.

"The problem of the Twentieth Century is the problem of the color line—the relation of the darker to the lighter races of men in Asia and Africa, in America and the islands of the sea . . .

"Negroes must insist continually, in season and out of season, that voting is necessary to modern manhood, that color discrimination is barbarism, and that black boys need education as well as white boys . . .

" . . . And the final product of our training must be neither a psychologist nor a brickmason, but a MAN. And to make men, we must have ideals, broad, pure, and inspiring ends of living—not sordid money-getting, not apples of gold.

"The worker must work for the glory of his handiwork, not simply for pay; the thinker must think for truth, not for fame . . . Before the Pilgrims landed we were here.

"Here we have brought our three gifts . . . a gift of story and song—soft, stirring melody in an ill-harmonized and unmelodious land; the gift of sweat and brawn to beat back the wilderness, conquer the soil, and lay the foundations of this vast economic empire . . . the third, a gift of the Spirit.

"Around us the history of the land has centered for thrice a hundred years . . . Actively we have woven ourselves with the very warp and woof of this nation . . . Would America have been America without her Negro people?"

"Golden Anniversary of the NAACP,"
Chicago Defender, April 11, 1959

This year the National Association for the Advancement of Colored People is celebrating its Golden anniversary, to culminate in its 50th

Jubilee Convention in New York City in July. These have been 50 golden years, each one a stepping stone in the forward march of the Negro citizens of the United States.

Cementing each stone with an amazing record of concrete achievement has been the day to day, week to week, month to month, year to year work of the NAACP, which is, to my opinion, the greatest social service organization in America. Certainly no future history of the United States can be written without including in its pages the National Association for the Advancement of Colored People.

Integration was a part of the NAACP from the very beginning. It has always been an interracial organization. Since its inception, Negroes and whites have worked side by side for greater democracy in our USA, and its board as well as various of its officers have been for 50 years of both races.

White men and women from Oswald Garrison Villard to Eleanor Roosevelt have helped guide and strengthen the NAACP both morally and financially. White legal talent as well as Negro legal talent have drawn the briefs which have led over the years to the recent history-making victories in the Supreme Court. White hands and black hands have helped to bring about educational integration across much of the South, partial though it now may be, but enormous in its potentialities.

There was never a time in my life when I did not hear of the NAACP from my childhood in Kansas to my manhood in Harlem. The only magazine that came by mail to my grandmother's house in Kansas, was *The Crisis,* the official organ of the NAACP, and as a very small child I noticed that most of the pictures in it were of people dark as I was dark.

Very early in life, *The Crisis* became my magazine, and I knew that its pages were my pages, its words about me. When I was old enough to read, the flaming words of the poetic and stirring, passionate and indignant editorials of Dr. W. E. B. Du Bois, editor of *The Crisis,* gave me my first knowledge of what power printed words can have when they are filled with integrity, social responsibility, and a deep caring for the basic values of human life.

For most of my life I have been a member of the NAACP, but sometimes when funds were low, or when I was out of the country, my membership lapsed. However, as soon as I have had a dollar or two, I renewed my membership in one branch or another throughout the country.

And the very first office I visited when I came to New York was that of the NAACP, to seek out the man whose words had meant so much to me in my youth, Dr. Du Bois. At the NAACP offices I met also the charming Jessie Fauset, then managing editor of *The Crisis,* Augustus Granville

Dill, the magazine's efficient business administrator, and the scholarly president of the organization and one of its founders, Joel Spingarn.

Later it was my privilege to know Arthur Spingarn, James Weldon Johnson, Walter White, and Roy Wilkins, men who have guided the NAACP through all its trials and tribulations to where it is today—an organization of monumental importance in American life.

Not only has the NAACP been a vital force in the betterment of conditions for Negro citizens, but it has helped to wash and rewash the rather sooty face of American democracy and make that face cleaner and brighter and better to look upon for all its citizens.

For its Golden Anniversary, let us endow the NAACP's Fighting Fund For Freedom with a million dollars in gold or—since the gold is all at Fort Knox—its equivalent in checks or currency. Let us all contribute generously this year to America's own National Association for the Advancement of Colored People.

"Remarks by Langston Hughes in Acceptance of 45th Spingarn Medal," LHP 3304, Beinecke (June 26, 1960)

To the NAACP, the Members of the Spingarn Medal Committee, and to Arthur Spingarn for his genial presentation, my thanks. But it would indeed be of the utmost conceit were I to accept this Medal in my name alone; or in the name of literature, which is my field. I can accept it only in the name of the Negro people who have given me the materials out of which my poems and stories, plays and songs, have come; and who, over the years, have given me as well their love and understanding and support.

Without them, on my part, there would have been no poems; without their hopes and fears and dreams, no stories; without their struggles, no dramas; without their music, no songs.

Had I not heard as a child in the little churches of Kansas and Missouri, "Deep river, my home is over Jordan," or "My Lord, what a morning when the stars begin to fall," I might not have come to realize the lyric beauty of *living* poetry.

Had I not listened to a blind guitar player on a Kansas City street corner singing, "Going down to the railroad, lay my head on the track— but if I see the train a-coming, I'll jerk it back"—had I not listened to songs like these, the laughter and sadness of the blues might never have become a part of my own poetry.

Had I not heard as a child such folk verses as:

> What a wonderful bird the frog are: When he hop he fly
>   almost.
> When he sit he stand almost. He ain't got no sense hardly.
> He ain't got no tail hardly neither where he sit—almost.

Had I not heard these, I might not have grasped the humor of the absurd incasing human as well as animal behavior.

Had I not listened to the old folks' memories of slavery told on front porches of a summer evening, there might not have been "The Negro Speaks of Rivers" written before I was twenty:

> I've known rivers: I've known rivers ancient as the world
> And older than the flow of human blood in human veins
> My soul has grown deep like the rivers.
> I bathed in the Euphrates when dawns were young
> I built my hut near the Congo and it lulled me to sleep
> I looked upon the Nile and raised the pyramids above it
> I heard the singing of the Mississippi when Abe Lincoln went
>   down to New Orleans
> And I've seen its muddy bosum turn all golden in the sunset
> I've known rivers: Ancient, dusky rivers. My soul has grown
>   deep like the rivers.

In the years following my childhood, had I not listened to the State Street stories, the Vine Street anecdotes, the Central Avenue complaints, Paradise Valley comments, the fun of South Street jokes whose humor is deeper than fun, and the Lenox Avenue tales and observations that eventually combined to create a composite character—born in the South but urbanized in the North—there would have been no Simple stories, no "Simple Speaks His Mind," or "Simply Heavenly," or "Simple Dreams a Mighty Dream."

There is so much richness in Negro humor, so much beauty in black dreams, so much dignity in our struggle, and so much universality in our problems, in *us*—in each living human being of color—that I do not understand the tendency today that some American Negro artists have of seeking to run away from themselves, of running away from *us,* of being afraid to sing our own songs, paint our pictures, write about ourselves—when it is our music that has given America its greatest music, our humor that has enriched its entertainment media for the past 100 years, our rhythm that has guided its dancing feet from plantation days to the Charleston, the Lindy Hop, and currently the Madison. Our problems have given intriguing material to writers from "Uncle Tom's Cabin" to Faulkner, from "The Octoroon" to Eugene O'Neill. Yet there are some of us who say, "Why write about Negroes? Why not be *just a writer?*" And why not—if one wants to be "just a writer"? Negroes in a free world should be whatever each wants to be—even if it means being "just a writer."

Some quite famous Americans of color are "just writers," their pages reflecting nothing of their ethnic background. Well and good! On the other hand, there is such a wealth of untapped material for writing in the Negro group, that it would be a shame were most of us to become "just writers." It would be an even greater shame if such a decision were made out of fear or shame. There is nothing to be ashamed of in the strength and dignity and laughter of the Negro people. And there is nothing to be afraid of in the use of their material.

Could you possibly be afraid that the rest of the world will not accept it? Our spirituals are sung and loved in the great concert halls of the whole world. Our blues are played from Topeka to Tokyo. Harlem's jive talk delights Hong Kong and Paris. Those of our writers who have most concerned themselves with our very special problems are translated and read around the world. The local, the regional can—and does—become universal. Sean O'Casey's Irishmen are an example. So I would say to young Negro writers, do not be afraid of yourselves. *You* are the world.

A very local literary character of mine, Jesse B. Simple, has gone from the corner of 125th and Lenox in Harlem to speak his mind around the world. He's read in Johannesburg, recited on the London radio, recreated on European stages by white actors in languages Simple himself never heard of. A Harlemite—from a very specific locale, in a very specific corner of a very specific city, and of a very specific color—black—is accepted in foreign lands thousands of miles away from the corner of 125th and Lenox as a symbol of the problems of the little man of any race anywhere.

I did not create Simple. He created himself. I merely transcribed him on paper. He is his own literature. In the South today—where children are going dangerously to school and teen-agers are sitting on stools before counters where no food is served them except the bitter herbs of hate—there is great material for literature. I hope there will soon be writers who will make great use of this material. Certainly in time, out of the Negro people there will come a great literature. Perhaps today the capital *P* with which some of us spell *problem* is larger than the capital *A* with which others would spell *art*. Nevertheless, I think it permissible that a poem pose a problem. In the case of many of my poems, the problem is that which the NAACP is seeking to solve. Once I presented it through the eyes of a child in a poem called "Merry-Go-Round."

When I wrote it, I imagined a little colored girl perhaps six or seven years old, born in the Deep South where segregation is legal. When she was about school age, her parents moved to a Northern or Western city, perhaps looking for better jobs, or a better school for their child. At any rate, in this new town—maybe a town like Newark, New Jersey, or Oakland, California, or even St. Paul or Minneapolis—one day this little girl goes to a carnival and she sees a merry-go-round going around. She wants to ride. But, being a very little girl, and colored, remembering the Jim Crowisms of the South, she doesn't know whether colored children can ride on merry-go-rounds in the North or not. And if they can, she doesn't know where. So this is what she says:

> Where is the Jim Crow section on this merry-go-round,
> Mister, cause I want to ride?
> Down South where I come from white and colored
> Can't sit side by side
> Down South on the train there's a Jim Crow car
> On the bus we're put in the back
> But there ain't no back
> To a merry-go-round:
> Where's the horse for a kid that's black?

Our country is big enough and rich enough to have a horse for every kid, black or white, Catholic or Protestant, Jewish or Gentile—and someday we will. Meanwhile:

> I, too, sing America
> I am the darker brother
> They send me to eat in the kitchen
> When company comes,
> But I laugh
> And eat well
> And grow strong.
> Tomorrow,
> I'll be at the table

When company comes
Nobody'll dare
Say to me,
"Eat in the kitchen,"
Then.
Besides,
They'll see how beautiful I am
And be ashamed—
I, too, am America.

Index